THE CHINA CHALLENGE

THE CHINA CHALLENGE

Sino-Canadian Relations
in the 21st Century

edited by
HUHUA CAO AND VIVIENNE POY

UNIVERSITY OF OTTAWA PRESS
OTTAWA

University of Ottawa Press
542 King Edward Avenue
Ottawa, ON K1N 6N5
www.press.uottawa.ca

uOttawa

The University of Ottawa Press acknowledges with gratitude the support extended to its publishing list by Heritage Canada through its Book Publishing Industry Development Program, by the Canada Council for the Arts, by the Canadian Federation for the Humanities and Social Sciences through its Aid to Scholarly Publications Program, by the Social Sciences and Humanities Research Council of Canada, and by the University of Ottawa.

LIBRARY AND ARCHIVES CANADA CATALOGUING IN PUBLICATION

The China challenge : Sino-Canadian relations in the 21st century /
edited by Huhua Cao and Vivienne Poy.

Includes bibliographical references.
ISBN 978-0-7766-0764-1

1. Canada--Foreign relations--China. 2. China--Foreign relations--Canada.
I. Cao, Huhua, 1961- II. Poy, Vivienne, 1941-

FC251.C5C55 2011   327.71051   C2011-901927-2

THE CHINA CHALLENGE

Sino-Canadian Relations
in the 21st Century

edited by

HUHUA CAO AND VIVIENNE POY

UNIVERSITY OF OTTAWA PRESS
OTTAWA

University of Ottawa Press
542 King Edward Avenue
Ottawa, ON K1N 6N5
www.press.uottawa.ca

uOttawa

The University of Ottawa Press acknowledges with gratitude the support extended to its publishing list by Heritage Canada through its Book Publishing Industry Development Program, by the Canada Council for the Arts, by the Canadian Federation for the Humanities and Social Sciences through its Aid to Scholarly Publications Program, by the Social Sciences and Humanities Research Council of Canada, and by the University of Ottawa.

LIBRARY AND ARCHIVES CANADA CATALOGUING IN PUBLICATION

The China challenge : Sino-Canadian relations in the 21st century /
edited by Huhua Cao and Vivienne Poy.

Includes bibliographical references.
ISBN 978-0-7766-0764-1

1. Canada--Foreign relations--China. 2. China--Foreign relations--Canada.
I. Cao, Huhua, 1961- II. Poy, Vivienne, 1941-

FC251.C5C55 2011   327.71051   C2011-901927-2

Acknowledgements

First of all, we would like to thank all the contributors for their extraordinary collaboration on this volume. It has given us a unique chance to work on this important project, examining the relationship between Canada and China during the past forty years. With the exception of the relationship with the United States, Canada's relationship with China is likely to be its most significant foreign connection in the 21st century. In that light, this book has the potential both to be very useful to those studying the relationship and to make an important impact on policy-makers in both countries.

We would also like to thank the Honourable Allan Rock, President and Vice-Chancellor of the University of Ottawa, for taking time to write the preface. His support will certainly encourage us to continue to contribute to the relationship between the two countries, and the series of which this book forms a part will contribute greatly to the University of Ottawa's efforts to increase awareness of its leadership on international issues.

We are also grateful for invaluable assistance in preparing the manuscript for publication that we have received from Carol Reichert, Policy Advisor to Senator Vivienne Poy; Jennifer Thomas, Manager, Communications and Special Projects of the Office of the President of the University of Ottawa; Marie-Eve Reny of the University of Toronto; and Ruibo Han, Matt Gaudreau, Yuanyuan Zhai, Jean-Francois Parent and Alex Payette of the University of Ottawa.

Contents

List of Tables, Figures and Maps

Tables

Figures

Chapter 16

Maps

Chapter 16

Foreword

Allan Rock

It has been more than forty years since diplomatic relations between Canada and the People's Republic of China were established by Prime Minister Pierre Elliott Trudeau. Throughout that time, China has undergone dramatic economic changes, and the country is now considered a key player on the global stage. China's emergence as an economic powerhouse, coupled with its successful efforts to expand its sphere of influence, have had a profound effect both on the development of international policy and on the global community as a whole. Meanwhile, Canada has worked steadily to strengthen cultural and economic exchanges with China, balancing strong trade against concerns such as human rights, the rule of law, climate change and the environment. While ebbs and flows in their bilateral relations have occurred, Canada and China continue to engage in collaborative efforts in political, commercial, cultural and academic arenas. Canada must not only persist in raising its profile as a contributing partner in this strategically important region, but also continue critically to examine its foreign policy toward China.

The China Challenge: Sino-Canadian Relations in the 21ˢᵗ Century is therefore a timely and relevant analysis of the history and future of the relationship between Canada and China. It examines topics such as Ottawa's foreign policy priorities, China's increasingly important position as an international policy-maker, China's growing economic clout and its potential implications for Canada's future prosperity, and the human and demographic aspects of bilateral relations. It offers readers perspectives from both scholars and Canadian government representatives, current and former, on why, from both a domestic and an international standpoint, China is more important to Canada than ever.

This book is the first in a series, China in the 21ˢᵗ Century, to be published by the University of Ottawa Press. The series will greatly contribute to the University of Ottawa's efforts to increase awareness of its leadership on international issues, a priority identified in Vision2020, the university's strategic plan for the future. It will also further advance the university's efforts to encourage collaboration between universities and governments.

Given the complex global issues facing the Canadian government today, it is critical that senior officials and elected leaders have access to thoughtful and fully developed knowledge and ideas from sources beyond their own departments. Universities, with their capacity for critical thought and independent research, can play an important part in the development of this information, and in nourishing an open and rigorous policy process as an important component in the future progress of bilateral relations with China.

With its rich cultural heritage, its tremendous economic influence, and the world's largest population, China will see its economic potential and its status among nations continue to flourish in coming decades. As it currently stands, China has made significant moves in trade relations with the United States, Australia, South America and Africa, is a leading force in the G20, has permanent membership of the United Nations Security Council, and is the second largest economy in the world after the United States. If Canada wishes to maintain a strong international presence, it must find ways to bridge the ideological differences that constitute foreign policy challenges in its relationship with China in order to reinforce its relevance and its capacity to develop new Canadian markets in Asia.

The China Challenge: Sino-Canadian Relations in the 21st Century and the subsequent books in the series China in the 21st Century will serve as valuable resources, providing policy-makers with expert knowledge, insight and opinions so that they may make the best decisions on how to enhance our nation's dialogue with China on vital issues of strategic interest for Canada.

Chapter 1

Introduction:
Canada's Response to China's
Increasing Role in the World

Huhua Cao

The international position of the People's Republic of China has undeniably changed since Canada became one of the first developed countries to recognize it, in 1970 (even before the People's Republic was admitted to the United Nations). When Mao Zedong declared on October 1, 1949, that China had finally "stood up" in the world, he had underestimated his country's potential to rise internationally. In 1949, China's ability to stand up implied its ideological move away from capitalism as the best instrument of struggle against "imperialism" and its "defenders" (see Friedman 1994 and Kirby 1994). The autonomy of the Chinese state was a product of its ability to resist the most influential capitalist world powers. In the 1960s, autonomy went as far as resulting in China's complete isolation from the international community, in a context where its relations with the two world superpowers were tense (see Gittings 1964, Kirby 1994, and Yahuda 1983). In no way did autonomy result in China's ability to influence the world scene. Indeed, China was to remain far from the centre of global political interests for several more decades. Up until October 25, 1971, it was denied membership in the United Nations, while Taiwan, under the name of the Republic of China, was the sole official representative of the Chinese nation.

During the Maoist era, one way in which the People's Republic regained autonomy in its foreign policy was "by dealing with foreign powers individually, not as a unit" (Kirby 1994, p. 17). This strategy, among other implications, meant that ideological differences would not be the unique

1

standard for defining the boundaries of China's relations with foreign partners. It opened the door to the possibility that China might have privileged
relationships of varying degrees with different western powers, based on
each country's ability to give and take. This strategy certainly played in
favour of bilateral relations between China and Canada under the leadership of Prime Minister Pierre Trudeau and since.

Following thirty years of remarkable economic growth since the end
of the 1970s, leading to China becoming the second largest economy in
the world after the United States (see Barboza 2010), its ability to "stand
up" today has a profoundly different meaning. While Deng Xiaoping, the
architect of China's economic reforms at the end of the 1970s, stressed that
China should "maintain a low profile and never take the lead" on international matters, the country's impressive economic growth over the past
thirty years not only has changed its economic status in the world, but has
also allowed the country to become a more and more important player in
the process of making important political and geopolitical decisions.

China has played a key mediation role in ensuring six-party talks to
find a peaceful resolution to security concerns resulting from the determination of North Korea to develop nuclear weapons. In Central Asia,
the Chinese government has been the key to the creation and hosting of
the Shanghai Cooperation Organization (SCO) since 2001. It has also in
recent years become an active participant in the Asia–Pacific Economic
Cooperation (APEC) forum, the Association of Southeast Asian Nations
(ASEAN) regional forum, and ASEAN-plus-three. The outstanding pace
at which its economy has grown has given China an important position in
the G20, and has planted the seeds for a potential "G2," comprising the
United States and China. China has become a "soft power," not in Nye's
military and security terms, but in the realms of popular culture, diplomacy
and participation in multilateral organizations, as well as development aid
(Kurlantzick 2007, p. 6).

China's presence and influence have also grown in Africa. Chinese leaders have sought to strengthen political relations with that continent by
establishing the China–Africa Cooperation Forum in 2000 (Kaplinsky,
McCormick, and Morris 2008, p. 14). One of the main commonalities
emphasized by China in its attempt to draw African interests closer to its
own has been an emphasis on their common imperialistic and neo-imperi-
alistic enemies (Taylor 2005, p. 5). According to the China–Africa Business
Council, China has become Africa's third largest trading partner. While
the value of its trade with the continent was only US$ 2 billion in 1999,

by 2005 that figure had risen to US$ 39.7 billion (Taylor 2005, p. 2). As Joshua Kurlantzick (2007, p. 6) maintains, "Beijing offers the charm of a lion, not of a mouse: it can threaten other nations with these sticks if they do not help China achieve its goals, but it can offer sizeable carrots if they do." Indeed, some countries in Asia, Africa and Latin America have cut off relations with Taiwan as a result of Beijing's "soft" influence (Kurlantzick 2007, p. 10). China is becoming more attractive than western countries as a foreign direct investor in some African countries, in part because the Chinese do not impose conditions relating to good governance and human rights. This has attracted criticism from the West, which sees China's exclusive focus on the commercial foundations of such investment as detrimental to universally accepted norms on sustainable development and human rights. Africa could well become a new arena for economic and other forms of rivalry between China and the West.

For Canada, bilateral relations with China between the 1970s and the 1990s may have been substantially confined to foreign policy, but China's emerging position in the world has also had profound effects on Canada's domestic policy. As Paul Evans (2006, p. 284) claims, the average Canadian's "trip to the gas station reveals how China's demand for energy is increasing prices for energy and natural resources; and a trip to the bank reveals how mortgage and interest rates are tied to China's purchase of US securities." Beyond the fact that China has bought a yearly minimum of US$ 80 billion worth of US government debt since 2005, the Chinese government has been crucial in the (still slow) recovery of the world economy from the recent crisis. Beijing made its largest purchase of US debt in June 2010, when the US Treasury sold China US$ 108 billion worth of Treasuries over a few days (see Kruger 2010). China's share of US imports has increased to approximately twenty percent of the total, and China has replaced Canada as the number-one trading partner. Canada's share of imports into the United States has fallen to fifteen percent (see Ratner 2010). Given China's position in today's globalized world, its financial choices undeniably have a profound effect on other countries' financial and commercial priorities. One week before the G20 Summit in Toronto in June 2010, President Hu Jintao announced that the People's Bank of China would interrupt the initially fixed 23-month peg in the yuan, which would allow for more flexibility in the movements of the currency (see Ratner 2010).

The facts set out above suggest that China is no longer just an international "policy-taker," but is increasingly playing a role as an international "policy-maker." As Paul Evans (2006) has pointed out, policy-makers around the world have to be concerned about what Beijing will do next. Similarly, Canadian policy-makers have yet to establish a comprehensive domestic and foreign policy strategy to deal with the growing Chinese influence at the global level. The first step toward dealing with this changing global situation is to understand better how China's identity, guiding philosophies, traditions, cultures, and domestic social, economic and political challenges affect its positions in the international community. This cannot be achieved without a close collaboration and sharing of knowledge between China scholars and Canadian policy-makers. Such collaboration may help Canada in formulating a better-grounded foreign policy strategy toward the Chinese economy. It may also help Canada to go beyond the foreign policy dead end created by an overemphasis on the social and human rights problems that still pervade Chinese society.

Redefining Canada's Foreign Policy toward the "New" China

The domestic challenges that the Chinese regime currently faces are numerous, and Canada may constitute a model that China may wish to examine and possibly adopt in order to address some of them.

Income disparities in China have grown considerably since the 1980s, not only across regions and provinces, but also between urban and rural areas and across social classes (see Cao and Bergeron 2010). In the context of growing social and economic grievances, and with a judicial system that comprises an ineffective and saturated system of petitions and complaints, collective protests frequently erupt in various parts of the country. A recent case among several others was that of a workers' strike for better work conditions at a Honda Motor Company parts factory in southern China in June 2010. Generally, despite some considerable progress with respect to citizens' economic and social rights, China's record on political rights has yet to improve significantly. According to the Human Rights Risk Atlas 2010, China fell to twelfth position in an index where Somalia was ranked at number one and the United States at 134.

The protests in Xinjiang on July 5, 2009, and the ways in which the authorities have responded to popular discontent, also indicate that ethnic tension remains, and command and control tactics are still the state's solution. While the state has manifested some signs of increasing willingness to accommodate civil society on some levels, its intentions as far as political reforms are concerned remain difficult to capture. Some legal reforms introduced since the year 2000 suggest that the government is making efforts to establish political transparency and a more rigorous rule of law, but it remains primarily concerned to maintain the survival of its own autocratic regime. In the current circumstances, democracy remains far from attainable.

China's environmental problems and the broader challenge of global warming have also been the target of concerns in the West. China has become the world's biggest emitter of greenhouse gases and, although it has made a formal commitment to cut the unit GDP carbon dioxide emission level by forty percent by 2020 (see Xin 2010), the need to maintain stable growth may make this target very difficult to reach.

The clashing positions of Canada and China on human rights in China have had a deteriorating impact on the two countries' bilateral relations, as China is becoming more resolute about its own distinctive political positions and ideology. Following the Tiananmen Square incident in June 1989, the Chinese government's attempts to maintain its own version of the Chinese national identity have relied upon emphasizing "Chinese values," defined in opposition to what it depicts as Western cultural frameworks. In some cases, Chinese nationalism has been manifested in the form of anti-Americanism. The Chinese regime has reached a position of economic influence in the world that allows it to choose what it wishes to accept from western powers, and ignore what it believes it does not need. In such circumstances, a bilateral policy attempting to impose what are seen as "Western values" upon the Chinese government is unlikely to generate satisfactory outcomes for either of the two parties. Some of the values that Western countries regard as universal are not necessarily interpreted with the same degree of importance by the Chinese regime. For example, Chinese policy-makers tend to place a greater emphasis on the right of nations to achieve development than on the civil and political rights of individuals. A more constructive dialogue among Canada's and China's scholars and policy-makers on contentious areas such as human rights and the proper treatment of minorities may lead to a Canadian foreign policy that emphasizes the exchange of ideas on the basis of equality and mutual benefit.

Establishing a good dialogue with China is the key condition for stable, fulfilling and profitable bilateral relations. In an attempt to explore the avenues that Ottawa might exploit in order to strengthen its ties with the People's Republic of China, this book discusses how Canada holds the potential to overcome the foreign policy obstacles posed by ideological differences with China. The two countries have had bilateral relations based on mutual respect and solidarity ever since the time of Pierre Trudeau, but more importantly, since the 1990s Canada has cultivated privileged ties with Hong Kong. Canada is demographically advantaged to the extent that four percent of the Canadian population is of Chinese origin, and it has become an important destination and centre of interest for the Chinese diaspora. Conversely, about 300,000 Canadians live in China today, which makes Sino-Canadian economic, cultural and political relations more important than ever.

The Structure of This Book

There are several reasons why a sustained dialogue between Canadian experts on China and practitioners is needed. First, before the 1980s, when China remained isolated from the centre of international politics, the number of China scholars was incomparably lower than that of scholars of other world regions, and the visibility of China scholarship remained severely limited. Today, as China's position in world politics has become central, understanding China is no longer confined to academia, but is also becoming a priority among government policy analysts and policy-makers across policy areas.

Second, in the past five years bilateral relations between China and Canada have been affected by inadequate policy-making and misunderstandings on the part of both Ottawa and Beijing. Mutually beneficial relations need to be based on well-grounded and attainable policy expectations. Due to their familiarity with Chinese culture, traditions and, in some cases, the languages, their extensive research, and their regular visits to the country, China scholars have the potential to make important contributions to the bilateral policy-making process on the Canadian side by offering policy-makers in-depth briefings on the evolution in the Chinese government's domestic and foreign policy priorities and challenges. Generally, well-grounded policies can be based only on multidisciplinary and multi-dimensional considerations, and the latter requires taking various opinions into account.

Hence, this book brings together a diversity of perspectives from both China scholars and Canadian government and non-government representatives on the history and future of Sino-Canadian relations, and addresses the ways in which Canada has redefined and will continue to readjust its foreign policy with respect to domestic and external policy changes in

China. Some of the chapters are written as speeches, hinting at the Canadian government's foreign policy positions on China, and others take the form of more standard analyses. This mixture of writing styles is illustrative of a broader diversity in approaches and perspectives. We hope that this volume will be of help to Canadian and Chinese policy-makers in developing a suitable bilateral strategy that could be beneficial for both countries.

The book is divided into five parts. The first part comprises the present chapter. The second part provides an overview of the history of Sino-Canadian relations from both practitioners' and scholars' perspectives. Fred Bild's chapter emphasizes the absence of patterns and linearity in the history of those relations, and explains, on the basis of concrete examples, that diplomatic ties since their inception have been the fruits of spontaneous initiatives or windows of opportunities, which had their own underlying intentions, depending on their nature, timing, and initiators. Charles Burton explores the domestic factors that informed Canada's foreign policy towards China from the 1970s to the early years of Stephen Harper's government, focusing on four key periods or events: the recognition of the People's Republic by the Trudeau government, Brian Mulroney's response to the Tiananmen incident, Jean Chrétien's "Team Canada" initiative, and the suspension of the Canada-China Bilateral Human Rights Dialogue in 2006. B. Michael Frolic accounts for the motivations underlying the creation of Canada's strategy toward China in 1987. Sonny Lo explores the foreign policy decisions of the Harper government in relation to China, compares them with the Mulroney government's relative coolness toward China in the 1980s, and argues that this change in attitudes to China results from Canada's need to adapt to a globally rising China, the Chinese Canadian diaspora's demands for improved bilateral relations, and strategic concerns on the part of the Canadian business elite. In a similar vein, Ming K. Chan explores the demographic and socioeconomic dimensions of the relationship between Canada and Hong Kong, and maintains that this historical bond has the potential to secure a relationship of trust between Canada and the People's Republic. Qiang Zha then discusses how Canada and China's bilateral relations have become more balanced and equitable as China's influence in the world has expanded.

The third part of the book comprises speeches made by current and former politicians, business leaders, and policy leaders, addressing the implications of, and conditions for, a growing demographic and economic interdependence between Canada and China. Yuen Pau Woo explores the ways in which China constituted a "bastion of stability" during the recent world economic crisis, compared to the United States, and suggests that Canada should draw from China's stable position in the crisis to diversify its sources of investments and increase financial and commercial cooperation with the country. Such a strengthening of bilateral relations would undeniably require moving beyond some of the negativity that has undermined Canada and China's relations in the past ten years. Senator Vivienne Poy stresses that Canada's emphasis on human rights has had negative implications, and suggests that Hong Kong and Taiwan should be the gateways into China for Canadian businesses. Perrin Beatty, a former Canadian federal minister, shares similar views, stressing that Hong Kong offers a legal and commercial environment that is ideal for Canadian companies seeking to expand ties with China. Thomas d'Aquino, a leading voice of Canadian business, claims that the recent world economic crisis should be viewed as a window of opportunity for greater multilateral cooperation based on mutual harmony between economic development and environmental protection, and explores the ways in which Canada's and China's bilateral relations could be a future experimental terrain for the realization of such an objective. Errol Mendes, switching from economic to legal issues in the framework of interdependence, describes the similarities between Canada and China when it comes to the rights of ethnic minorities, and argues that Canada should serve as a global constitutional model for China and other multiethnic states that face important constitutional problems related to social stability.

The fourth part of the book concerns the Chinese diaspora in Canada. Kenny Zhang claims that, unlike most countries, whose relations with China boil down to investment deals and trade agreements, Canada, with its significant and highly diversified Chinese Canadian population, has the opportunity to take bilateral ties a step further by reaching agreement in the area of human capital. In their chapter, Ghazy Mujahid, Ann Kim and Guida Man maintain that as China's population grows and ages, the Chinese diaspora in Canada is likely to have more frequent exchanges with the People's Republic for longer periods of time. The authors examine three dimensions of the relations between migrants and their families in China: the care that migrants extend to their parents in China, the care that grandparents in China provide for young children sent back to China, and mutual support as a result of elderly parents immigrating to Canada under sponsorship arrangements. Jack Jedwab stresses that Canadians who speak Chinese as well as English and/or French will reinforce the collective capacity for building cultural bridges between people in the two countries. Huhua Cao and Olivier Dehoorne address the evolution of the geographic distribution of Chinese immigrants to Canada over the past one hundred and fifty years. Not only have Chinese immigrants to Canada become better represented in smaller cities, there has been a shift away from settling in Chinatowns to settling in suburban areas. The authors address the policy implications associated with retaining skilled economic immigrants under an increasingly flexible economy. Tony Fang addresses some of the downside of deepened demographic ties between Canada and China, namely the fact that Chinese nationals immigrating to Canada are increasingly more educated than Canadian-born workers and yet their incomes tend to be lower.

Finally, in the fifth part of the book Jeremy Paltiel suggests that Canada should move away from a foreign policy based on a "frame of teacher and pupil." It may be more appropriate for both Canada and China to use each other as a mirror, as opposed to a model, in order to analyze each other's practices and to see how the latter may be adapted and improved.

References

Barboza, David. (2010, August 16). "China Passes Japan as Second-Largest Economy." *New York Times*. Online at http://www.nytimes.com/2010/08/16/business/global/16yuan.html?_r=1&hp [consulted January 14, 2011].

Cao, Huhua, and Sabrina Bergeron. (2010). *Disparités régionales et inclusion des minorités : Les défis de la Chine de l'après Jeux Olympiques de Beijing* [Regional Disparities and Minority Inclusion: China's Challenges after the Beijing Olympics]. Quebec City: Presses de l'Université du Québec.

Evans, Paul. (2006, March 1). "Canada, Meet Global China." *International Journal*, 283–97. Online at http://www.asiapacific.ca/editorials/speeches-and-presentations/canada-meet-global-china [consulted January 14, 2011].

Friedman, Edward. (1994). "Reconstructing China's National Identity: A Southern Alternative to Mao-Era Anti-Imperialist Nationalism." *Journal of Asian Studies* 53:1, 67–91.

Gittings, John. (1964, January). "Co-operation and Conflict in Sino-Soviet Relations." *International Affairs*, 40:1, 60–75.

Kaplinsky, Raphael, Dorothy McCormick, and Mike Morris. (2008). "China and Sub Saharan Africa: Impacts and Challenges of a Growing Relationship." SAIS Working Papers in African Studies. Baltimore, MD: African Studies Program of the Paul H. Nitze School of Advanced International Studies at The Johns

Hopkins University. Online at http://www.sais-jhu.edu/academics/regional-studies/africa/publications.htm [consulted January 14, 2011].

Kirby, William C. (1994). "Traditions of Centrality, Authority and Management in Modern China's Foreign Relations," in *Chinese Foreign Policy: Theory and Practice*, ed. David Shambaugh and Thomas W. Robinson. Oxford: Clarendon Press, 3–29.

Kruger, Daniel. (2010, June 21). "China Backs Obama as Treasury Holdings Rise to $900 Billion." Bloomberg. Online at http://www.bloomberg.com/news/2010-06-20/china-backs-obama-with-u-s-treasury-securities-rising-3-to-900-billion.html [consulted January 14, 2011].

Kurlantzick, Joshua. (2007). *Charm Offensive: How China's Soft Power is Changing the World*. Yale University Press.

Ratner, Jonathan. (2010, June 20). "China Loosens Currency Peg." *Financial Post*. Online at http://business.financialpost.com/2010/06/20/china-loosens-currency-peg/ [consulted January 14, 2011].

Taylor, Ian. (2005). "Unpacking China's Resource Diplomacy in Africa." Working Paper No. 19. Hong Kong: Center on China's Transnational Relations at The Hong Kong University of Science and Technology.

Xin Benjian. (2010, August 6). "China's Emission Reduction Pledge and Global Response." *People's Daily*. Online at http://english.peopledaily.com.cn/90001/90780/91345/7096279.html [consulted January 14, 2011].

Yahuda, Michael. (1983). *Towards the End of Isolationism: China's Foreign Policy After Mao*. London and Basingstoke: Macmillan.

EVOLUTION OF

CANADA-CHINA RELATIONS

Chapter 2

Canada's Staying Power:
A Diplomat's View

Fred Bild

It is a particularly unrewarding task to try to find patterns in Canada's relations with China. To maintain that they evolve through a sort of subconscious thread leading from discovery to mutual exploitation, through disappointment, before eventually attaining a level of "maturity," results in nothing more than an academic exercise for ordering ephemeral conclusions. Besides, as Norman Bethune, Canada's most famous adventurer into war-torn China, demonstrated, such searches for leitmotifs are often founded on preconceived notions (in his case, political ones). Using solid 19th-century logic, the great doctor saw any country's venture into another as being rooted in imperialistic urges. According to Bethune, it normally got into gear after a succession of missionary explorations, followed by capitalist entrepreneurs, who were soon afterwards reinforced by military and diplomatic personnel. Here I will seek to show that such linear reasoning had nothing to do with the relationship as it evolved between Canada and the Orient, least of all China, but rather that what seemed to dominate most often were spontaneous initiatives, each with its own specific underlying motivations, depending on the time and the chief actors involved.

During my stay in China I discovered, however, that the imperialistic mindset that Bethune described did find some echo in some of our Chinese counterparts. The best example of this occurred several years after my departure, when a PhD student in 2004, at the Beijing Institute of Contemporary International Relations showed me what he called a policy document of the 1960s, which indicated that in earlier times Canada's

Asian policies were viewed as nothing less than part and parcel of US strategy for the encirclement of China. As he read them out to me in translation, these included Canada's assistance to nations in Southeast Asia, its participation in the Korean War and subsequently in the International Commissions for Supervision and Control in Indochina, its recognition of Taiwan, and even its acceptance of immigrants from Hong Kong. I'm not sure I was entirely successful in disabusing this young researcher of this interpretation but I tried to explain to him that, with carefully designed Ptolemaic epicycles, this sort of reasoning could purport to show contradictory policies—such as Canada's uninterrupted relations with Communist Cuba, its outspoken criticism of US policy in Vietnam in the 1960s, and even its negotiation of diplomatic relations with the People's Republic long before the Nixon–Kissinger initiative—as nothing more than manoeuvres inspired by Washington.

As a former practitioner of the art of diplomacy, rather than as an academic, I am struck by the ways in which categories applied to human endeavours can confuse just as much as they can elucidate. Academics, presumably, are engaged in combing through the remnants of past activity to detect the true roots or causes of contemporary reality. The practitioners, primarily preoccupied with the here and now, delve deep into their archives only occasionally for clues to present-day problems. Yet I find that, when discussing yesterday's or today's China, both worlds, the more practical as well as the more detached, tend to examine the subject with far too little regard for the past and within excessively restricted frameworks. My experience tends to show that, contra the logic of grand strategy or overarching schemes, Canada's relationship with China has been conducted from simultaneous, overlapping and sometimes contradictory motives, and managed with the best of intentions by harried but professional diplomatic staff. This visceral knowledge resists the glib categorization of academic researchers. That the short history of relations between Canada and China might be driven by shifting contingencies and irregular interventions of chance is a view that many seekers after patterns eschew.

Having spent some time in recent years examining various epochs of Canada's relationship with China, I am struck by the diversity of motives and approaches of all those steeped in that highly eventful and turbulent country. I suppose that, if one were to view the relationship from the viewpoint of view of missionaries, government officials, politicians, business people or ideologically driven activists, one could easily come up with handy labels to describe each group's distinct motivation. The examples provided would, however, reflect much generalization and selectivity. On the question of recognition of the People's Republic, for example, Lester Pearson seems to have been prompted initially by a desire to move quickly, before US policy became too unyielding and enshrined non-recognition as a NATO doctrine. His successors on this subject, Paul Martin Sr. and then Pierre Trudeau, proceeded according to their own calculations of Canada's interests. The former was determined to convince Washington to take the bull by the horns, rather than wait for the Third World vote at the United Nations to seat the People's Republic over US objections. The latter, on the other hand, was confident from the outset that it was a matter of first changing the mindset within the Ottawa policy establishment and then finessing the US position. One could argue that each of these three actors faced different situations when they played their roles on the stage, and that they faced three different sets of obstacles and political climates. It is none-theless clear that, while they all pursued the same objective, their personal motivations were significantly different.

Similar differences can be found among diplomats or other government officials, although their professional requirement of obedience to their political masters usually serves to paper over any individual distinction in personal outlooks. Even between activists of the same ideological persuasion, such as James Endicott and Norman Bethune, one can find serious differences of approach and basic motivation. This is not to say that comparisons are odious, but rather, more simply, that lumping people together into ready-made categories is a futile exercise. The same applies to the "phases" of the Sino-Canadian relationship.

Early Contacts

One can go back to the earliest trans-Pacific contacts and see that the unpre-dictable often played a determinant role. I sometimes wonder whether mere accident interfered with the promotion of a more robust channel of com-munications and commerce from our western shores. After all, After all, the earliest recorded trade between Canada and China was that of the Haida Gwai otter pelts worn by Captain James Cook's crew on their way to the Bering Sea, who would not have pursued their voyage to the China coast if their captain had not been murdered during their stopover in Hawaii. Yet it was as a result of this contact that the Hudson's Bay Company joined the fur trade with China and that, as early as 1788, a certain Captain John

Meares started to import Chinese labourers to the west coast of Canada (see Gough 2000). On the other hand, political timetables and sheer venality contributed to the development of "the Chinese fact" in Canada. Such speculation does not lead far, but it does serve to illustrate the web of disasters, hardships and determination that fashioned the beginnings of our dealings with the people of China.

Following these initial contacts, a whole century went by before Canada brought in thousands of Chinese labourers to do the hardest and most dangerous work in the construction of the western segment of our transcontinental railway. It happened, again quite by accident, just in time for the Canadian Pacific Railway (CPR) to partake of an unexpected bonanza from the transport of Chinese silks headed for New York and European markets. In the mid-19th century a silkworm disease had devastated silk manufacture in Europe and, as a result, textile mills were competing for rapid and low-cost supplies of Chinese silks. With the completion of the rail link to Vancouver, the cross-Canada route to New York turned out to be the fastest. It was a trade that saw the vessels of the CPR's own White Empress Line unloading tonnes of bales of silk onto newly outfitted "silk trains" in Vancouver, to be sped virtually non-stop to Montreal and New York in four days flat, an exploit that lasted into the 1940s, to the great profit of the CPR (but with scarcely a mention in our history books). On the other hand, if white Canadians, newly settled in British Columbia, had not given vent to their rabid racist tendencies at the time, Canada might well have had far greater numbers of hard-working Chinese and Japanese, and their industry and enterprise might have helped the country avoid much of the economic depression of the end of the 19th century.

Such questions abound throughout the evolution of our early foreign relations and, to my mind, underline the random nature of much of these. Most of the time, there was no one, neither actor nor thinker, who had any notion that they were participating in what was to be an ongoing link with a part of the world that would one day be of critical importance to Canada.

Governments and Asian Trade

Although there was a significant missionary presence in China, and there were even a few industrialists there by the late 19th century, it was not until the beginning of the 20th century that solid foreign relations ("hard power" as opposed to "soft power") started to affect the relationship. Not surprisingly, the Anglo-Japanese alliance of 1902, of which Canada, inescapably, was a participant, had a direct effect on relations with China. While the alliance provided the coast of British Columbia with some Japanese naval protection during the First World War, this was not judged reason enough after the war for admitting sizeable numbers of Japanese migrants seeking employment. By implication, the already strong rejection of Chinese labourers was intensified. Objections to the treaty of 1902, which was renewed in 1905 and 1911, eventually led Prime Minister Arthur Meighen to propose that it be replaced by a multilateral agreement. He thereby opened the way to the Washington naval and disarmament conferences of 1921–22. Thus the British role in the Far East was responsible, at least in part, not only for the strengthening of anti-Asian sentiment in British Columbia, but also for Canada's discovery of the joys and challenges of multilateralism and Anglo-Saxon solidarity. Both of these starting points turned out to be important for the evolution of some of the long-term characteristics of Canada's foreign policy, even though at this stage they were still some distance away from guiding Canada's relations with Asia, and particularly with China.

Blocking immigration and promoting trade were the dominant themes of Canadian relations with the whole of Asia throughout the first half of the 20th century, but the advent of the Great Depression soon made the latter a moot point. The flare-ups created by Japan in Manchuria and elsewhere in China commanded a certain amount of attention from Canadians concerned about foreign affairs, particularly as there were obvious divergences emerging between British and US policies in the region, but as the spectre of another war in Europe loomed ever larger, Canadian eyes were riveted eastward. Apart from a small segment of public opinion on the west coast, the country lost interest in the Pacific theatre and would heave a sigh of relief after Pearl Harbor ensured that the United States took on that burden. Canada's contribution of around 6,000 soldiers to the war effort in the Pacific was in no way comparable to the scale of its commitment to the European theatre.

Canadian Activism in Asia

In the post-war euphoria Canadians hardly noticed at first that their country had emerged as the second strongest economy in the world. The fact that Canada also had considerable political influence was, however, a reality that Lester Pearson and his small cohort of talented Foreign Service officers were not slow to exploit, although it required agility, *sang froid* and resourcefulness to do so. It started in Japan, where a select group of Asia specialists played a very active role in advising General Douglas MacArthur on the reconstruction and democratization of the country. More generally, however, the main institutions through which Canada conducted its post-war relations with Asia were the very institutions it had helped to shape: the United Nations and the Commonwealth, and the latter's newly minted Colombo Plan. If Canada had not played a significant part in these developments, its subsequent outlook on East Asia would no doubt have been quite different, yet it cannot be said that these initiatives all fit together in an overall plan. They happened piecemeal. Only when one looks at them together, many years later, can one propose that there was a theme to all this "helpful fixer" activity, as Pierre Trudeau labelled it many years later.

Again, if the Korean War had not erupted when it did, in June 1950, Canada's relations with China would have been quite different throughout the Cold War (Ronning 1974, p. 179). Indeed, some claim that the Korean emergency need only have started six weeks later for Canada's position in relation to China to have been radically altered. That strikes me as far-fetched. Mutual recognition might well have been established with Beijing at that time, but it would probably not have hindered or delayed our participation in the UN-approved multinational force under US command. It certainly would not have been a propitious beginning for renewed bilateral relations. Even though it might have given Canada easier access to Beijing as the war progressed, it is doubtful that it would have changed much in the *déroulement* of that war. As it was, Lester Pearson failed to dissuade MacArthur from crossing the 38th Parallel and heading towards the Yalu River, nor could he restrain the latter's nuclear sabre-rattling against China (Pearson 1973, pp. 159–64). Much more evident is the fact that Canada's Cold War stance, in spite of its insistence that the North Atlantic alliance had no relevance to East Asia, reflected a mindset that determined a readiness to bear arms in the face of open aggression against non-Communist regimes. In other words, the Cold War became the thematic backdrop for much of Canada's intentions and actions in the Far East (Stairs 1974, pp. 128–30).

How Did We Get Here?

If there are trends to be drawn from this brief outline of Canada's meandering into the politics of East Asia, they certainly do not denote a determined attempt at developing a Canadian policy toward China, much less a strategy. The 1950s, and more specifically the Korean conflict, marked an hour of awakening. For the first time, Canadians were forced to conclude that the British and US approaches were not reconcilable. Moreover, neither seemed to fit into any scenario that would suit Canada's objective of keeping the situation from deteriorating into a long-term confrontation between East and West. In particular, Canadian leaders came to the conclusion that the US approach risked spreading war to China and the rest of Asia. In 1954, when the first Taiwan Straits crisis erupted, Ottawa found itself pleading that Quemoy and Matsu did in fact belong to the People's Republic, which represented no threat to the West (Geoffrey Pearson, p. 132). In September the same year, when the United States created SEATO, a collective defence pact modelled on NATO with the Philippines, Pakistan, Australia, New Zealand, France, Taiwan and the United Kingdom, Canada's participation was not sought, nor did Canada wish for it. By this time the Canadian government had begun to have serious doubts about the wisdom of the US strategy in Asia.

In less than twenty years, tumultuous though they were, Canada's view of East Asia had gone from a passing interest, through a distant concern, to a current and persistent headache. The Geneva Conference held in 1954 to settle the conflict in former French Indochina seemed for a moment to hold out a promise of some *détente* in Cold War animosity. It was short-lived, however, and it saddled Canada with a role about which decision-makers had serious reservations. The three International Commissions for Supervision and Control for Vietnam, Laos and Cambodia, on which Canada was to serve alongside India and Poland, were not under UN direction, and the United States had made it clear that it would not consider itself bound by the Commissions' findings or recommendations. In addition to the cost in human resources, the resultant delay in opening official relations with China was even more regrettable. It is ironic to note here that not long after Lester Pearson had been subjected to a violent harangue by President Lyndon B. Johnson at his Texas ranch, Pearson's foreign minister, Paul Martin Sr., undertook yet one more vain effort to seek an acceptable form of recognition of the People's Republic (English 1991, p. 141).

Recognition at last

Both the Indochina fiasco and the recognition conundrum had to await the arrival of new actors on the scene before they could be tackled conclusively.

For Canada, the principal new figure was Pierre Elliott Trudeau. Caught up in the new optimism of the 1960s and contemplating, somewhat prematurely, a radically changed world, Trudeau called for a rethinking of Canadian foreign policy. He imposed a new questioning of previous stances: Had previous policies been too narrowly defined by fear of the Soviet menace? Had Canada been hoodwinked into seeking security under US leadership? Had Canada been too oblivious to the overbearing friendliness of its southern neighbour? These questions underlay Trudeau's prescription of a foreign policy rooted in domestic concerns. Economic growth and the quality of life were objectives that were thus dutifully enshrined in a (multicoloured) "White Paper," *Foreign Policy for Canadians* (see Department of External Affairs 1970). It caused quite a stir when it was published in 1970, especially since it implied criticism of Pearson's approach and policies.

In the final analysis, however, despite some trendy new management jargon in the paper and some exaggerated calls for new forms of action, Trudeau's government innovated in only two areas: China and NATO. The latter generated much heat in Ottawa and other capitals, but in the end resulted in no major change. The former was successful and at long last normalized Canada's relationship with China, just in time, some would say, to keep Richard Nixon from taking all the credit for China's opening to the West. Canadians have been understandably upset that in the United States and, indeed, the world over, the Nixon–Kissinger bombshell completely obscured Canada's achievement in clearing the way to ending the isolation of the People's Republic. Why did Canada get credit for this pioneering work only in Beijing and among a handful of Canadian scholars who study diplomatic history? The main reason is, of course, that the repercussions of Nixon's move marked a sea change in US geopolitical strategy and the first step towards a *détente* of a different order than that which was proving so tenuous with the Soviet Union in Europe. Hardly a single US commentator noticed that, by the time Nixon visited China, the Canadian Embassy in Beijing had been open for business for more than a year. It took Washington and Beijing another seven years before they were able to upgrade their liaison offices in each other's capitals to full-fledged embassies. In the meantime, no fewer than sixty-six other countries had established relations with Beijing, most of them using the Canadian "take note" formula regarding Taiwan.

The United States, of course, had to amend the Canadian formula, not only because of the pressures from its Taiwan lobby, but also because it sought to maintain most of the military ties it had forged with Taiwan since 1949. The Japanese, who negotiated recognition in 1972, were up against even more formidable difficulties resulting from the tragic past of their actions against China from 1894 to 1945, and the need to sign a peace treaty. The latter was negotiated over six years after the exchange of ambassadors in 1972. If one looks closely at these two agreements, both of them much more elaborate than the one with Canada that was their forerunner, what shines through clearly is the shared Japanese and US objective of preserving as much as they could of their former special ties to Taiwan. Both countries have since succeeded in doing so, to a certain extent, but only in exchange for a more clear-cut recognition of Beijing's claims to the island. It turned out, some twenty years later, to be a non-trivial point, since those who followed the Canadian formula are now in no way committed to withholding recognition from an eventual independent Taiwan. Such are the dynamics of diplomacy.

However world-shaking all this may have seemed at the time, there were hardly any immediate changes to be seen in bilateral relations, either after the Canadian breakthrough or after the signing of the Shanghai Communiqué by the People's Republic and the United States. When Trudeau undertook his first official visit to China, in 1973, the Chinese media greeted him warmly as a *lao pengyou*, an "old friend." Agreements were signed for the opening of consular missions, as well as for trade under most-favoured-nation terms. None of this, however, was to have any immediate effect. China first had to struggle through the last years of the Cultural Revolution, and the changing of the guard after the deaths of Zhou Enlai and Mao. It was not until Deng Xiaoping's reforms got under way that economic relations started to move into a higher gear. In 1983–1984 agreements were signed on launching aid through the Canadian International Development Agency (CIDA) and on the protection of investments. Trade accelerated, and investments grew in such fields as telecommunications, hydroelectric power and mining technology. Canadair and de Havilland, Alcan and Nortel all made their way into the Chinese mainland. The days when all trade had to be conducted at the semi-annual Canton Trade Fair were gone. The barometer for the relationship between Canada and China was at last set fair.

Tiananmen and After

All of this seemed to come crashing down with the disastrous events in and around Tiananmen Square in June 1989. The growth of trade slowed, investments from Canada plummeted, and non-commercial exchanges entered a difficult phase. Most of China's newfound partners, at least those outside Asia, asked themselves whether China was a country with which they could build a long-term future. On learning of Deng's subsequent intransigence, many people called for China to be punished. Canada did not follow the example of some of its allies by imposing significant trade sanctions, but it did curtail some CIDA programmes, especially those involving government agencies such as the security services and the police. Visits by senior officials were kept to a minimum and ministerial visits were ruled out for the time being (see Clark 1989). In Chinese eyes, however, Canada's most unpardonable act was to declare all Chinese studying in Canada at that time eligible for landed immigrant status. According to a classified briefing paper prepared by the Department of External Affairs in 1990, over eighty percent of them seized the opportunity thus offered.

I arrived in Beijing to take up my assignment as Ambassador in October 1990, in the midst of this period of deliberate coldness. It happened to be the week of the twentieth anniversary of the establishment of diplomatic relations. The only instructions I had were to refrain from any celebratory statements: "marking" the event was all we were doing. I couldn't help asking myself whether this was what we could have foreseen in the days when we were elaborating China policy pursuant to the Trudeau initiative. Had no one entertained the notion that Chinese reforms might someday lead to upheavals and that the regime would resort to violence to retain its hold on power? Indeed, I do recall some memorandums of the early 1980s in which such possibilities were raised, but Deng's smiling face and his reassuringly pragmatic approach to modernization, combined with the rise of Gorbachev, the fall of the Berlin Wall and the liberation of Central and Eastern Europe, had mesmerized most Western governments into the belief that Communist regimes, on every continent, were on the way out.

One year earlier I had had the privilege of attending the political meetings of the annual G7 summit, that time in Paris. When it came to discussions of how to show disapproval of what had happened in Beijing just a few weeks before, there was a consensus that each member country should institute some sort of sanctions; each being left to choose the type and intensity. The United States was unwilling to limit its military cooperation with China because it did not wish to jeopardize its listening posts on Soviet activities to the north and west of China. The British, fearful of how Beijing might react to the gigantic public demonstrations in Hong Kong, sought to keep their own reaction muted. Listening to the earnest and shocked entreaties from Margaret Thatcher and George Bush Sr., and the extensive discussions that followed, none of my Canadian colleagues nor I imagined that within a very short time this entente would be broken by more than one of the participants. In fact, two weeks before the meeting in Paris the United States had already secretly sent two emissaries, National Security Advisor Brent Scowcroft and Deputy Secretary of State Lawrence Eagleburger, to assure Deng that President Bush wished for the close relations between China and the United States to continue (Suettinger, pp. 79–83). Less than five months later, the United Kingdom sent its own secret envoy on a similar mission. Japan, on the other hand, reluctant from the outset to impose any sanctions at all, was the first to lift the economic and aid restrictions it had imposed, and did so by the end of the year. What happened to the mood of the Pearson and Trudeau years, when one dared to dream of "participatory internationalism"?

A "Mature Relationship"

Up to that point Canada had caused the Chinese government few problems, indeed none that had raised more than the occasional eyebrow in the Chinese leaders' compound in Zhongnanhai. No one there harboured any serious doubts about Canada's sincerity in striving to develop ever more cooperative relations. During some ministerial visits, and even during the visit of Governor General Jeanne Sauvé in 1987, qualms had been expressed regarding human rights, but never with much insistence, and certainly with no implication that the subject might harm the future of our relations. All that had changed on June 4, 1989, and bilateral ties entered a new, more mature phase. Maturity is usually an irreversible process, but does it mean that previous levels of trust and cooperation can never be recovered? The future was to answer both "Yes" and "No" to this question.

At this juncture, I must confess that the official coolness in our relations paradoxically afforded me and my team at the Embassy a certain latitude in action that we would not have had under the more hectic pace of bilateral visits and incessant requests for information that had characterized the period before Tiananmen. I was able to proceed without interruption to get acquainted with my staff, learn the special features of our mission's *modus operandi*, and call on many diplomatic colleagues, several of whom were in Beijing on their third or fourth assignment. All the Western-oriented ones gave me valuable insight into the ways in which they were coping with the strained relations between our hosts and their respective headquarters. Least expected was the eagerness with which major government officials, including Politburo members, were prepared to grant me interviews, not simply to reiterate the message I had been hearing loud and clear since landing at the airport—that "China's reforms and opening to the outside will continue unabated"—but also to encourage any contact and activity that could give the appearance of normal relations and business as usual.

Executives from the relatively few Canadian firms that had remained active in China during these troubled times were delighted to find that, with less than forty-eight hours' notice, I could take them to call on virtually any Chinese minister to make representations on whatever venture they were encountering difficulties with. Years later, when things had returned to "normal," they referred to this period as the "halcyon" days. Relations did not, of course, return to normal that quickly, nor for that matter did China's economic development, but by 1991 trade figures were up from the previous lows. Our CIDA officers managed without difficulty to reorient their objectives so as to favour more grassroots activities and even the immigration branch was able, through the drop in two-way traffic, to refurbish its appallingly overcrowded and understaffed premises.

I soon became aware, however, that the mutual striving for "normal relations" was a two-edged sword. The Chinese side could hardly maintain for long their extremely polite and productive demeanour while bemoaning that there were no high-level visits between our two countries. On our side, I asked myself how one could continue to take advantage of this positive atmosphere while trying to introduce human rights issues into bilateral discussions. I wrote in my diary at the time:

> The mission is beginning to work at cross purposes. The political section remains eager to track human rights violations, while the trade section calls for discretion, lest their trade promotion activities be hampered. Tomorrow I'm to make a *démarche* on the Minister of Industry on behalf of a Canadian company that feels aggrieved by the uneven playing field on which it is having to face other foreign competitors. Obviously that's not the moment to bring up the forthcoming trial of a well-known dissident. (See Bild, p.4).

Nonetheless, the political section of the Embassy kept close track of the human rights situation, particularly as the dissidents of 1989 were brought to trial one after the other. We made representations to the Foreign Ministry and lost few opportunities to impress upon our various Chinese interlocutors the opprobrium that China was reaping through the harsh sentences being meted out. I even took the message to the provinces, figuring that local officials would be more susceptible to such representations. At the outset, I quite relished the exercise and, while sitting next to some local potentate at a lavish banquet, would whip out a list of political prisoners alleged to be in his province's jails. This rude behaviour tended to startle them, but only rarely elicited anything other than the standard reply: "the only people in prison are criminals, not political activists, and local governments cannot intervene or even raise questions about names on a list, since that would infringe upon the independence of the judiciary." The experience was sometimes amusing, usually a bit chilling, and always without any noticeable effect. My efforts to enlist the cooperation of like-minded members of the diplomatic corps in this exercise were largely unsuccessful. A few tried to emulate my antics, only to become disillusioned. At a more junior level, however, we did manage to get a cooperative tracking and light harassment activity organized. Stalwart young officers from a few Western embassies took turns making early morning visits to the Ministry of Justice, where the day's upcoming trials were posted. Whenever a known dissident's name was on the list, one of these courageous young diplomats would knock at the courthouse door and ask for permission to attend. Rebuffed every time, they nevertheless persisted for several months until the series of trials came to a close.

While this painful internal process was going on, the smiling face of China was being beamed to all its neighbours. The foreign minister, Qian Qichen, undertook a series of visits to all the countries of the region. Mutual recognition was restored with Indonesia and Singapore, and diplomatic relations were established with Brunei. China was now in position to seek the status of a dialogue partner of the Association of South-East Asian Nations. (See Deng and Yang, pp. 113-116). North Korea was manoeuvred into accepting the "two Koreas" solution for membership in the United Nations. India agreed to resume boundary talks (the only ones that would not be settled definitively). Vietnam finally accepted China's terms for normalizing relations. South Korea switched its recognition from Taipei to Beijing. Cross-border trading posts were opened with Russia and the recently independent republics of Central Asia. Qian Qichen was able to boast, in a speech to the diplomatic corps at the Foreign Ministry in June 1991, that his "policy of good neighbourliness has created harmony throughout Asia."

Meanwhile, Canadian policy on China remained unmoving, not to say stagnant. Instructions from Ottawa became less and less clear. Rumours reached us of divisions within the Cabinet, with the ministers bearing economic portfolios calling, though not loudly, for a resumption of high-level visits for the benefit of the business community. The Canadian foreign minister at the time, Barbara McDougall, who seemed to have made China-bashing her favourite pastime, insisted on keeping China in Coventry (according to one of the first high-level Canadian dignitaries to resume contact with China in 1992). None of this was enough to frustrate my team of exceptionally enterprising officers, except on such rare occasions as when three Members of Parliament, Beryl Gaffney (Liberal), Svend Robinson (NDP) and Geoff Scott (Progressive Conservative), descended on Tiananmen Square with the deliberate intention of creating a scene. Disregarding our clear instructions not to organize any kind of public event unless they wanted to land in jail, they went ahead and invited foreign media, through open-line telephone calls, to attend their placing of a wreath in memory of the victims of June 4. I won't recount our representations at the Foreign Ministry except to say that, after the trio had been expelled *manu militari*, I was able for several months thereafter to embarrass my hosts with veiled references to the high regard that Canadians have for elected representatives visiting us from afar. The area hit hardest, however, by this frosty Canadian approach was arts and culture. The business community in Ottawa still had enough clout to keep some export credit assistance alive, and CIDA had managed through bureaucratic momentum to keep most of its programmes in China afloat, but when it came to publications on Canada, orchestral tours or literary exchanges, budgets were at zero.

What distinguishes Foreign Service staff in the field from desk-bound bureaucrats at headquarters is that the former are not afraid to use their ingenuity. In this case, they encouraged Canadian study centres at some twenty-two Chinese universities to undertake translations of major Canadian works or organize scholarly conferences on Canadian subjects. They even managed to stage a Sino-Canadian conference, in Spring 1992, to discuss modern media challenges. A dozen Canadian producers, directors and distributors were brought together for a week with their Chinese counterparts. They came away with at least an inkling of the market opportunities then opening in China. The Chinese, for their part, gained a better idea of what could be obtained from "Hollywood North."

Take-Off Resumed

It was pure coincidence that this flight into the media arts happened as the Chinese economy regained its thrust. I wrote the following in my diary in 1992:

> Ever since May I've been involved almost full-time in commercial matters.... the number of Canadian visitors ...seems to be doubling by the week.... is this how trends affect policy? ...one deals with public relations only when nothing more immediate is at hand? ...In the commercial area trends appear so much more clearly.... after all, what was the impetus that brought the Canadian business community back to this side of the Pacific? ...hardly the speeches I made to Chambers of Commerce across Canada.... no, it was the eighty-eight-year-old Deng Xiaoping's "Nan Xun," his grand tour of the South, that did it. He exclaimed that the results of market reforms were spectacular and must be continued. Business took off again almost immediately and the investment queue never slackened again. The "almost" in the preceding sentence denotes a six-week hiatus between reports of Deng's declarations in the Guangdong press and an acknowledgement in the *People's Daily*. Future historians will tell us what occurred in that period.... the battles at the apex of the hierarchy must have been epic ...but it was a fine example of power, timing, and skill at staging a media event.

The brakes that had been put on economic reform in the immediate aftermath of Tiananmen were suddenly loosened. By the end of 1992 bilateral trade was at a high of 4.6 billion dollars, with capital goods accounting for more than half the total. Canadian investments had doubled over the previous year.

With all these positive developments, yet another serendipitous occurrence put us on a new human rights track. In early 1993, some of our Chinese university acquaintances suggested that we give some thought to joint university research projects in the area of institutional reform and democratic development. The idea apparently had support in inner councils in Beijing. The five scholars eventually chosen, supported by CIDA funds, left for a six-week study trip to examine Canada's democratic institutions and practices. The report they submitted to the State Council seemed to have had some effect, since it was mentioned to me on several occasions by senior officials whom I met at social functions. In the planning of China's fiscal reforms, they said, the Canadian tax system was being referred to frequently. It was still some distance from more liberating subjects, such as freedom of assembly or *habeas corpus*, but we thought it might be a start. Lo and behold, a few weeks later the Royal Society of Canada was invited to send a group of scholars to China to discuss "the transition from feudalism to the rule of law." This was to be the beginning of an ongoing dialogue among officials and experts on how to modernize state institutions, the dialogue that the present Canadian government unfortunately decided to cancel "for lack of results." It is not for me to comment on the progress in these exchanges after I was no longer on the scene, but what seems to have been overlooked in the hasty condemnation of one of the more successful projects of enlightenment is that these first steps of 1993 led in the same year to the training of Chinese judges at the Université de Montréal. Since then, according to CIDA (reporting in May 2010), more than 275,000 prosecutors, judges and criminal lawyers have received training in the application of Canadian and international legal and human rights standards. Only simplistic or ideologically twisted reasoning could refuse to recognize that such exposure of future generations of Chinese jurists will inevitably have an effect on China's reform of its legal system. I never encountered anyone in China who rejected the idea that legal and political modernization was necessary: the question to which no one had ready answers was how it was to come about. It is precisely this question of "how" that these programmes were addressing.

At the same time, Canada took initiatives to extend China's involvement in multilateral affairs. The Embassy pursued a dialogue at the highest levels of the Foreign Ministry on questions such as nuclear non-proliferation, regional security and restraints on the export of missile technology, as well as on the future of China's participation in the various Asia–Pacific cooperation bodies.

Thus it was that in the waning days of the Mulroney era had left the foreign ministry portfolio, the larger picture of Canada's interests in China once again came to the fore. The list of ministers waiting to visit China suddenly became overcrowded and more than our mission could handle. The Canadian Embassy in Beijing in 1988 had boasted a total of eleven commercial officers, the largest such complement of the entire Foreign Service. After June 1989, this number was reduced to six, not to grow again, except briefly before the Team Canada exercise in November 1994. Ad hoc infusions of assistance permitted us to cope. The air was not cleared, however, until the election of a new government in Ottawa and the statement by Prime Minister Jean Chrétien, on March 19, 1994, that no one should expect him to tell the Chinese government what to do when he could not even make any of the provincial governments toe the line. André Ouellet, the new Liberal foreign minister, thus had a ready-made platform for explaining the new government's revised approach on human rights: individual cases and particular problems would continue to be dealt with directly, but in private. In a wider context, however, human rights objectives were enshrined in the government's statement entitled *Foreign Policy on China: A Four-Pillar Partnership*. They would be advanced through cooperative constructive projects seeking to develop good government and the rule of law.

Who could have predicted that, a mere five years after the tragedy of Tiananmen, the Prime Minister of Canada, accompanied by nine provincial premiers, two territorial leaders, and close to 500 business people, would fill the Great Hall of the People, along with some 1,200 Chinese guests, including many provincial leaders, cadres and most of the *Who's Who* of the new Chinese business class? From then on, with Ottawa determined to forge an ever friendlier and more mutually beneficial relationship with Beijing, relations went from strength to strength. In 1997, Chinese and Canadian leaders agreed to build a "21st-century framework for partnership." By 2003 they had put in place a whole panoply of agreements to enhance political, economic and cultural collaboration in areas as diverse as animal and plant inspection and quarantine, shipping, air transport, potash, petroleum and nuclear energy development, and collaboration between judicial systems. China announced that it would establish a research facility at the vice-ministerial level on Sino-Canadian relations and coordinate positions on major international issues, as well as in the areas of energy, environmental protection and telecommunications.

In 2005, when Prime Minister Paul Martin Jr. made his first official visit to China, the two countries had already had some differences of view regarding Chinese mineral and petroleum acquisitions in Canada. Nonetheless, they signed a joint statement on energy cooperation, promising to work closely on oil sands, energy efficiency, the environment and related matters. When President Hu Jintao visited Canada later that year he talked of "upgrading the China–Canada comprehensive partnership." These were not just well-chosen words: they reflected actions that were already under way, as well as future intentions. Both governments had realized that if the world's environmental problems were to be taken seriously, they needed close cooperation on protecting the planet and developing greener technology. The advances being made in China today in new, environmentally friendly methods and machinery demonstrate that those policies were on the right track.

The long honeymoon was to sour thereafter, as several issues seemed to spell more trouble for the future of the relationship, including Canada's apparent inability to extradite Lai Changxing, whom China regards as its most wanted criminal; China's detention of the Uighur Canadian Huseyin Celil without recognizing his Canadian citizenship and associated consular rights; Ottawa's intervention in Chinese attempts to buy major interests in Canadian mining and oil companies; Beijing's refusal to grant official tourist destination status to Canada; and Ottawa's granting of honorary citizenship to the Dalai Lama. Of course, as a friend of mine used to say, the past is behind us, the present is uncertain and the future is always full of hope, but the recent past, despite current deliberate attempts to patch things up, has opened several areas whence misunderstanding, mistrust, and recrimination can reappear in old or new guises.

Conclusion

I trust that this narrative of Canada's evolving approach to foreign policy conundrums will have demonstrated that an absence of overriding strategic objectives was generally the rule. While the search for trade and investment opportunities was often a dominant motive, for a long time relations were mostly of an exploratory or hopeful nature and, when they were successful, it was more a result of luck rather than of precise planning. On the other hand, economic opportunities were frequently missed simply because of conflicting short-term political aims, as when racism on Canada's west coast coincided with inadequate labour supply. Indeed, one could point to similar conflicts today between political short-sightedness and longer-term fruitful relations with China.

None of the above is meant to underestimate Canadian foreign engagements. I am quite certain that a similar stock-taking of any other world power, major or secondary, would not be able to boast better batting averages. Such is the foreign affairs beast. What I do mean to underline, however, is that circumstances, the irrationality of some players, unpredictable events and sheer chance have fashioned our so-called policies more often than not. What ought to be obvious to any practitioner of the art is that the numerous foreign policy papers, whether they speak of "pillars" or "patterns," have hardly ever had any influence on what went on in practice, nor did they guide any policy-maker more than for a few hours after their publication. To point to Canada's obvious desire, from the early 20th century onward, to avoid having to chose between the United Kingdom and the United States, or to its later striving to become less dependent on either of them for trade, is no more enlightening than stating that a rat caught in a cage has as its first objective to get out and, second, to feed itself. If we must label the various stages of our relations with China, I would prefer to divide them into two major categories: those where there was a clearly evident policy line, applied with some consistency, and those where confusion and haphazardness were dominant. A superficial examination of Canada's relations with China over the past forty years would tend to place most of them in the second category. Since the "mature" relationship dates only from 1989, with the latter segment representing few mature features, one would have to conclude that the major part of this period should be classified as unclear. Coincidence, after all, is the vernacular of history.

References

Bild, F., article, Canada's Response to China in the 1990s: A View from the Field, *Journal CETASE*, Univ. de Montréal, 1996.

Canadian International Development Agency. (2010). "China Program" prepared by Asia Bureau, 4 May 2010.

Clark, Joe. (1989, June 30). "China and Canada: The Months Ahead." Ministerial Statement by the Secretary of State for External Affairs.

Creighton, Donald. (1976). *The Forked Road: Canada 1939–1957*. Toronto: McClelland & Stewart.

Deng, Y., Wang, F., (eds.) (2005) *China Rising: Power and Motivation in Chinese Foreign Policy*, Rowman & Littlefield, Lanham MD. 69-71.

Department of External Affairs. (1970). *Foreign Policy for Canadians*. Ottawa: Information Canada.

English, John. (1991). "Lester Pearson and China," in *Reluctant Adversaries: Canada and the People's Republic of China, 1949–1970*, ed. Paul M. Evans and B. Michael Frolic. Toronto, Buffalo, NY, and London: University of Toronto Press, 133–47.

Gough, Barry M. (2000). "Meares, John," in *Dictionary of Canadian Biography Online*. Toronto: University of Toronto, and Quebec City: Université Laval. Online at http://www.biographi.ca/009004-119.01-e.php?&id_nbr=2552&in

terval=25&&PHPSESSID=o362fe0mehbneb8jc4eif14qe4 [consulted January 14, 2011].

Pearson, Geoffrey A.H. (1993), *Seize the Day: Lester B. Pearson and Crisis Diplomacy*, Carlton University Press, Ottawa, 132.

Pearson, Lester B. (1973). *Mike: The Memoirs of the Right Honourable Lester B. Pearson*. Vol. 2: *1948–57*, ed. John A. Munro and Alex I. Inglis. Toronto, Buffalo, NY, and London: University of Toronto Press.

Ronning, Chester. (1974). *A Memoir of China in Revolution: From the Boxer Rebellion to the People's Republic*. New York: Pantheon Books.

Stairs, Denis. (1974). *The Diplomacy of Constraint: Canada, the Korean War, and the United States*. Toronto, Buffalo, NY, and London: University of Toronto Press.

Suettinger, Robert L. (2003). *Beyond Tiananmen: The Politics of U.S.–China Relations, 1989–2000*. Washington, DC: Brookings Institution Press.

Chapter 3

The Canadian Policy Context
of Canada's China Policy since 1970

Charles Burton

Commentary on relations between Canada and China relations tends to lament the shortcomings of Canada's response to the challenge of China's dramatic rise to power over the past thirty years. The perception is that Canada is not sufficiently politically and economically committed to China for Canada fully to realize Canadian interests in China. The focus of this analysis has been on the very dynamic changes in China since China embarked on policies of "opening and reform" in 1978. The argument is that China is transforming dramatically year by year through a staged process of sloughing off the legacy of Marxist ideology and Leninist organization that informed the People's Republic of China from 1949 until the inauguration of the new paradigm of "opening and reform" in late 1978. This line of argument maintains that Canada is not keeping up with innovative policy and greater commitment of government resources to engage China in ways that adequately meet the imperatives of China's ongoing transformation and expansion.

However, this kind of analysis is based on a narrative that is "China-led," in the sense that China is seen as highly active in the dynamic, while Canada is depicted as a largely static and passive entity. It tends to downplay the dramatic transformation of the international context as a whole and Canada's commensurate reinterpretation of its own position and role in international relations since 1970. It also does not take into account core aspects of China's political, economic and social system that are fundamental to the regime, and therefore are not amenable to reform so long as the current regime remains in place.

The Trudeau Era: Rapprochement with China, 1968–1984

The establishment of diplomatic relations between Canada and China in 1970 was a highly controversial political decision for Canada in the context of the times. Due the xenophobic imperatives of the "anti-imperialist," "anti-colonialist" Marxist discourse that legitimated the assumption of state power by the new Communist regime after the establishment of the new People's Republic of China in 1949, interaction between Canada and China in all aspects had been very much reduced. Soon after the new Communist government came to power it had ordered nearly all the resident Canadian business people and missionaries, including doctors and teachers, many of whom had been resident in China for many years, to leave the country and resettle elsewhere. Those expelled included the children of Canadians who had been born in China. Only a very small handful of Canadian Communist fellow travellers were allowed to stay on in the "New China."

China's entry into the Korean War engaged Canada and the People's Republic in direct hostilities that, for the first time in our countries' histories, saw Canadians and Chinese confronting each other on the battlefield. In the years that followed there was a common perception in the West, exacerbated by US McCarthyist fear-mongering, that the Russian-dominated Soviet Union and "Red China" secretly shared a foreign policy agenda to "liberate" all the nations of the world through "revolutions" informed by Marxist-Leninist ideology. The fear was that Communist subversion might ultimately transform Canada into a totalitarian dictatorship answerable to the Soviet Union. As the West and the Soviet Bloc vied for the allegiance of the post-colonial Third World, a new fear of a "domino effect," in which one Asian nation after another succumbed to Communism, seized the imagination of US policy-makers. Many interpreted this in terms of the "Soviet alliance" gradually moving toward achieving a critical balance of power in the Cold War. The future of Canada as a Christian nation, loyal to the British Crown and based on principles of liberal democracy and private enterprise, was perceived as being under severe threat.

The Chinese Nationalist regime in exile in Taiwan, fighting to regain its control of the Chinese mainland, was seen as a beacon of hope for a reversal of this ominous trend. The Nationalist regime, despite being in effective political control only of Taiwan and a few other islands off the southern Fujian coast, was diplomatically recognized by Canada as the sole legitimate government of the whole of China. On that basis, the Nationalist regime occupied China's permanent seat on the UN Security

Council. Reports of economic chaos, famine and severe political repression in China through the 1950s and 1960s enhanced the urgency that many Canadians felt about continuing to support the remnant Nationalist regime's thin aspirations to "gloriously retake the mainland" from the "Communist bandits," despite the fact that almost the entire population of China lived securely within the People's Republic. The authority of the Chinese Communist Party was well consolidated by the early 1950s, after a series of political campaigns had effectively decimated any political opposition. Canada's lack of any formal institutional relations with the most populous nation on Earth was a highly irregular state of affairs. The diplomatic conundrum was that neither the Republic of China based in Taiwan nor the People's Republic would abide any cross-recognition of "two Chinas."

In 1970, after years of negotiations, the governments of Canada and the People's Republic managed to finesse this point, and thereby remove a significant barrier to formal diplomatic relations and the exchange of embassies. The "Canadian formula" with regard to the mainland regime's claims over Taiwan was that the Canada "takes note of" them. This formed the basis for Canada's recognition of the People's Republic in October 1970 and was subsequently adopted by many other nations that recognized the People's Republic in the years following (see Canada, Foreign Affairs et al. 2010). Nevertheless, there was much political resistance in Canada to the requirement, negotiated between Ottawa and Beijing, that the diplomats of the Republic of China be made to close its Embassy and return to Taiwan before diplomatic relations between Canada and the People's Republic could finally be established (Evans and Frolic 1995, pp. 241–52).

This is not to say that Canada had not had any contact with mainland China at all between 1949 and 1970. In fact, Canada began a very significant trade with China in the form of wheat sales, starting in 1958. At that time China was suffering from a very severe food shortage due to the disastrous policies of the "Great Leap Forward" campaign. In 1961, an agreement was signed to ship CA$ 422 million worth of wheat to China over two and a half years (see Canada, Foreign Affairs et al. 2010). This initiative was undertaken at the behest of Alvin Hamilton, the Minister of Agriculture in the Progressive Conservative government of Prime Minister John Diefenbaker. These sales to China were much opposed at the time by supporters of Canada's role in the Commonwealth, who felt that supplying China with so much wheat would have the effect of aiding China in its very serious conflict with India, one of Canada's Commonwealth partners.

Moreover, the United States had a very strict embargo on trade with the People's Republic at this time.

This major Canadian trade initiative with China amounted to an audacious challenge to the China policy of the United States. Alvin Hamilton's initiative was seen as a signal that Canada's foreign policy would be made in Canada and would promote Canadian values in international affairs. Canada was anxious to make it clear to the United States, to the world and to Canadians themselves that Canada would not simply follow in lockstep with the foreign policy doctrine of the United States. As Canada became much less a functionary of Britain in the post-war period, questions of Canadian identity had assumed new urgency. The cultural imperative for Canada to distance itself from the United States was deeply felt by much of the Canadian population in those years. (Today the main public function room in the Canadian Embassy in Beijing is named the Alvin Hamilton Room in honour of his contribution to the development of relations between Canada and China.)

The Diefenbaker government's "wheat diplomacy" with China set the stage for Canada's initiatives in the 1960s and 1970s, aimed at growing closer diplomatically to the People's Republic. It is important to note that Canada's approaches to China under Prime Minister Lester Pearson, and then under Prime Minister Pierre Trudeau, took place at the height of the Vietnam War. At that time China was supporting the regime of Ho Chi Minh with arms and logistics, so that, as Canada was negotiating formal diplomatic relations with the People's Republic, Chinese-supplied guns, bombs, and grenades were killing the young drafted soldiers sent to Vietnam by Canada's neighbour and close ally the United States. It was also at exactly this time that China was engaged in the highly anti-American ideological campaign that formed part of its "Cultural Revolution." Canada's approaches to the Chinese regime to establish formal diplomatic relations allowed Canada's Liberal government to continue to "play the China card," and thus very explicitly and forcefully assert its foreign policy as being independent of that of the United States. From the Canadian point of view, this can be paired with Trudeau's outreach at the same time to Fidel Castro's regime in Cuba, another arch-enemy of the United States.

Reflecting on the motives for Canada's decision to formally recognize the People's Republic in October 1970, it now seems clear that engagement of China through formal diplomatic relations would reduce China's diplomatic isolation, and lead to China becoming a more active and responsible member of the community of nations (see Evans 2009). Moreover, one might today look to Trudeau's watchword of "reason over passion" as an explicatory factor. The Nationalist government in Taipei controlled territory occupied by just one sixtieth of the Chinese population, so it made rational sense to change to having diplomatic relations with the government in Beijing, which was in control of the territory occupied by the other fifty-nine sixtieths of the Chinese population.

By the late 1960s as the People's Republic celebrated twenty years of stable, albeit ruthless, Communist rule, many Canadians no longer perceived the regime in Taiwan as a beacon of hope for the "free world," but rather reinterpreted it as one of many morally bankrupt and corrupt right-wing military regimes throughout the world supported by the military and economic might of the United States. These ranged from the "banana republics" in Central and South American to the regimes of Mobutu Sese Seko in Zaïre and of Ferdinand Marcos in the Philippines. Mao Zedong's regime was apparently identified with the interests of workers and peasants, and committed to comprehensive social justice, including egalitarian distribution of China's national wealth. It was seen by many in Canada as offering an exemplary developmental model for Third World development.

Arguably of greater significance, these diplomatic initiatives can be seen as responding to the strain of thought in Canada at the time that the global spread of US technology and capital would have a profound impact in transforming domestic economic and political institutions, and might even destroy their soul, culture, spirit and identity. This idea was articulated at length by the distinguished Canadian "Red Tory" philosopher George Grant (see Grant 1965), and had strong currency among leftist Canadian nationalists, whose political stance was strongly anti-American. These leftist Canadian nationalists were entranced by the idea of Mao's China forging a Chinese response to the crisis of modernity on Chinese terms, being beholden neither to the Soviet Union nor to the United States, and thus allowing the Chinese people to be, as these Canadians understood it at least, more truly human. It goes without saying that there was much misinformation and naïveté about the true nature of the Chinese "Cultural Revolution" in Canada in those years.

Trudeau's visit to China in 1973 was important symbolically, in that Trudeau met at length with Premier Zhou Enlai and more briefly with Chairman Mao Zedong, and travelled in China accompanied by Zhou and the recently rehabilitated Deng Xiaoping. However, the visit had few substantive results, beyond a consular agreement that led to some Chinese citizens being permitted to reunite with family in Canada, and some sports and public health exchanges.

Overall, in these first ten years of relations Canada was not able to do much to realize its interests in China. Levels of trade, except for wheat, remained very low. Bilateral and multilateral relations in other areas were also quite constrained by China's xenophobic ultra-ideological policies of those years. Movement of people back and forth between Canada and China was also very limited. Canada's entire immigration programme in China was handled by a single clerk on a part-time basis. Canadians resident in China in the 1970s amounted to a small number of diplomats, fewer than twenty Canadian exchange students, a handful of Canadians working as translators and teachers, and no business people at all. They could all be easily gathered around the Embassy swimming pool in Beijing on Canada Day.

The level of activity between Canada and China was low, but relations were "friendly," as many Canadians were strongly supportive of the policies of the Chinese Communist Party during these years. Canada–China Friendship Associations sprung up all over Canada, and the emphasis was on Canadians "learning from China." This "friendship" was not a mutual interaction, in the sense that the base-line assumption of this friendship was that Chinese socialism was morally superior to Canadian capitalism.

The Chinese Communist Party's decision in December 1978 to repudiate the policies of the Cultural Revolution as "ten years of disaster," and in general to abandon the "movement politics" and "socialist economics" of China's Marxist era after the death of Chairman Mao, was something of a shock to the pro-Maoist political pretensions of the Canadian "friends of China." However, after China's adoption of policies of "opening and reform," the possibilities for deepening relations between Canada and China became much heightened, and there was much enthusiasm for this development on both sides. In 1979, Canada extended a $2 billion line of credit to encourage expansion of economic relations under the new conditions. A small development aid programme run out of the Canadian Embassy in Beijing began in 1981. A general agreement on development cooperation was signed in 1983, a major step forward as under Mao China had refused developmental assistance from Western nations. The Canadian International Development Agency (CIDA) was to help China to "build international linkages and learn from foreign expertise by supporting people-to-people contacts and education programs in Canada and China" (see Canadian International Development Agency 2005). Twinning agreements between Canadian and Chinese provinces and municipalities also grew apace, with high levels of activity back and forth (see Canada 2009).

In January 1984 the Chinese Premier Zhao Ziyang became the first Communist leader to address a joint session of the Canadian Parliament. The degree of effusiveness with which Zhao was greeted in Canada could not have been greater. In his introductory remarks, Prime Minister Pierre Trudeau noted that "our bilateral relations have achieved such variety, depth and warmth," and effused about his "most valued memory" of his visit to China in 1973, when he had discussed politics with Zhou Enlai "far into the night." In thanking Premier Zhao, the Speaker of the House of Commons, Lloyd Francis, referred to a parliamentary delegation that visited China in 1983, noting with evident enthusiasm that "all members of the delegation were absolutely delighted with their visit" (see Parliament of Canada 1984). It is puzzling today to try to comprehend how elected members of the legislature of a liberal democracy such as Canada could have been "delighted" by an authoritarian one-party state whose legislature meets for only two weeks a year in a committee of the whole to rubber-stamp approval for the often repressive rule of the Chinese Communist Party. It appears that Canadian concerns about pervasive reports of human rights violations in China were not raised while Zhao Ziyang was in Canada, despite Trudeau's determined championing of the new Canadian Charter of Rights and Freedoms only two years before.

The newly elected Progressive Conservative Government of Brian Mulroney was probably less pleased by Zhao's meeting for ninety minutes in Zhongnanhai, the government compound in Beijing, with René Lévesque, the leader of Quebec's separatist Parti Québécois, in October 1984, but this had no impact on relations overall.

Canada's Response to China under Brian Mulroney after June 4, 1989

The tone of relations between Canada and China was dramatically transformed after the Tiananmen incident in 1989 (see Brook 1992). Many Canadians had been elated by the "democratic spring" in Beijing that year, identifying it with recent "people power" movements along the lines of Solidarity in Poland or the People Power Revolution that had toppled the authoritarian regime of Ferdinand Marcos in the Philippines in 1986. The televised images of the military suppression of the movement in Beijing after June 4, 1989, brought home to Canadians the powerful reality of the Chinese Communist security apparatus, which was jarringly dissonant with the naïve warmth with which most Canadians had previously approached China's authoritarian regime.

On June 5, the Parliament of Canada held an emergency debate on the situation. Bullets had come through the window of the Canadian diplomatic staff quarters at Jianguomenwai. Canadian students in Beijing were encamped on the grounds of the Embassy compound awaiting evacuation. Joe Clark, Minister of Foreign Affairs, made a statement on behalf of the government: "I know that all members of the House of Commons and, indeed, all Canadians, share a deeply felt sense of horror and of outrage at the events that have unfolded over the last few days in China" (as quoted in Mulroney 2007, p. 665). In a statement to the press, Prime Minister Brian Mulroney said: "We are appalled by the tragedy that has been visited upon young people in China seeking greater democratic freedoms within the system. It's a calamity for them and it's a calamity for the breath of fresh air that was a democratic impulse running throughout China" (quoted in Mulroney 2007, pp. 665–66). As Mulroney recalls in his autobiography (Mulroney 2007, p. 666):

> I also spoke in Vancouver just a few days after the Chinese attack on the students. "I say to those young heroes: 'Do not despair, victory must eventually be yours because liberty cannot be denied.' Canada abhors the great tragedy that has been inflicted on those brave young leaders in Tiananmen Square. Indiscriminate shooting have [*sic*] snuffed out the precious human lives, but they can never snuff out the fundamental urge of human beings for freedom and democracy." …Joe [Clark] hauled in the Chinese Ambassador to Canada to register our disgust.

Fearing continuing civil unrest, many Canadian firms closed their representative offices in Beijing after repatriating Canadian staff. The Canadian Ambassador, Earl Drake, was withdrawn to Ottawa for prolonged consultations. All Chinese nationals in Canada were eventually granted Minister's Permits and allowed to remain in Canada permanently if they wished. Most of them did so, causing considerable complaint from the government of China, particularly in respect of those scholars who had come to Canada on Chinese government funding. Canada banned sales to China of weaponry and other goods deemed to have military applications, CIDA suspended negotiations with China's Ministry of Commerce for development aid projects worth a total of about CA$ 60 million, and CA$ 11 million worth of ongoing programming was scrapped, since China would not send participants to Canada for training as they would likely not return to

China. A moratorium on high-level contacts between the governments of Canada and China was also announced (see Gecelovsky and Keenleyside 1995). In 1990 the reduced Canadian Embassy in Beijing was directed by Ottawa that there should be "no celebratory activities" marking the twentieth anniversary of the opening of diplomatic relations.

In fact, this stated policy of shunning the Communist government of China was not strictly observed. In the months and years that followed, a series of cabinet ministers met with their Chinese counterparts in Beijing and took part in bilateral consultations at international meetings in other countries. There was a strong policy undercurrent that supported continued engagement of China as the most effective way to realize Canada's aspirations for that nation (see Gecelovsky and Keenleyside 1995). In April 1992 a trade delegation led by Michael Wilson, Minister for Industry, Science and Technology and Minister for International Trade, marked the restoration of normal government-to-government relations between Canada and China. The Canadian policy of shunning China had effectively failed and had had no significant impact on the Chinese regime, which carried on the *status quo ante*. Canadian dreams of Chinese democracy had crashed on the shoals of Chinese Communist authoritarian reality.

Jean Chrétien's "Team Canada": Engagement with China, 1993–2003

Liberal Prime Minister Jean Chrétien subsequently led "Team Canada" trade missions to China in 1996, 1998 and 2001. The last was the largest trade mission in Canadian history to date. Chrétien was accompanied by close to 600 business participants, eight provincial premiers, three territorial leaders, the Minister for International Trade, Pierre Pettigrew, and the Secretary of State (Asia–Pacific), Rey Pagtakhan. On the economic front, the strategy was to send a critical mass of Canadian business people, buttressed by the highest level of political support, to induce Chinese state-owned enterprises and smaller businesses to consider contracting for Canadian products and services. As for Canada's agenda of promoting liberal democracy and respect for human rights in China, Chrétien evidently shared the opinion of many in Canada's business community that economic opening would eventually produce political democratization (see Evans 2009), and that directly raising Canadian concerns over human rights abuses in China could have a negative impact on Canada's economic interests in China. Indeed, in 1994, after his meeting with the Chinese President, Jiang Zemin, Chrétien made a high-profile public statement that he was skeptical of the efficacy of directly raising human rights concerns with the Chinese leadership: "I'm the Prime Minister of a country of twenty million people. He's the President of a country with 1.2 billion. I'm not allowed to tell the Premier of Saskatchewan or Quebec what to do. Am I supposed to tell the President of China what to do?" He reiterated this policy stance, which must have been very well received by the Chinese Communist leadership, in 2008 (see Gee 2008).

Chrétien visited China six times while he was in office and forged close personal ties with China's Communist leaders (see Chrétien 2007, pp. 339–43). His son-in-law, André Desmarais, is honorary Chairman of the Canada–China Business Council, President of the Power Corporation, which has extensive interests in China, and a director of the China International Trust and Investment Corporation (CITIC), a Chinese state-owned conglomerate. Some suggest that Chrétien's stance on human rights in China, which he maintained after leaving office, has been "heavily freighted with personal and private interests" (see McParland 2008). In November 1998, when he was still Prime Minister, and leading one of his Team Canada missions, Chrétien did make a strong statement on human rights in a speech at Tsinghua University in Beijing, saying: "I would be less than frank if I did not say directly to you that many Canadians are disturbed when we hear of people being arrested or in prison for expressing political views different from the government" (Chrétien 2007, p. 343). Nevertheless, Chrétien's policy on promotion of good governance, democratic development and human rights was managed in an ambiguous way that sent out mixed signals to the Chinese authorities on Canada's commitment to this aspect of the bilateral relationship.

Despite these very proactive initiatives undertaken in the Chrétien era, Canada's trade and investment in the Chinese market have not been as strong as those of other nations. According to numbers given in the United Nations Commodity Trade Statistics Database, in 1997 only 0.93 percent of Canada's total exports went to China, and this amounted to 1.41 percent of China's total imports. However, Canada's share of China's imports dropped overall to 1.06 percent in 2003, even though this amounted to 1.61 percent of Canada's total exports. Thus, while Canada's absolute amount of exports to China increased, its share of China's import market decreased significantly. Canada's share of the Chinese import market bottomed out at 0.97 percent in 2006. After the Conservatives under Prime Minister Stephen Harper assumed power, Canada's share of Chinese imports modestly increased to 1.12 percent in 2008 and the total proportion of Canada's exports that went to China reached a new high of 2.71 percent. Canada has a huge merchandise trade deficit of about four to one with China, and it has generally been widening over the past fifteen years. In sharp contrast to Canada, Australia has achieved a modest surplus in its trade with China: Australia's exports to China grew by 45.4 percent in 2008, compared to growth of only 19.5 percent in China's exports to Australia (see Australia 2010). Moreover, according to a report published in the *Globe and Mail* in 2009, there were 130,000 Chinese students studying in Australia, compared to 42,000 studying in Canada, even though Australia has ten million fewer people than Canada (see Wheeler 2009).

The factors that have led to Canada's relatively disappointing performance in the Chinese market have been articulated along three main lines of interpretation. First, the interpretation put forward by the Federal Government Policy Research Initiative is that the trade imbalance reflects the structural characteristics of the Canadian economy in relation to China's within the global economy. This interpretation implies that there is no need for government to see this trade imbalance as a problem, since it is a phenomenon reflecting global market economic principles (see Ghosh and Wang 2006). Second, other observers attribute Canada's weak performance to specifically Chinese factors, such as manipulation of currency exchange rates to keep Chinese exports cheap and imports expensive, hidden subsidies to Chinese state-owned enterprises and local government subsidies to local businesses, local government connivance in preventing Canadian businesses in China from repatriating profits through theft of intellectual property, unfair adjudication of disputes with local partners, and other non-tariff barriers, including secret non-market, politically based decisions to give business to firms from countries other than Canada because of the regime's unhappiness with the government's "unfriendly" political engagement with the Chinese central authorities. Third, still other observers argue that the problem lies in the "culture" of Canadian business, which lacks vision and drive, and is conditioned by "coddling" from government subsidies and incentive programmes. The Canadian Chamber of Commerce, for example, has said that "many companies are small, 'unworldly' and risk-averse, with limited knowledge of the Chinese market" (see Canadian Chamber of Commerce 2006).

This last explanation appears to be the most convincing overall, but another important factor that is difficult to square with any of these three interpretations is that there are proportionately five times as many people of Chinese ancestry in Canada as in the United States, so Canada should have a significant advantage in terms of language, cultural understanding and willingness to function in a Chinese environment.

Canada's Engagement of China Today

There is a high degree of consensus across all the Canadian federal parties that Canada's priorities with regard to China are, first, to promote prosperity through trade and investment, and, second, to encourage high-quality Chinese immigrants to move to Canada. According to the most recent Census, conducted in 2006, of the 31.2 million residents of Canada 1.2 million identified themselves as Chinese. That amounts to about four percent of Canada's total population. Chinese is now the third most widely spoken language in Canada, after English and French.

Canada also wants to collaborate with China on matters of mutual concern that arise in a rapidly globalizing world, such as fair trade, environmental sustainability, limiting the spread of diseases, respect for human rights and fighting transnational crime. There is little room for partisan disagreement on any of this. Moreover, Canadians of all political stripes are concerned by reports of alleged human rights violations in China. Canada's foreign policy stands for freedom of expression, the right to religious and political freedom and the right to private property free from expropriation through corrupt deals. Even a "sensitive" political initiative such as extending honorary Canadian citizenship to the Dalai Lama received unanimous support in the Canadian House of Commons. Internationally, China's close relations with what Canada regards as unstable and repressive regimes in Burma, Sudan, North Korea, Zimbabwe and elsewhere are of concern to the government of Canada. Whoever forms the next government in Ottawa will likely continue to respect Canada's fundamental interests in its relations with China. The main factor distinguishing the Liberal Party from the Conservative Party, the NDP and the Bloc Québecois is the question of human rights. Lloyd Axworthy, who was foreign minister in the Liberal government of Jean Chrétien, initiated a confidential bilateral dialogue on human rights in 1997. The Liberal Party continues to support this "quiet diplomacy" approach to human rights engagement with China (see Liberal Party 2008). In 2006, however, Canada suspended this dialogue because it was seen as ineffective in furthering human rights in China (see Burton 2006 and 2009). Canada is concerned that, for example, China shows few signs of moving toward ratification of the International Covenant on Civil and Political Rights, which it signed in 1998. However, Canada is currently in discussions with China on a new mechanism for human rights engagement on terms that would be acceptable to both governments.

In general, Canada hopes to rethink and reinvigorate the way it engages China along many dimensions in the years ahead. For example, most of the younger Chinese diplomats in Canada have near-fluency in English or French, and many have graduate degrees from universities in Canada, the United States, Australia or Britain. Canada needs to send comparably qualified Canadians to China, preferably people who have done advanced study in China, but Canada is not yet doing to a sufficient extent, and is less effective in realizing its interests in China as a result. Canada also needs to overhaul the way Ottawa does its trade promotion in China. Canada needs a clear strategy for better access to the Chinese market, one that factors in the distinct characteristics of Chinese culture and Canada's comparative advantage in that market.

Finally, China requires comprehensive engagement. In the United States, Canada does not focus on the State Department alone. Canada's Embassy in Washington engages Congress, the President and all the elements of political power. This multifaceted approach is informed by a policy decision, taken more than twenty-five years ago, recognizing that diversified engagement is necessary in order to enhance Canadian interests in Washington. Likewise, Ottawa must engage Chinese policy-makers in both the government and the Communist Party, all of whose decisions have implications for Canada's interests. The focus of Canada's Department of Foreign Affairs and International Trade on China's Ministry of Foreign Affairs should be expanded to a more comprehensive engagement of the Chinese system. Canadian diplomats need to better recognize that many of the most influential players in the Chinese system are in Communist Party institutions.

In December 2009 Prime Minister Stephen Harper made an official visit to China, following the eighteen ministerial visits made to China since Harper formed his government in 2006. One notable accomplishment on this visit was that Canada was finally able to negotiate "approved destination" status for Chinese tourism to Canada, something that had not been achieved despite considerable efforts by the two previous prime ministers, Jean Chrétien and Paul Martin. While he was in China Prime Minister Party Harper articulated a theme about which there is a large degree of consensus in Canada: "Now is the time to enhance and expand our relationship, to build upon our mutual successes, and to use the authority these successes have afforded us to set an example for others in the world" (see Canada 2010). The Prime Minister also observed before leaving China that "Canada has made a real significant impact here, [but] at the same time we all sense we are only scratching the surface" (see CBC News 2009).

References

Australia. Department of Foreign Affairs and Trade. (2010). "China Fact Sheet."
  Online as http://www.dfat.gov.au/geo/fs/chin.pdf [consulted January 14, 2011].
Brook, Timothy. (1992). *Quelling the People: The Military Suppression of the Beijing
  Democracy Movement.* Toronto: Lester.
Burton, Charles. (2006). *Assessment of the Canada–China Bilateral Human Rights
  Dialogue.* Department of Foreign Affairs and International Trade. Electronic
  version online as http://spartan.ac.brocku.ca/~cburton/Assessment%20of%20
  the%20Canada-China%20Bilateral%20Human%20Rights%20Dialogue%20
  19APR06.pdf [consulted January 14, 2011].
Burton, Charles. (2009). *A Reassessment of Canada's Interests in China and Options
  for Renewal of Canada's China Policy.* A Changing World: Canadian Foreign
  Policy Priorities No. 4. Toronto: Canadian International Council. Electronic
  version online [membership required] at http://www.canadianinternational-
  council.org/research/canadianfo/areassessm [consulted January 14, 2011].
Canada. Department of Foreign Affairs and International Trade. (2009, November
  12). "Canada–China Twinning Relationships." Online at http://www.canadain-
  ternational.gc.ca/china-chine/bilateral_relations_bilaterales/twinning_relation-
  ships_relations_jumelage.aspx?lang=eng [consulted January 14, 2011].
Canada. Department of Foreign Affairs and International Trade. (2010). *40 Years
  of Canada–China Relations.* Online at http://www.canadainternational.gc.ca/
  china-chine/bilateral_relations_bilaterales/booklet-brochure.aspx [consulted
  January 14, 2011].
Canadian Chamber of Commerce. (2006). "China and Canada: The Way
  Ahead, Strategies and Solutions for Addressing Barriers to Enhanced Trade and
  Investment with China. Online [membership required] as http://www.chamber.
  ca/cmslib/general/china-e3.pdf [consulted January 14, 2011].
Canadian International Development Agency. (2005). "China: Governance."
  Online at http://www.acdi-cida.gc.ca/CIDAWEB/acdicidansf/En/JUD-
  31111939-M6C [consulted January 14, 2011].
CBC News. (2009, December 6). "Hong Kong to Accept Canada's Beef: Harper."
  Online at http://www.cbc.ca/world/story/2009/12/05/china-harper-hong-
  kong.html [consulted January 14, 2011].
Chrétien, Jean. (2007). *My Years as Prime Minister.* Toronto: Knopf Canada.
Evans, Paul. (2009, December 11). "Harper in China." *Toronto Star.* Online
  at http://www.thestar.com/comment/article/737389 [consulted January 14,
  2011].

Evans, Paul, and B. Michael Frolic, ed. (1991). *Reluctant Adversaries: Canada and the People's Republic of China*. Toronto, Buffalo, NY, and London: University of Toronto Press.

Gecelovsky, Paul, and T. A. Keenleyside. (1995, Summer). "Canada's International Human Rights Policy in Practice: Tiananmen Square." *International Journal* 50:3, 564–93.

Gee, Marcus. (2008, August 22). "C'mon, Mr. Chrétien, Our Voice on China Does Matter." *Globe and Mail*. Online at http://v1.theglobeandmail.com/servlet/story/RTGAM.20080821.wcogee22/BNStory/International/# [consulted January 14, 2011].

Ghosh, Madanmohan, and Weimin Wang. (2006). "Is Canada Underperforming in Foreign Direct Investments and Exports to China?" *Horizons* 9:2. Ottawa: Government of Canada Policy Research Initiative. Online as http://www.policyresearch.gc.ca/doclib/HOR_v9n2_200608_e.pdf [consulted January 14, 2011].

Grant, George. (1965). *Lament for a Nation: The Defeat of Canadian Nationalism*. Ottawa: Carleton University Press.

Liberal Party of Canada. (2008, January 16). "Chinese Ambassador Confirms Strained Canada–China Relationship." Press release. Online at http://charlesburton.blogspot.com/2008/01/liberal-party-china-policy-press.html [consulted January 14, 2011].

McParland, Kelly. (2008, August 22). "Jean Chrétien and the Power of China." *National Post*. Online at http://network.nationalpost.com/np/blogs/fullcomment/archive/2008/08/22/kelly-mcparland-jean-chretien-and-the-glory-that-is-china.aspx [consulted January 14, 2011].

Mulroney, Brian. (2007). *Memoirs, 1939–1993*. Toronto: McClelland & Stewart.

Parliament of Canada. (1984). "Address of Zhao Ziyang, Premier of the People's Republic of China to Both Houses of Parliament in the House of Commons Chamber, Ottawa on Tuesday January 17, 1984." Appendix to *House of Commons Debates Official Report* 1, 509–13.

Wheeler, Carolynne. (2009, October 7). "Canadian Universities Falling Behind in Drawing Students from China." *Globe and Mail*. Online at http://www.globecampus.ca/in-the-news/article/canadian-universities-falling-behind-in-drawing-students-from-china/ [consulted January 14, 2011].

Chapter 4

Canada and China:
The China Strategy of 1987

B. Michael Frolic

By 1985, fifteen years after Canada had recognized the People's Republic of China, relations between the two countries had reached a level of maturity. Trade was steadily expanding and China ranked as Canada's fifth largest trading partner. A growing number of high-level visits marked an apparent tightening of relations between the two governments. In early 1984 China's Premier, Zhao Ziyang, became the first leader of a Communist country to address the Canadian House of Commons. Both sides continued to invoke the spirit of Dr. Norman Bethune in declaring that they had developed "a special relationship." A fledgling aid programme administered by the Canadian International Development Agency (CIDA) had emerged as a promising link, and a family reunification programme, established during Prime Minister Pierre Trudeau's visit to China in 1973, had brought to Canada over 25,000 Chinese trapped during the Cold War to rejoin their families. China was now casting off the fetters of revolutionary socialism and self-imposed isolation, and was engaging with the outside world. In 1978, Deng Xiaoping had declared that China was "opening up" (*kaifangle*), and that modernization, not class struggle, had become China's top priority. Foreigners were invited in to revitalize a flagging economy, and Chinese were encouraged to *xiahai*, to jump into the sea of markets and join the outside world. By 1985, then, a new China was emerging, one that had abandoned collectivized agriculture, was actively soliciting foreign investment and technology, and was promoting entrepreneurship and free market principles.

Foreigners, remembering the China of the 1970s, initially were wary of this sudden turn in direction. While Deng was the spokesman for a new type of Chinese economy and a more open relationship with the outside world ("It does not matter if the cat is black or white as long as it catches mice."), his opponents within the Chinese Communist Party resisted these ideological changes. The struggle between reformers and "hardliners" continued throughout the 1980s, lending a measure of uncertainty to the long-term stability of the post-Mao reforms. Could China succeed in so abruptly changing course, moving from a planned socialist economy to one that willingly embraced Western (capitalist) market principles? Had China given up its commitment to supporting international revolutionary movements? Could it be trusted to take on a responsible role in conventional international institutions? The split between China and the Soviet Union had produced an emerging multipolar world. The Cold War was winding down and China was searching for a significant place for itself in this changing world order, where the new Sino-American relationship was becoming the gold standard for measuring foreign reactions to Chinese policies and behaviour.

Since the 1960s Canadians had articulated the idea that Canada had a mission to bring China into the community of nations, thus ending its isolation. In 1970, the Canadian government made a formal commitment to help China gain admission to the United Nations at the expense of removing Taiwan as a member. One of Canada's tasks in the 1970s was facilitating China's entry into multilateral regimes and institutions. By the mid-1980s China had acquired membership in the World Bank and the International Monetary Fund, and Canada had pledged to assist its entry into the General Agreement on Tariffs and Trade. Canada actively promoted China's participation in arms limitation talks and in international nuclear non-proliferation and testing regimes. In 1983, Trudeau attempted to create a multilateral "peace initiative" bringing together the Soviet Union, the United States and China.

The first fifteen years, therefore, represented an ambitious undertaking in the midst of far-reaching international and, in China, domestic transformation. No one was exactly sure about the course of China's new path, but there was an air of optimism that engagement with China was a major step forward. For the most part, however, while not opposing closer relations with China, the majority of Canadians paid scant attention to the construction of closer ties. A small policy community of bureaucrats and politicians, occasionally joined by academics and a few others, created and administered China policy. The attention of most Canadians lay elsewhere, primarily on the weakened state of the economy, the love–hate relationship with the United States, the effects of the oil crises, and the constitutional issues involving the muffling of Quebec separatism and the reassertion of Canadian national identity.

Brian Mulroney and Canada's China Policy

In September 1984, the election of a Progressive Conservative government led by Brian Mulroney heralded a shift in Canadian politics. After twenty-one years of Liberal rule, barely interrupted by Joe Clark's short-lived government of 1979, the Conservatives were ready to put their stamp on Canada. Electors had voted in a party that favoured big business, advocated a reduced role for government, sought to water down restrictions on foreign investment in Canada, was intent on dismantling Canada's national energy policy, and was determined to forge a better relationship with the United States. The party also contained within its ranks an anti-Communist group that supported Taiwanese autonomy, was suspicious of China and publicly criticized Chinese abuses of human rights.

The expectation was that Mulroney would move quickly to distance himself from Liberal foreign policy. This certainly was the case with his immediate shift to more positive relations with the United States. However, the impact on Canada's China policy was limited. While Mulroney met with Ottawa mandarins and pointedly asked, "What makes you think I should take your advice?" (Globe and Mail 1984) his government's policy initially appeared to be one of continuity rather than change. Mulroney had a full domestic and international agenda in other areas, and China was not a top priority. While the Conservatives wanted to develop Canada's trade in the Asia–Pacific region, as did the Liberals, the main target remained Japan, not China. Like the Liberals, the Conservatives, despite their criticism of Canada's "one China" policy and their support for Taiwan, remained committed to that policy. In the House of Commons on October 11, 1985, Mulroney said: "I have indicated to the Premier of China and the President of China the fact that the intention of this Government is to pursue the policy set out by my predecessor, Mr. Trudeau, with which I agree. We have honoured that in all circumstances" (Government of Canada 1985).

In March 1986, eighteen months after taking power, Mulroney made a visit to China (as reported in the Globe and Mail, May 13, 1986). The time had come to focus on China and put his imprint on Canada's China policy.

Mulroney had visited China in 1979 as a private citizen and the contrast seven years later was palpable. He commented:

> I was struck by the tremendous changes in the last six or seven years, tre-
> mendous progress that we can see visibly on the streets.... There is a greater
> sense of well-being, a greater consumer reality that is there, that seems to
> be shared by the Chinese population.... As Chairman Deng said the other
> day, the Chinese are trying to be realistic. They have an enormous problem,
> unique in the world, in terms of inherent difficulties that arise because of
> [the size of] the population itself. (Globe and Mail 1986)

During Mulroney's visit, Canada announced the expansion of concessional financing to promote trade, an additional CA$ 350 million to blend
with the CA$ 2 billion worth of credit that had previously been extended
by the Export Development Corporation (EDC). CIDA's aid programme
was doubled to CA$ 200 million over the next five years. Canada presented
China with a bulk fertilizer blending plant worth CA$ 300 million to pro-
mote Canadian potash sales. Canada also won assurances that it would
remain a favoured supplier of wheat. The Chinese encouraged Canadian
business to invest in China, including participation in the Three Gorges
hydroelectric project, which was most attractive to the Canadian power
industry. In a meeting with Canadian businesspeople in Beijing, Mulroney
"promised to cooperate with businessmen and the Chinese government to
make the next century 'the age of the Pacific'" (Globe and Mail 1986).

In his meetings with China's leaders, Mulroney received assurances that
China would remain committed to the "open door policy" and was developing a trading regime that conformed to international practices in protecting commercial rights and intellectual property. With respect to human
rights in general, Mulroney made a significant public departure from past
Liberal policy by openly dwelling on human rights in his farewell meeting
with Premier Zhao Ziyang, commenting later:

> My meeting with Premier Zhao was entirely devoted, by and large, to the
> human rights issue.... No one can challenge the right of a duly elected
> government to raise any issue with a friend, even though I recognize the
> traditional Chinese position that this is an internal matter. I didn't raise
> it in a spirit of hostility. I raised it as the kind of subject that can be dis-
> cussed between friends whose friendship is maturing and open to that
> kind of discussion. (Globe and Mail 1986)

In the months following the Prime Minister's visit the primary focus was on trade. While China had "opened up" and Canada seemingly was poised to expand its commercial links, trade was sluggish, failing to meet Canadian expectations. The Chinese market was slow to open up. Canada faced increased competition from foreign challengers, Canadian business people complained that Canada needed to expand its trade promotion and commercial presence. China was hesitant in offering foreign companies intellectual property protection. Canadian companies were lobbying for greater participation by the government in securing deals, and the large concessional financing fund was underused by the Chinese. Canada continued to have a trade surplus with China, but the gap was narrowing and Canada continued to remain heavily dependent on resource-based exports, primarily of wheat.

The China Strategy of 1987

Aside from trade concerns, the bilateral relationship in late 1986 needed to take into account a number of other developments. In the fall of that year the government instructed the Department of Foreign Affairs and International Trade (DFAIT) to develop a strategic plan for China. While the primary goal was to increase trade, the eventual "Canadian Strategy for China," as set out in a Memorandum to Cabinet, was intended to fulfill a number of other objectives (Cabinet of Canada 1987). First, it would consolidate and focus the various Canadian instrumentalities that had grown up over the first fifteen years. The Strategy could pull together the many bilateral components and provide a managerial basis for these initiatives. Thus high-level visits and trade could be linked more tightly together, CIDA's aid programme could be used to facilitate trade, and policies on culture and immigration could be attuned to economic and trade interests.

Second, as a follow-up to the Prime Minister's visit, the Strategy could put Mulroney's imprint on Canada's China policy as he sought to distance his government from Trudeau and the Liberals in foreign affairs. One officer in DFAIT observed:

> We were ready to do this. The Prime Minister's Office told us right after Mulroney's trip that he needed a key 'deliverable' to establish his China credentials and implement the initiative announced in Beijing. We were already working on the components of an action plan when we

received official notice from the politicians to put the document together. (Interview 1996)

Third, behind the scenes the Canadian foreign policy bureaucracy was in the throes of major change. In 1983, the Department of External Affairs (DEA) and the Department of Industry, Trade and Commerce (ITC) had been reorganized into a single body, essentially to cope more effectively with their increasingly complex tasks. This merger of Canada's two main internationally focused political and economic bureaucracies created both opportunities and tensions, as Ottawa mandarins struggled to adapt to new roles and expectations. The China Strategy served as a testing ground for the new partnership, bringing together sixteen ministries and departments under the aegis of a new department, eventually to be headed by three ministers, for foreign affairs, international trade and development, and development assistance. To the former "political" mandarins at the DEA, it was an opportunity to maintain their leadership and to resist challenges to their fading pre-eminence in the foreign policy arena. According to one DFAIT officer, interviewed in 1996, "It was a chance for us to retain our dominant role in the coordination and implementation of foreign policy. Putting together a China Strategy was a test of our abilities" (Interview 1996).

Finally, the Strategy served to emphasize the increased importance of Canada's relations with China. It was the only country that received special treatment, with a strategic plan devoted to strengthening a bilateral relationship. While continentalism and trade relations with the United States were the primary foreign policy objectives of the Mulroney government, it was clear that China was emerging as another priority, soon to contend strongly with Japan. Implementing the Strategy also implied that Canada continued to be relatively optimistic about the long-term stability of China's economic and political transformation, even as factional struggles persisted at the highest echelons of the regime.

Organizations have their formal and informal histories, and DFAIT is no exception. While the official nod from the politicians and the Prime Minister's Office (PMO) to draft a China Strategy occurred in the fall of 1986, informally the process had begun earlier, in the waning days of the Trudeau era. A senior official, John Hadwen, having just returned from an ambassadorial posting abroad, put together a paper proposing that Canada develop a China strategy, consolidating what had been achieved and providing a guideline for the future.

There's a key document you won't find in the files—I wrote it in 1983. It was entitled 'Why Canada Should Now Make a Major Effort in China.' I sent it up and no one ever sent me a reply. After a while, I just went ahead and did it. And that was that.… How to get it organized? I circulated it to everyone in the Department and consulted widely, with a heavy emphasis on trade.… I went to China with EDC in late 1983 to find out why the Chinese were shying away from our two-million-dollar line of credit.… I soon realized that while other government ministries and departments had increasing interests in China, DFAIT could put it all together. We had to be the manager and coordinator. (Conversation 1994)

Beginning in 1984, DFAIT organized an interdepartmental China Working Group (CWG) to help to coordinate China-related activities. Trade was the main focus, but discussions also centred on evaluating China's political stability, linking trade and aid, coordinating high-level visits, and bringing in perspectives from academics and non-governmental organizations. According to Hadwen, "The China Working Group used to meet at night under my direction. We met at 7 p.m. and I ordered in sandwiches, wine and beer. Sometimes we met two to three times a month" (Conversation 1994).

I attended CWG meetings in 1985 and 1986. It was noted at the meeting in 1985 that there was a "broad consensus" that China's modernization was going to continue and was presenting Canada with greater opportunities. How to focus and coordinate the sudden surge in China related activities? How to maximize our trade potential? How to be optimistic, yet maintain a cautious perspective? At the meeting in 1986, we received a debriefing on the Prime Minister's visit to China, as well as those of several cabinet ministers, and updates on concessional financing (from CIDA and EDC), agricultural cooperation (from Agriculture Canada), and thermal and hydroelectric power (from the Task Force on the Hydro-Electric Power Sector). I had the impression that we were processing a great deal of information about China and, within the constraints of time and resources, trying to develop a coherent China strategy. One DFAIT official who also participated in the CWG commented in 1986, "It's like herding cats. Too many independent-minded departments, egged on by business and political interests. Too many egos. It's a big challenge" (Conversation 1986).

In the fall of 1986, DFAIT was instructed by the PMO to prepare a submission to Cabinet on relations with China. A drafting team was assembled to liaise with concerned parties: the various government departments, the

CWG, the Embassy in Beijing and selected members of the policy community. The final stage of the process, the drafting of the Memorandum to Cabinet, was launched at a meeting of the CWG on January 17, 1987. Copies of the draft were sent to the ministers involved by March, and then forwarded to the Cabinet Committee on Foreign Affairs and Defence Policy at the end of the month. Cabinet approved the Strategy in early April 1987 (Cabinet of Canada 1987: Volume 38, File 20-1-2).

In the drafting process DFAIT was guided by a number of recommendations made by the drafting team. The basic issue, it said, was "how to capitalize on Canada's fascination with China to seize opportunities created by its modernization drive and to position ourselves for the year 2000, when China should have the world's third largest GDP after the United States and Japan" (Cabinet of Canada 1987). The Strategy recommended that all ministerial visits henceforth should target priority government objectives, in order to stanch the excessive flow of officials beset by "China fever" and making questionable journeys. The remaining recommendations were:

- to elevate the China dialogue on key Asian strategic concerns and global arms-control issues to the ministerial level;
- to develop a cadre of Chinese-speaking officials and specialists to deliver programmes in China;
- to promote better partnership between government and the private sector, in order to promote long-term objectives;
- to have high-level visits target economic objectives;
- to convene periodic meetings of leading business, academic and other China specialists "to ensure that Canadian strategy is based on national consensus";
- to establish working committees to link federal, provincial and private-sector groups to promote trade objectives;
- to increase Canada's use of the "China connection" through Hong Kong;
- to pursue co-financing arrangements with international financial institutions to lever greater procurement opportunities for Canadian companies;
- to extend academic, cultural, professional, sports, media and other exchanges, in order to increase the number of Chinese students in Canada, to promote people-to-people contacts, to enrich Canada's multicultural heritage, and to project Canada's image as a highly developed and open society.

The rationale for the China Strategy underlined the growing political and strategic importance of China to Canada. For example, according to the document, "China is a dominant Asia power. Canada has a stake in China's stability. Canada's recognition of the Asia–Pacific region as key to Canadian security and economic interests requires that our political dialogue be strengthened." The document noted that Canada had positioned itself to meet "increasingly fierce competition" in the China market, and that a careful "Canada Inc." approach to China was "vital to commercial success." In an accompanying press release, the government referred to a "focused," "orchestrated" and "aggressive" strategy to cope with "our fascination about China," which often is "undertaken without a sufficient assessment of real potential benefits to Canada." It asserted that there was now "an urgent need for more timely and incisive knowledge of developments in China" and for "better management of Canada–China relations through improved consultative and cooperative mechanisms."

What was the reaction of those on the ground in China, the officials in the Canadian Embassy in Beijing? The Ambassador, Richard Vessot Gorham, who had been at the post since May 1984, was generally supportive of the exercise. In his view, while foreign observers should not be deluded into thinking that China will emerge as some sort of mirror image of Western democracy, with full freedom of political expression, a free press or respect for individual rights and liberties, nonetheless the reforms appeared "to have legs," and "the excellent state of Canada–China relations puts Canada in a favoured position to take advantage of China's opening up and modernization" (Cabinet of Canada 1987: Volume 38, File 20-1-2). In a telegram dated February 6, 1987, the Ambassador reminded Ottawa that it should proceed with caution and temper optimism with a measure of realism:

> A hardnosed look would lead us to conclude that the return on our investment (over and above Chinese expressions and sentiments of friendship and goodwill) have not been impressive, other than a sustained market for our wheat (which the Chinese buy because they need it) and recent encouraging sales of high tech end products. We can cite no evidence that the lustre of the Maple Leaf or the memory of Norman Bethune, despite all our efforts and our investment of human and financial resources, have persuaded Chinese negotiators to opt for sourcing their requirements in Canada. (Cabinet of Canada 1987)

The Ambassador "welcomed the general thrust" of the draft Strategy, "especially the mandate to coordinate more effectively the new interests

of the various government departments and agencies that previously were
not involved with China." He was critical, however, of several parts of
the draft. In his opinion, targeting ministerial visits to sectoral priorities
was a good idea, but would be almost impossible to achieve. In addition, "dialogue will not produce Chinese recognition of Canada as a
world power. If we want to improve our knowledge of China and train
more Chinese-language speakers, we need to provide substantially more
resources to move out of the quill pen era." The Strategy recommended
that Canada should help to promote Chinese exports to Canada, in
order to reduce the large Canadian surplus in trade with China, but the
Ambassador wondered whether this was a useful strategy, since Canada
would be building up China's capacity to become our trade competitor. He also thought that the comments about China's rapid economic
development were oversimplified. China's absorption of Western technology and management principles required social and political liberalization, and China would encounter many difficulties in disengaging from
its authoritarian past and present. He noted that "the principles which
have governed Canada's relationship to China remain valid" and that the
Strategy could build on what had already been achieved. Nevertheless, he
cautioned Ottawa: "Don't be mesmerized by the sheer size of China and
this current shift in PRC policy."

Selections from the Text of the China Strategy

The document is an impressive summary of informed Canadian thinking
about China at the time, with an equally convincing set of assumptions and
policy recommendations for future action. In this section I present a few
highlights from the document.

On China's commitment to reform:

> China's modern history has been marked by a realization that it cannot
> become a major power without accepting foreign technology and manage-
> ment techniques, and also by a deeply xenophobic reaction to the penetra-
> tion of western ideas and philosophy.... The long-term durability of the
> reform programme is not to be taken for granted.... China is unlikely to
> waver from its objective to become a modern industrial power in the short-
> est possible time.... To achieve this status is a matter of urgency and pride
> for all Chinese, "reformers" and "conservatives" alike.

On China's key political and strategic role:

A nuclear weapon state, China is a major military power, a key player in the Asia–Pacific region, which is increasingly vital to Canada's long-term security and economic prosperity. China's relations with the United States have become increasingly warm, although United States policy towards Taiwan, including arms sales, hinders Sino-American cooperation. The situation in Asia remains volatile. The Soviet Union, perceived by China as its main threat, occupies Afghanistan, subsidizes an expansionist Vietnam, arms Filipino rebels, and is increasingly close to a dangerously unpredictable North Korea.... Annual ministerial-level consultations on security issues are essential to promote a growing convergence of security interests with China.

On Canada's relations with Taiwan:

The one-China policy has been the cornerstone of Canada's mutually beneficial relationship with the PRC since 1970. Canada does not maintain official relations with Taiwan, but the government encourages people-to-people contacts. The recent establishment by the Canadian Chamber of Commerce of an office in Taipei should result in better access to a potentially lucrative market.

On Canadian development assistance to China:

CIDA's involvement in China was a logical step in the construction of Canada's bilateral relationship. Development assistance responds to real needs in China, particularly in the area of technology transfer and human resources. Canada's programme is now one of the largest in China, ranking second only to Japan's. CIDA's philosophy is to build upon China's open-door policy designed to acquire Western technologies and skills ... in jointly identified sectors where Canadian expertise meets Chinese priorities, for example, agriculture, energy, and forestry, as well as telecommunications and transportation. CIDA also provides pre-project studies through its Industrial Cooperation Division. These provide substantial opportunities for Canadian companies with commercial interests.

On trade issues:

The composition of Canada–China trade has undergone major changes. Over the past two decades Canada has enjoyed a large surplus in our bilateral trade, largely as a result of strong grain and resource exports. The gap has shrunk in recent years.... Large rapid gains in the sales of Chinese clothing and textiles account for the declining deficit with Canada.... Negotiations to renew the clothing restraint schedules ended without an agreement this January.... Chinese textile exporters still have room to manoeuvre, moving "up market" or into unrestrained categories. Grain sales have been the core of Canada's exporting success in China.... As China's wheat production has increased in the early 1980s, Canadian sales have declined.... The dramatic recent drop in world wheat prices slashed receipts to Canada by almost one half. New suppliers have entered the fray and competition is felt from expanding Chinese production capacities.

Overall conditions for doing business in China are becoming increasingly complex (decentralization of decision-making, financial reform, the evolving regulatory environment, are examples of this trend).... To launch joint ventures in a complicated and unfamiliar environment, where foreign exchange is scarce, Canadians must be well-informed, persistent, and adaptive. Hence, government support should be directed in a selective fashion to those Canadian companies that have products/technology/expertise that respond to China's priority requirements, and the "staying power" to weather both economic ups and downs, and the slow approval process—we are seeing encouraging progress in our capital goods sector. For example, Babcock & Wilcox have sold steam generators worth 203 million dollars, and are in close pursuit of similar contracts. Oil and gas equipment sales were [worth] almost 120 million dollars in 1986. Super heavy mining vehicles represented some 70 million dollars of exports.

On competition in the China market:

China is a fiercely competitive market. Japan, the United States, Hong Kong, and Germany are the most important exporters to China, with Canada ranking a distant fifth. Japan's remarkable success in China is based on a corporate culture which recognizes the need for long-term commitment, the presence of over 250 trade offices throughout China, and an industrial and trading house capability that can deal with Chinese requirements for counter trade and commodity trade purchases for export sales.

The Americans sell fewer consumer durables than the Japanese, but successfully compete in China in the heavy industry, oil and gas, mining, and transportation sectors ... a result of the proven quality of American technology and the staying power of the multinationals. The Australians have adopted a successful trade strategy which targets limited public and private resources to sectors where Australian companies are internationally competitive, for example, iron and steel, wool, textiles, non-ferrous metals, transportation, communications, and coal. This targeted and pragmatic approach is more relevant to the Canadian situation.

(It should be noted that in 1983 Australia had adopted a China Action Plan, which in several respects was similar to the Canadian China Strategy. Four years later, Canadian officials consulted with their Australian counterparts when drafting the Canadian Strategy.)
On Canadian government activities in China:

Various federal line departments and agencies have been active in China for several years. While the Programme for Export Market Development and the Promotional Projects Programme are the prime programmes for export promotion, the federal government has recently provided funding for new tools specifically targeted to China. These include the 350-million-dollar concessional financing facility administered by EDC. The CIDA Technical Cooperation Programme is designed to provide funding for feasibility studies. The National Trade Strategy, which was adopted in the fall of 1985, supported the opening of the Shanghai Consulate and the resources to create two new trade officer positions in Beijing.

While appreciative of government assistance, business groups are concerned about the lack of focus of government efforts and the potential duplication of federal, provincial and municipal programmes.... Business groups have also voiced a need for more in-depth analysis and identification of commercial opportunities. Federal government financial assistance should be channelled into sectors where it can make the greatest difference, i.e., energy, agriculture, communications, transportation, and resource development.

On academic, community and non-government organizations:

Many leading Canadian academics are actively involved in the promotion of exchange programmes with China, often as advisers to provincial or municipal governments. Several have served in our Embassy in Beijing and have maintained close ties with the federal government. Their advice is regularly sought. Several NGOs (Amnesty International) are increasingly active in pursuing human rights and other questions in China. Continued consultations are under way with them to ascertain the appropriate means to conduct a useful dialogue on such sensitive issues with the Chinese government.

The Strategy did not mention human rights other than in these two brief sentences, even though Prime Minister Mulroney had confronted Zhao Ziyang on these issues in Beijing in 1986, and his government had signalled its intention to elevate the discussion of human rights issues to a more prominent place in the bilateral relationship.

In the first of two annexes to the Strategy the government discussed how to improve its links with the private sector. Separate meetings were held with executives of the Canadian Export Association, the Canadian Chamber of Commerce, the Canada–China Trade Council and eleven companies that traded with China. The business associations flagged the following concerns: "an urgent need for better control over the growing number of visits to China; insufficient knowledge of the China market; the need for long-term corporate and financial commitment; learning how to set up joint ventures [and] how to utilize government programmes." They also reaffirmed the value of "carefully selected and timed visits to China by federal ministers attuned to trade objectives," and recommended better, more competitive financing arrangements and a "Canada Inc." approach to China that would link government and business more closely together.

In a second annex the government attached its communications plan, stating that "Canadians appear to regard China as a country of priority foreign policy importance." However, it would be

> a challenge for Canada to channel Canadians' general and sometimes romanticized notions about China along more realistic and constructive lines.... Public opinion would support a government initiative to make our relations with China more productive, particularly one directly linked to furthering Canadian economic interests and generating jobs for Canadians.

The annex added that the growing Chinese ethnic community in Canada "would support new government initiatives with respect to China." Canadians were to be given the following message by the government as it carried out the provisions of the China Strategy:

It is in the interest of all Canadians that relations with China be concluded in the context of a national strategy that gives coherence to exchanges taking place at all levels of government, by NGOS and by the private sector.... A successful further development of relations with China means potential prosperity and jobs for Canadians.

The senior staff at the Canadian Embassy in Beijing would be enlisted to go on comprehensive speaking tours across every region of Canada, and "a slide show, emphasizing and standardizing our message, will be developed for use by government speakers at service clubs, trade organizations, and other targeted audiences." Canadian media would have to be briefed to support the new China Strategy:

> The government will conduct seminars and background sessions for Canadian journalists.... Some elements of the Canadian media may seek to criticize extensive ministerial travel to the PRC as envisaged in the work plan. One way to attenuate such criticism is to ensure that visas are linked to specific and identified goals, and cast as part of a coherent approach to China.

In April 1987 the Strategy was announced quietly, without much fanfare, through a press release concerning a future visit to China by Pat Carney, Minister of International Trade. Carney and Joe Clark, the Minister for Foreign Affairs, were to speak at various venues in support of the Strategy, as would other ministers,

> before and after their planned trips to the PRC.... Members of Parliament and Senators are to be briefed on the Strategy, and information suitable for use in their constituencies [is to be] made available to them.... Minister Clark will send a letter to the Chairman of the Parliamentary Standing Committee on External Affairs and International Trade and to the Caucus Foreign Affairs Committee outlining the elements of this more strategic approach to relations with China.

The Strategy in Historical Perspective

The China Strategy is an impressive document. It aptly summarizes the state of relations between Canada and China at a key point in time, and outlines an action plan to provide focus and substance to the future relationship. To my knowledge, Canada has never since produced a similar document, although over the past twenty-three years DFAIT has occasionally attempted less ambitious strategic planning exercises involving China. In 1987, its officials took pride in what they had accomplished. The Strategy, in their view, maximized Canada's trade objectives, strengthened government-to-government links and solidified the new Department's position as the coordinator and implementer, if not the originator, of China policy (Personal Interview 2009).

To be sure, the Strategy overemphasized trade relations with China and devoted minimal space to other aspects of the bilateral relationship, in particular human rights, immigration, consular affairs and people-to-people links. Since 1987, these areas have become more central and now occupy a substantially larger portion of the relationship. In 1987, however, trade was the main issue motivating the creation of the Strategy. These other issues gained more prominence in the 1990s, after the Tiananmen crisis of 1989.

In addition, the Strategy put Prime Minister Mulroney's imprint on Canada's China policy. For twenty-one years China had belonged to Trudeau and the Liberals. After Mulroney's visit to China the Strategy provided an opportunity to separate the Conservatives from the Liberal past. One therefore might have anticipated a China policy that downplayed the role of government, sought to elevate Canada's diplomatic relations with Taiwan, expressed suspicion of China as a Communist country, and made criticism of China's failings on human rights a central element. In fact, however, the Strategy did none of these things. If anything, it advocated a stronger role for government, openly engaged China, reaffirmed the "one China" policy and omitted any criticism on human rights. In the words of one DFAIT official whom I spoke with in 1991, "What we saw, and what we were told, was continuity, with almost no change. To be frank, in retrospect, we hardly missed a step in the transition from Trudeau to Mulroney" (Personal Interview 1991).

In essence, Canada's China policy before the Tiananmen crisis maintained its cross-party nature. What divided Liberals and Conservatives domestically appeared not to do so with respect to relations with China. Canadian domestic politics had a minimal impact on the bilateral relationship in the 1980s. One can argue that the focus on trade development was in good part designed to provide an economic boost to Canada ("jobs, jobs, jobs"). However, economic recovery was an all-party goal and China policy was never an election issue. After Tiananmen, the Conservative human rights agenda brought a new dimension to the relationship, but the other parties supported this shift. When the Liberals returned to power in 1993 and made trade the main thrust of the relationship, giving human rights a lower priority, the Conservatives held back and essentially followed along. Only with the Harper government after 2005 did the consensus on China policy break apart, as the Conservatives called into question several of the key principles that had underlain the policy for many years.

The China Strategy made it clear that China was important to Canada and that trade was the main link. It recognized that post-Mao China had embarked on a new course and that it was possible for Canada to expand its relationship with this "new" China. At the same time, the Strategy tempered its optimism with caution, pointing out that expectations for increased bilateral trade and for political openness inside China might not easily be fulfilled. In this respect, the document was prescient. Even with bilateral trade running at CA$ 50 billion, almost twenty-five times the level of 1986, the economic relationship has not fully met Canadian expectations. Those who have wished for dramatic changes in the area of human rights and democracy have equally been disappointed.

When the Conservatives took power in 1984, they intended to clean house at the top levels of the public service. The rationale was that, after twenty-one years of Liberal rule the bureaucracy had become a handmaiden of the Liberal Party in power. As noted earlier in this chapter, Mulroney had asked the mandarins in Ottawa, "What makes you think I should take your advice?" In fact, with respect to China policy the Conservatives did just that. They worked closely with the mandarins to put together the new China policy. The China Strategy was drawn up by the bureaucrats at DFAIT in consultation with their political superiors, yet it was very much a product of departmental expertise. The politicians gave the signals and the bureaucrats fell in line.

The ongoing reorganization of the Canadian foreign affairs bureaucracy played an important role. As DEA, once the "golden child" of foreign affairs, saw its former prominence tarnished, its powers diluted and under attack, it rose to the occasion, taking charge of the merger with ITC, the international trade arm of the bureaucracy. Putting together the Strategy under DEA's direction showed that the Ottawa political mandarins could respond to the challenge, at least with respect to formulating China policy. One DFAIT official whom I interviewed in 1994 commented:

My background was on the political side. When I got involved in the China Strategy, I had to widen my horizons, working with trade-oriented officials who sometimes lacked political and diplomatic smarts, and I, in turn, needed to focus more sharply on the bottom line, on dollars and cents. (Personal Interview 1994)

While organization and institutions absolutely mattered in the process of preparing the China Strategy, so too did the work and ideas of individuals. The interplay of these two forces was a central element in the construction of the Strategy. As noted earlier, one official on his own began the process in 1983 and continued for three years developing agendas, coordinating mechanisms, and expanding the horizons of the Strategy-in-the-making. The Prime Minister stepped into the process in 1986 with his visit to China, and then, as another DFAIT official observed, "The PMO shaped the next stage of the process." Subtle encouragement was also provided by key Chinese officials, who were consulted both in Ottawa and in Beijing (Interviews 1987-1995). It is worth noting that the consultative process was wide, and included groups and individuals not normally part of the foreign policy-making process. Several round tables were convened under the aegis of the Foreign Minister and senior officials, and a number of meetings of the CWG were opened to "outsiders." This was one of the rare occasions when bureaucrats and politicians permitted the widening of the foreign policy community during the preparation of a policy agenda. Later, after Tiananmen, the China policy community again broadened to include groups and individuals galvanized by that crisis, notably the media, which were suddenly more attentive and critical, persistent human rights activists, and newly politicized members of Canada's Chinese communities.

The Strategy met a surprising fate. While it served as a broad framework for Canada's relations with China, in particular the work of the federal government and its partnership with business, the Strategy was hardly noticed at the time by the public. One DFAIT "China hand" commented that he did not know much about it and, while he agreed with the general thrust of the document, he had, in fact, never seen the complete document (Personal Interview 1992). As Canada began to implement many of the provisions of the Strategy, it was eclipsed by the events at and around Tiananmen Square on June 4, 1989. High-level visits, a key component of the Strategy, were formally suspended for three years. Some CIDA projects were frozen or cancelled. A pall settled over the relationship. Human rights, conspicuously missing from the Strategy, suddenly became a principal public focus of relations until 1994, when the Liberals, back in power and led by Jean Chrétien, once again made trade the basis of the China relationship, with a visit by a large delegation of business people and federal, provincial and territorial leaders to Beijing and Shanghai.

Today, forty years after diplomatic relations with China were established and almost twenty-five years after the China Strategy was created, both Canada and China have changed in many respects. Nevertheless, what was constructed in 1986–87 remains an important reference point in the evolution of the bilateral relationship, reminding us of what was accomplished in the past and of the issues that continue to affect the relationship today.

Acknowledgements

This chapter is part of a book-length study of relations between Canada and China since 1970. It relies heavily on interviews with Canadian and Chinese officials, and materials from the Canadian Department of Foreign Affairs and International Trade. The author wishes to thank officials in both countries for their generous cooperation.

References

Bellchambers, Glenn. (1988). "A Review of the China Action Plan," in Dunn, H. A. and Fung, Edmund S. K. (eds.) *Sino-Australian Relations, The Record, 1972-1985*, Centre for the Study of Sino-Australian Relations, Griffiths University, 135-141.

Cabinet of Canada. (1987, February 10). "Canadian Strategy for China," Memorandum to the Cabinet of Canada, PNRE-0194. File 20-1-2 China, Volume 38, 1987.

Globe and Mail. (1984, December 10).

Globe and Mail. (1986, May 13). "Greater sense of well-being evident in China, PM says." Toronto, Ontario, A.5.

Government of Canada. (1985, October 11). House of Commons Debates, 7584-7585.

Interviews

Conversation with DFAIT official, Ottawa, 1986

Conversation with John Hadwen, Ottawa, 1994

Interviews with officials from the Chinese Ministry of Foreign Affairs in Beijing, and several Chinese Ambassadors to Ottawa, 1987-1995.

Personal Interview, DFAIT Official, Ottawa, 1991

Personal Interview, DFAIT Official, Ottawa, 1994

Personal Interview, DFAIT Official, Ottawa, 1996

Personal Interview, Ottawa, 2008

Chapter 5

The Politics of Soft Power in Sino-Canadian Relations: Stephen Harper's Visit to China and the Neglected Hong Kong Factor

Sonny Shiu-Ling Lo

While conventional wisdom regards the visit of the Canadian Prime Minister Stephen Harper to China in December 2009 as a turning point, heralding warmer relations between Canada and China, a silent process involving China's increasing "soft power" over Canada has been looming for some time. This chapter examines the various dimensions of Sino-Canadian relations since Harper's visit, including trade, immigration, tourism, cross-border crime and sociocultural exchanges. At the same time, with hundreds of thousands of Canadians residing in Hong Kong, Canada's soft power over China has been relatively neglected, an important issue that will also be discussed in this chapter.

The political scientist Joseph Nye invented the concepts of "soft power" and "hard power" to discuss the ways in which the foreign policies of the United States evolved, and to delineate how other countries in the world perceived US military, economic, cultural and political power (see Nye 2004). "Hard power" refers to the military and economic might that a country possesses, but, as Nye emphasizes, these are not the only determinants of a nation state's success in world politics. In addition, "soft power," which can co-opt others, is an influential tool with which foreign policy objectives can be achieved without the need to resort to coercion. As Nye has pointed out (2004, p. 5):

> Hard power can rest on inducements ("carrots") or threats ("sticks"). But sometimes you can get the outcomes you want without tangible threats

or pay-offs. The indirect way to get what you want has sometimes been called "the second face of power." ...it is also important to set the agenda and attract others in world politics, and not only to force them to change by threatening military force or economic sanctions. This soft power—getting others to want the outcomes you want—co-opts people rather than coerces them.

Nye stresses that soft power is not simply the same as influence, because it represents the ability to attract others through one's culture and values, and "the ability to manipulate the agenda of political choices" (Nye 2004, p. 7). While hard-power resources entail command behaviour, including force, sanctions and payments, soft-power resources embrace culture, values, institutions and policies (Nye 2004, p. 8). Using these concepts developed by Nye, this chapter argues that China's soft power over Canada has gradually increased since Harper's visit, but on the other hand, Canada's soft power over China has not yet been fully used, even though the values and behaviour of Canadian citizens residing in Hong Kong could shape China's policy toward Canada.

Stephen Harper's Visit to China: Normalization of Bilateral Relations

Harper's visit to China had significant implications for the development of Sino-Canadian relations. First and foremost, his visit was widely viewed, not only by Chinese leaders but also by Chinese commentators in Canada, as a long-overdue move that repaired the frosty relations between China and Harper's Conservative government, which had come to power three years before.

Up to the eve of his visit to China Harper had adopted a far more aloof attitude toward China than any of his predecessors. The government of the Liberal Prime Minister Pierre Trudeau had recognized the People's Republic in 1970, making Canada one of the first Western countries to do so. In 1994, another Liberal Prime Minister, Jean Chrétien, had led a trade delegation to China and signed bilateral agreements covering projects to a total value of CA$ 90 billion. In 1998 Chrétien had visited China again and made several more trade agreements. Three years later he led yet another trade delegation to forge commercial and trade agreements worth CA$ 57 billion. Finally, in 2005, Liberal Prime Minister Paul Martin had visited China and made eighty trade and bilateral deals, laying the groundwork for both sides to discuss an approved destination status agreement in relation to Chinese tourists visiting Canada.

In contrast, Harper had long been seen as relatively anti-Communist, if not necessarily anti-Chinese, primarily because the ideology of Harper's Conservative Party sees socialist regimes as undemocratic and ideologically incompatible. Most importantly, under the Conservative government Canada appeared to see China as a threat, and had offered support to the Dalai Lama, who is seen by the Chinese government as fostering separatist sentiment in Tibet. Harper did not attend the opening ceremony of the Beijing Olympics in 2008, a decision that was taken as a sign of a disrespectful attitude toward China and a lack of understanding of the concept of *mianzi* ("face" or honour; see Schiller 2009a). China had also taken note of the Canadian media's frequent claims about Chinese spies in Canada, interpreting them as signs of mutual distrust between the two countries.

In February 2009, in response to a question as to why Harper had not visited China after he became Prime Minister, Stockwell Day, Minister of International Trade, argued that Harper had had to deal with the global financial crisis in 2008, as well as pressing domestic issues and a general election. The frosty relations between China and Canada were broken by the visit of the Chinese Foreign Minister Yang Jiechi to Ottawa in June 2009, when he invited Harper to pay a visit to China. Harper accepted Yang's invitation and his eventual visit was widely viewed as a watershed in resuming a more normal and harmonious relationship between Canada and China.

Harper's visit led the Chinese Premier Wen Jiabao to make some public criticisms of Canada's tardiness in maintaining friendship with China, saying that the visit "should have taken place earlier" and that he hoped "we are able to fix our problem of mutual trust" (as quoted in Schiller 2009b). In the *Toronto Sun* Michael Den Tandt (2009b) reacted strongly to Wen's remarks in an editorial piece headed "Standing Up for Canada":

> The Chinese premier took the "unprecedented step" (gasp!) of upbraiding Prime Minister Stephen Harper (cringe!) at a press conference. What does it mean? ... Will trade with China suffer? The Chinese Premier ... was in a press conference with Harper to begin with because China needs Canada. China continues to require access to the North American market, which includes Canada. China continues to require access to our natural resources. Canada is a sovereign nation, one of the wealthiest on

the planet, with a proud, able people, blessed with values and institutions that are the envy of the world. China's governing elite, in particular, could learn a lot from Canada.... Trade? By all means. But we don't need to take dictation from any foreign leader, certainly not Premier Wen Jiabao. Let him sputter. Now let's carry on, advancing our values and interests, as always.

Indeed, China does need Canada, but Canada also needs China's huge economic market. From the perspective of the Chinese leadership, Harper should have visited Beijing much earlier to demonstrate Canada's eagerness to treat China as a friendly state. Wen's comment could be seen as a sign that he did not give *mianzi* (face) to Harper, just as Harper, whose advisers were apparently ignorant of this Chinese tradition, had failed to give *mianzi* when he skipped the Beijing Olympics. The *Ming Pao*, a Chinese-language newspaper in Toronto, argued (December 4, 2009) that Wen's remarks were "not a sign of China making Harper lose face," but the reality is that the question of face is critical in Chinese political and cultural tradition. The Liberal Party leader Michael Ignatieff was not the only observer who thought that Harper had indeed lost face when Wen reprimanded him.

Chinese leaders also perceived Harper's Conservative government as being too close to the Republican administration of George W. Bush in the United States, in that both governments saw China as a threat rather than as a cooperative partner. Following the victory of the Democratic candidate Barack Obama in the U.S. presidential election in November 2008, the Conservative government in Canada gradually shifted toward a more Realpolitik, less ideological approach to China. The wind of political change in Sino-Canadian relations in late 2009 was to a large extent a reflection of Obama's victory. After all, Canada's mainstream political currents are often shaped by the political transformations of its giant neighbour.

Despite the lateness in resuming a more friendly relationship between the two countries, China conferred a "gift" upon the Harper government by granting Canada approved destination status, which meant that the number of Chinese tourists visiting Canada would increase by 40,000 to 50,000 a year, with a likely boost in annual tourist revenues of CA$ 100 million (see Schiller 2009b). The Canadian tourist industry warmly welcome this move, as at least 70,000 Chinese tourists would visit Toronto each year and the knock-on effects on the property market, the retail sector, restaurants and casinos would be tremendous. In particular, many more Chinese would visit friends and relatives in cities such as Vancouver,

Toronto and Calgary. With 1.2 million ethnic Chinese residing in Canada, many of them have their family roots entrenched in Canadian soil, but retain family and emotional ties with Greater China (understood here as comprising mainland China itself, Hong Kong, Macau and Taiwan). The granting of approved destination status to Canada represents a landmark, not only in the further acceleration of human interactions between the two countries, but also in the strengthening of the family, identity and emotional bonds between the Chinese in Greater China and the ethnic Chinese in Canada. Harper's visit undoubtedly was a watershed in the deepening of human interactions between Canada and Greater China.

Harper's visit also symbolized belated Canadian recognition of the rapid economic and global rise of China. In a speech delivered in Shanghai to the Canada–China Business Council and the Canadian Chamber of Commerce (*Ming Pao*, December 5, 2009), Harper said that the orientation of Canada's trade had shifted to East Asia, that the promotion of free trade was his government's policy, and that the ethnic Chinese had played a positive and significant role in the construction of the Canadian Pacific Railway. Clearly, Harper was trying to acknowledge the positive contributions of Chinese to Canada and to reorient Canadian trade policy toward the global emergence of China, which has become a lucrative market for Canadian business. Harper also announced in Shanghai that Canada would set up four additional trade offices in China. The rapid global emergence of China has forced the Harper government to become far more pragmatic than before.

President Hu's Visit to Canada in June 2010

In June 2010, President Hu Jintao visited Canada to discuss five areas for further cooperation (*Sing Tao Daily*, June 25, 2010): the expansion of bilateral trade involving high-technology products, with both Canada and China attempting to elevate the value of this trade to US$ 600 billion; the promotion of bilateral investment in building ports, railways, telecommunications networks and other infrastructure projects in China's western, central and northeastern provinces; the deepening of cooperation in the use of nuclear power and natural gas; the development of new frontiers of cooperation, such as high technology, service industries and the "green economy"; and opposition to any form of protectionism.

The focus on cooperation in high-tech development and energy is note-worthy. China lacks sufficient supplies of technical expertise and energy to sustain its rapid pace of economic development, and Canada, with its endow-ments of technical education and natural resources, serves as a very critical source of both. In September 2009, for example, PetroChina had announced plans to invest CA$ 19 billion in acquiring sixty percent of the ownership of certain oil sands projects in Alberta (*Sing Tao Daily*, September 1, 2009). The strategic aspect of Hu's visit to Canada was clear, although its implications seem to have been neglected by many Canadian observers. Significant break-throughs were also achieved in other dimensions of Sino-Canadian relations. China announced that it would set up Chinese cultural centres in Canada, and both sides agreed on enhancing the numbers of Chinese tourists vis-iting Canada; promoting educational exchanges; increasing cooperation on environmental protection, energy-saving, food inspection, crime control and oil sands; establishing cooperation between the Chinese Import and Export Bank and Canada's telecommunication industry; creating a partnership between Guangdong's nuclear power enterprise and its Canadian counter-part; and collaborating on mining and resource extraction.

Hu's visit was recognized by the Canadian mass media as a crucial turn-ing point, signalling the return to the good old days of Sino-Canadian relations. As the *Toronto Star* on June 25, 2010 remarked in an editorial of "China's leader reaches out":

> Hu spoke of wanting to "further scale up cooperation" and "move for-ward the strategic partnership" between China and Canada. That's stan-dard, polite rhetoric, but it is nonetheless reassuring after a period of chilly relations…. China is now playing a larger role in the G20…. [It] is the new "indispensable" country. Beijing bolstered the G20 consensus on stimulus that helped avert a depression. It supports reform of the finan-cial system. China's move to revalue its undervalued currency is a positive (if fledgling) signal that it takes its leading role seriously. Politically, China can help thwart the nuclear ambitions of North Korea and Iran. It is also a big power in African development and in managing climate change…. To be sure, Canada's disagreement with Beijing on democracy, human rights, and espionage are still deeply felt. Indeed, our own spy chief triggered an ill-timed ruckus on the eve of Hu's visit by all but confirming that China is one of several countries trying to influence our policy-makers…. But disagreements, however profound, need to be managed, not exacerbated. That's something the ideologically driven Conservatives took a long time

to recognize. Modern Canada/China ties now go back forty years, to the
Trudeau era. Hu's idea for an enhanced partnership could usher in an
even more productive fifth decade.

The Fear of Chinese "Espionage" in Canada

Before Hu's visit Richard Fadden, head of the Canadian Security Intelligence
Service (CSIS), claimed that China had infiltrated a number of spies into
political circles in Canada at the federal, provincial and municipal levels.
Fadden's claims were met with criticism by some Canadian commentators,
who believed that the accusations had no concrete basis, and also provoked
heated discussions within the Chinese community in Canada. One retired
political scientist, Reg Whitaker, told the *Toronto Star* (June 24, 2010):
"For CSIS to make unspecified allegations on national television without
apparently contacting the provincial government and federal government is
something you and I, and the general public, shouldn't hear about." Olivia
Chow of the New Democratic Party told the *Sing Tao Daily* (June 25,
2010) that Fadden's remarks were "irresponsible."

In fact, analysts familiar with China's "united front" strategy, which
is aimed at winning the hearts and minds of Chinese and non-Chinese
alike, do not see it as having any subversive impact on Canadian security.
China sets out to make friends with foreign officials, politicians, and overseas Chinese, as well as Chinese compatriots in Hong Kong, Macau and
Taiwan (see Lo 2008 and Loh 2010). Lobbying Canadian officials and
politicians, and even Canadian Chinese community leaders, is a normal
use of "soft power" in the Chinese political tradition. Nevertheless, some
Canadian commentators and politicians see such work as subversive. One
Conservative member of Parliament, Rob Anders, claimed that two other
members of the House of Commons had received business favours and
sexual services from Chinese agents (*Ming Pao*, July 31, 2010). Critics
responded that, unless he could point out specific examples, such claims
appeared to exaggerate the impact of China's efforts on the behaviour of
Canadian politicians.

From a conservative security perspective, the Canadian fear of potential Chinese espionage is understandable. Canada is the neighbour of its
superpower friend and long-term ally the United States, and is endowed
with strategic natural resources. China's ability to influence Canada's policies and tap its high-tech developmental skills, commercial knowledge and

energy resources, is arguably indispensable in the augmentation of China's soft power not only in relation to Canada but also in relation to the United States. However, any security threat from China is often overstated in the Canadian media and political circles, which are influenced, to some extent, by anti-Communist and anti-China sentiment emanating not only from within Canada but also from the United States. Huge controversy was aroused, for example, in September 2009, when three Chinese community groups, Canada ALPHA, BC ALPHA and Toronto ALPHA, went to court to seek an injunction against *Nest of Spies: The Startling Truth about Foreign Agents at Work within Canada's Borders*, a book in which Fabrice de Pierrebourg, a journalist, and Michel Juneau-Katsuya, a former officer of CSIS, made allegations about industrial espionage conducted on behalf of a number of countries, including China. In a settlement of the case in November, the publisher HarperCollins Canada agreed to remove certain sections of the book that were deemed to be "defamatory."

The establishment of Confucius Institutes has also aroused some controversy (see Little 2010). Since 2004 the Chinese government has supported the establishment of about 300 Confucius Institutes in various parts of the world, including seven at McMaster University, the University of Waterloo and other locations in Canada (*Ming Pao*, June 26, 2010). These institutes can be seen as part of an effort by the Chinese government to shape perceptions of China through the propagation of Chinese culture, language, literature and art. The use of cultural and other non-political means of influencing the ways in which foreigners and overseas Chinese view China is nothing new. Confucius Institutes have been supported by the Ministry of Education inside China, and it is not surprising that the instructors sent out to work in them are politically acceptable to the government. However, as long as Canadian students and other members of the public attending these institutes are politically independent and retain their capacity for critical thinking, any effort made by an instructor to subject them to political propaganda would be futile, and might well elicit negative reactions from those who support the idea that human rights and democratic values are universally applicable.

Human Rights Concerns

Perhaps the most prominent difference between Stephen Harper's Conservative government and the Chinese regime is over human rights.

Harper's sympathetic support for the Dalai Lama and his reiteration of the importance of human rights, the rule of law and freedom during his visit to China in December 2009 are sufficient indications of this difference. Critics have pointed to what they regard as inconsistency on this issue, as, for example, when the Canadian government appeared to appease the Chinese regime by preventing New Tang Dynasty TV and the *Epoch Times* from attending President Hu's public appearance in Ottawa in June 2010 (see Delacourt 2010). However, this incident was an exception, and contrasted with Canada's longstanding practice of expressing concern for human rights in China. In February 2009, for example, the Canadian immigration authorities issued a permit for a Chinese dissident journalist, Jiang Weiping, to enter Canada. Jiang had been arrested in China in December 2000 and released from detention in January 2006 (*World Journal*, February 10, 2009). According to Jiang, he was thrown into prison because of his investigative reports on a corruption case involving the Mayor of Shenyang, a city in northeastern China. His case aroused the concern of some overseas Chinese human rights activists in Canada, whose efforts on his behalf helped to ensure that he and his family could immigrate to Canada. Jason Kenney, Canada's Minister of Citizenship, Immigration and Multiculturalism, insisted that Jiang's case did not really affect Sino-Canadian relations (*Today Daily News*, February 8, 2009).

Concern about human rights is also articulated by some ethnic Chinese and Tibetan groups in Canada. Before Harper's visit to China the *Canadian Chinese Express* reported (November 27, 2009) that some Canadian Chinese groups had lobbied the foreign minister, Lawrence Cannon, in favour of a more assertive policy on the protection of human rights in China. According to the *Today Daily News* (December 2, 2009), these groups included the Toronto Association in Support of China's Democratic Movement, the Free Tibet (Canadian) Association and the Canadian branch of Amnesty International. While the Liberal Party's international trade commentator Scott Brison criticized the Conservative government for paying too much attention to human rights issues rather than trade, a public opinion survey conducted by Angus Reid on December 1 and 2, 2009, showed that, of 1,006 respondents, sixty-eight percent agreed that Canada should devote more attention to human rights than to trade with respect to countries known for human rights violations, including China (*Ming Pao*, December 3, 2009). Hence, the Conservative government's emphasis on human rights in China is a policy in conformity with the mainstream values of Canadian society. This explains why Harper insisted that he would not give up on human rights issues for the sake of trade with China, even though his stress on the supremacy of human rights did not meet with applause from his audience in Shanghai. Similarly, when Hu Jintao visited Ottawa in June 2010, Harper insisted that he would raise human rights with the Chinese President. Critics and skeptics may question whether such political gestures are of any use, yet the Canadian government's position is that, in expressing concern for human rights, Harper and other Canadian politicians are expressing the values of most Canadians, who cherish multiculturalism, civil liberties, human rights, the rule of law and political tolerance.

In a speech delivered at Tsinghua University in Beijing, Michael Ignatieff, the leader of the Liberal Party of Canada, said that Canada could contribute more to the promotion of human rights and the strengthening of the rule of law through human interactions than through diplomatic activity, and emphasized that the Chinese people themselves, rather than foreigners, were responsible for resolving issues of human rights, religious freedom, economic liberalization and the use of the death penalty (*Ming Pao*, July 6, 2010). Ignatieff thus appears to have adopted a more diplomatic approach to the sensitive issue of human rights than Harper, even though he had been Director of Harvard University's Carr Center for Human Rights before his return to Canada in 2006. Ignatieff also said that Canadians should admit the progress made by China in the area of human rights protection, including its efforts at reducing poverty. It may be argued that, from the perspective of managing *mianzi* and understanding Chinese culture, Ignatieff is ahead of Harper, but critics have maintained that the Liberal Party is all too often "soft on China" (see, for example, Den Tandt 2009a). In any case, the Canadian political elite in general cannot shy away from concern for human rights in their interactions with China, and the differences with Beijing on this issue will certainly persist in the foreseeable future.

The Lai Changxing Case and the Politics of Extradition

The case of Lai Changxing illustrates the dilemmas faced by the Canadian government in coping with China. On the one hand, the Canadian government has to respect the human rights of individuals, including Lai, who escaped from the province of Fujian to Canada, by way of Hong Kong, in 1999. The Chinese authorities accused Lai of financing a multi-billion-dollar operation smuggling cigarettes and fuel into Fujian, bribing officials and military officers, and avoiding taxes, but, after a long process of legal actions, Lai was allowed to stay in Canada, on the grounds that, if he were sent back to China, he would face the death penalty. In compliance with the Canadian court's judgment, the authorities granted Lai a work permit, a move that aroused the anger of the Chinese government. The Chinese Foreign Ministry spokesman Jiang Yu said: "The Chinese government is unwavering and consistent in its position that the fugitive Lai Changxing return to face trial under Chinese law. We have already made serious representations to the Canadian side." Another complex immigration case involved two brothers who worked in a branch of the People's Bank of China in Harbin. They were regarded by the Chinese government as "corrupt elements," but after both men entered Canada their lawyer argued that, if they were sent back to China, they would face physical abuse or even the death penalty. The Supreme Court of Canada was not convinced by the risk assessment submitted by the immigration authorities, and the brothers were detained. The court also said, however, that the argument against Canadian protection of the two brothers was weak, and ordered that a new risk assessment should be conducted by another group of immigration officials. Their assessment favoured the two brothers, who then applied for landed immigrant status in Canada. Both these cases demonstrated not only the independence of Canada's judicial system, but also the determination of the Chinese authorities to have those it regards as criminals tried and punished. The two cases also prompted both China and Canada to look into the possibility of negotiating an extradition agreement, although Lai has said that he is not afraid of such an agreement because he is not a criminal.

Both China and Canada are signatories of the United Nations Convention Against Corruption. The official Chinese view is that if corrupt individuals escape from China to other parts of the world, including Canada, the Chinese government has a duty to prevent the outflow of the proceeds of these individuals' crimes. A formal extradition agreement would bring about the return of criminal suspects from Canada to China, but an agreement on the proceeds of crime would close the legal and practical loopholes that, according to the Chinese government, allow criminals to take state assets with them when they leave China. From the Canadian perspective, having formal agreements in place on extradition and the proceeds of crime would help to prevent Canada from becoming a haven for Chinese criminals, especially now that economic liberalization has stimulated an increase in cross-border crime across Greater China (see Lo 2009). Accordingly, in December 2009, the two governments agreed on a joint declaration on cross-border crime, and in January 2010, the Canadian government made the unprecedented decision to return to China a Chinese citizen, Cui Zhili, who was accused of involvement in an insurance fraud worth CNY 16 million in Beijing in 2002, and who had escaped to Canada in January 2003. The return of Cui to China raised the question whether Lai Changxing might also be extradited, but, more importantly, the Cui case showed that it was possible for both sides to use administrative arrangements to tackle the issue of cross-border crime.

The Neglected Hong Kong Factor in Enhancing Canada's Soft Power over China

When Stephen Harper visited Hong Kong in December 2009 he remarked that, with 200,000 Canadians residing there, Hong Kong was actually the largest Canadian city outside Canada. In total, 292,000 Canadians reside in Greater China. Moreover, about 100,000 people from Hong Kong have studied in Canada. The Canadian Chamber of Commerce has a membership of 1,200 in Hong Kong, making it the largest Canadian business organization outside Canada. In 2009, immigrants from Hong Kong to Canada topped the three categories of economic migrants, immigrants to Quebec and other provinces, and family reunions, outstripping the numbers of immigrants from mainland China and Taiwan. In many respects, then, Hong Kong occupies a central place in Canada's relations with Greater China.

Nevertheless, the Canadian government has not yet tapped the human resources and "soft power" connected with the Hong Kong factor in Sino-Canadian relations. Many politicians in Hong Kong, especially the democrats, have Canadian linkages or heritage to some degree. For instance, Albert Chan Wai-yip, the leader of the League of Social Democrats, studied in Canada and was a Canadian citizen before he renounced Canadian citizenship to participate in legislative elections in Hong Kong during the 1990s. Cyd Ho, a member of the legislature, also studied in Canada, while the deputy minister Greg So was formerly a lawyer practising in Canada, and also renounced Canadian citizenship when he became one of the appointed officials of the Hong Kong Special Autonomous Region. The former health official Margaret Chan studied at the University of Western Ontario (she is now Director General of the World Health Organization). The current Financial Secretary, John Tsang, formerly worked in Canada, while the former treasury chief Frederic Ma Si-hang also resided in Canada before he returned to work in Hong Kong. Many Canadians participated in the mass protests and parade against the maladministration of Tung Chee-hwa's government on July 1, 2003 (as the former Canadian Consul General, Tony Burger, pointed out to

me during a meeting and discussion in June 2004). Given these and other
close linkages between Hong Kong and Canada, it is at least arguable that the
Canadian government should reassess its lack of a policy for using the soft
power of Hong Kong Canadians in relations with China.

The absence of a clear and explicit Canadian policy on the Hong Kong
element in Sino-Canadian relations is attributable to several factors. First and
foremost, the human resources of the Canadian Consulate in Hong Kong are
weak and inadequate for handling any "united front work" comparable to
what the Chinese government is doing in Canada. Second, while the Harper
government realizes the significance of Hong Kong as the "largest Canadian
city outside Canada," it has no concrete policy measures, not to mention
policy advice, on how to translate the hidden soft power of Canadians in
Hong Kong into an effective instrument for articulating Canadian interests.
Canada lacks Hong Kong experts to balance the influence of those Sinolo-
gists who tend to view mainland China as being far more significant than
Hong Kong. Third, a few diplomats in the Canadian Foreign Service may
identify the hidden influence and soft power of Canadians in Hong Kong,
but since they are often rotated to work in different places, their expertise and
knowledge on Hong Kong are constantly lost or underused. As a result, the
Hong Kong factor has been largely neglected by the Canadian political and
diplomatic establishment. The human resources of the Canadian Consulate in Hong Kong need to be increased so that more staff can be devoted to
networking with Canadian individuals and groups in Hong Kong, organizing activities and sharing information so that a strong network and database
can be established. This potentially powerful Canadian community would
be able to influence various Chinese policies not only toward Hong Kong
itself but also toward Canada. The existing Canadian groups in Hong Kong,
including the Canadian Chamber of Commerce and the Canadian Club,
should not be complacent, but should expand their membership, and educational exchange programmes and cultural cooperation projects should be better organized under the leadership of Canadian officials. The talents available
in Greater China can be identified and tapped so that they can contribute to
the specific needs of Canada's rapidly changing society.

Conclusion

Since December 2009, the Conservative government of Canada has belat-
edly established more friendly relations and cooperative partnerships with

the Chinese government in a number of areas, including trade, tourism and crime control. This shift in Canada's foreign policy has also triggered an unintended dialectical process of enhancing Beijing's soft power over Ottawa. Canada is geopolitically located beside the United States, whose relations with China have oscillated ever since the founding of the People's Republic in 1949, and it is therefore understandable that China has sought to augment its soft power over Canada, if only as a means to influence opinion in the United States.

Engaging China should not be seen as simply having a subversive impact on Canada, as the constant fear of Chinese espionage in Canada suggests. Rather, engaging China means that Canada can and should maintain its tradition of supporting human rights development in the world, and that Canada must reassess its lack of any "united front" policy toward the Chinese residing in Greater China, notably in Hong Kong, where so many Canadian citizens live, work and raise their families. A new Canadian policy toward Hong Kong and, by implication, toward China as a whole, should ideally be adopted, in order to win the hearts and minds of Hong Kong Canadians and non-Canadians through enhanced cultural, social and educational exchanges and improved diplomatic organization and coordination. Given that many Chinese in Greater China appear to have a favourable perception of Canada as a country endowed with political tolerance, economic affluence, educational quality and social stability, adopting a more proactive policy toward Greater China would enhance Canada's soft power over China in the long run. Such reciprocal moves to enhance Canada's soft power in response to the gradual rise in Beijing's soft power over Ottawa should not be seen as politically sinister. In the real world of politics, seeking to influence the behaviour and policies of other nation states is normal. If the Canadian political and diplomatic elite can reassess their lack of a policy for enhancing Canada's soft power in Greater China, the time is ripe for its members to ponder a more proactive, long-term and strategic policy change in the coming years.

References

Delacourt, Susan. (2010, June 25). "Harper Helps Hu Keep Critics Away." *Toronto Star*, A10.

Den Tandt, Michael. (2009a, December 4). "Grits Soft on China." *Toronto Sun*, 20.

Den Tandt, Michael. (2009b, December 5). "Standing Up for Canada," *Saturday Sun* (Toronto), 18.

Little, Matthew. (2010, July 16). "Confucius Institutes: Getting Schooled by Beijing." *Epoch Times*.

Lo, Sonny Shiu-Hing. (2008). *The Dynamics of Beijing–Hong Kong Relations: A Model for Taiwan?* Hong Kong: Hong Kong University Press.

Lo, Sonny Shiu-Hing. (2009). *The Politics of Cross-Border Crime in Greater China: Case Studies of Mainland China, Hong Kong, and Macao.* Armonk, NY: M. E. Sharpe.

Loh, Christine Loh. (2010). *Underground Front: The Chinese Communist Party in Hong Kong.* Hong Kong: Hong Kong University Press.

Nye, Joseph S. (2004). *Soft Power: The Means to Success in World Politics.* New York: Public Affairs.

Schiller, Bill. (2009a, December 3). "PM's Tough Beijing Balancing Act." *Toronto Star*, A6.

Schiller, Bill. (2009b, December 4). "Harper Scolded for China Snub." *Toronto Star*, A25.

This chapter also draws on news reports and editorial pieces in the *Toronto Star*, the Toronto *Sun* and five Chinese-language newspapers: the *Canadian Chinese Express* (Toronto), the *Ming Pao* (Toronto), the *Sing Tao Daily* (Hong Kong), the *Today Daily News* (Toronto) and the *World Journal* (Toronto and Vancouver).

Chapter 6

Friends across the Pacific: Links between Canada and Hong Kong in Historical and Contemporary Perspectives

Ming K. Chan

The extraordinarily intimate, multifaceted and mutually beneficial trans-Pacific bond between Canada and Hong Kong is not predicated on political-administrative ties such as those between a colonial power and a dependent territory, nor on war, conquest or military alliance, or a collective economic mode, and it is definitely not a case of necessity between neighbours sharing a border. Rather the extensive relations between Canada and Hong Kong stem from deliberate choices built upon common interests and shared values. Until 1997, membership of the Commonwealth underlay the relationship, but since Hong Kong's retrocession to China in that year Canadian links with Hong Kong have grown with a new dynamism.

More than one million Chinese now live in Canada, over half of them being of Hong Kong origin or with direct Hong Kong ties. These Hong Kongers proliferate through all the ten provinces and three territories of Canada, though there is a heavy concentration in the largest cities: according to the Census of 2006, Metropolitan Toronto, with a total population of 5.1 million, had absorbed 486,000 Chinese, while Vancouver hosted 380,000, Montreal 72,015, Calgary 66,375, Edmonton 47,200, Ottawa 45,060, Winnipeg 13,750, Victoria 12,325, Saskatoon 4,245, Regina 3,340 and Halifax 3,105. Since the 1990s, Vancouver has been nicknamed "Hongcouver." Within forty kilometres of downtown Toronto a dozen Chinese shopping malls punctuate Greater Toronto, each filled with Hong Kong-style restaurants, supermarkets, bookstores, beauty salons, and fashion boutiques. Canadians in major cities routinely encounter persons or businesses with Hong Kong connections.

One prominent Hong Kong-linked icon in the Canadian business landscape is HSBC Bank Canada. HSBC's original name, the Hong Kong and Shanghai Banking Corporation, reflected its birth in Hong Kong in 1865 and its later branching out into Shanghai and other Chinese treaty ports, as well as the former British territories in Southeast Asia. Its Chinese name, Huifeng ("abundance of remittance"), indicates its role in handling remittances from overseas Chinese (Liu 2006, p. 18). HSBC landed in Canada in 1981 as the HongKong Bank of Canada. Since then, through acquisitions such as its takeover of the Bank of British Columbia in 1986 and its expansion among the fast-growing Canadian Chinese population, it has become a major bank, particularly in British Columbia and Ontario. Headquartered in Vancouver and with 260 offices, including 140 branches, throughout Canada, HSBC Bank Canada ranks seventh among Canadian banks in terms of assets, at CA$ 70.5 billion, and had total deposits of CA$ 49.6 billion as of August 2009 (see Lazarus 2003). From British Columbia to the Maritime Provinces, there are HSBC branches in Asian malls and Chinatowns, often with mostly Chinese tellers serving mainly Canadian Chinese clients. Inside these HSBC branches, other than transactions in Canadian currency, one might almost feel as if one were in Hong Kong, as Cantonese is the language most commonly spoken, and waiting customers read Canadian editions of Hong Kong's two major dailies, the *Ming Pao* and the *Sing Tao*. They are among the more than forty Chinese-language dailies or weeklies published in Canada, at the core of the country's thriving Chinese-language media alongside numerous radio and television channels serving Chinese communities across five time zones.

Historical Migration to Canada

The roots of Canada's links with Hong Kong and Guangdong Province in southern China date from 1858, soon after the British took Hong Kong as a colony in 1842 following the Opium War. Linked by the British empire's shipping and economic networks and buttressed by their strategically located natural harbours, Hong Kong and Vancouver soon became major ports on the trans-Pacific route for goods and "coolie" immigrant traffic. The Canadian Pacific Railway drew more than 17,000 Chinese workers to Canada during the construction of its main line in the western provinces between 1881 and 1886. Chinese labourers in Canada were mostly Cantonese who sailed from Hong Kong to Vancouver (see Li 1998). Canadian Pacific's links with Hong Kong lasted for decades: its shining White Empress ocean liners can often be seen in pre-war photographs of Hong Kong Harbour (see Lamb 1991) and the Canada goose, symbol of Canadian Pacific Airlines, was a familiar sight on billboards in Hong Kong in the 1950s and 1960s.

Some of the Cantonese labourers brought in to work on the railway or in the mines settled in the western provinces and built Canada's earliest Chinatowns in Victoria, Vancouver, Calgary and Edmonton. Their progress was disrupted after 1923, when the federal Parliament passed the Chinese Immigration Act, specifically banning further Chinese immigration, and was not resumed until after that Act was repealed in 1947. In 2006 the Canadian government issued an official apology and token compensation to the surviving victims of the head tax levied on early Chinese immigrants, symbolically closing a sad chapter in Sino-Canadian relations, and partially redeeming the dark legacy of the white state's actions against ethnic minorities in Canada's collective conscience. First imposed in 1885, at fifty dollars, the head tax was increased to 500 dollars in 1903. A total of CA$ 23 million was collected from the 82,000 Chinese who reportedly arrived between 1886 and1923 (see Ng 1999).

The post-war era saw only limited numbers of Chinese immigrants arriving in Canada, and Cold War politics, with the absence of diplomatic relations with Beijing until 1970, ensured that they came overwhelmingly from Hong Kong rather than the mainland. Major political events on both shores of the Pacific also shaped the Chinese influx into Canada. Violent disturbances launched by pro-Beijing activists engulfed Hong Kong for five months in 1967, partly fuelled by the Cultural Revolution in mainland China and Portuguese capitulation to Chinese demands over nearby Macao after similar riots there in 1966. Stern police measures, supported by the local Chinese majority, helped the British authorities to restore order (see Bickers and Yip, eds. 2009). Losing confidence in the colony's future as radicals waged militant anti-West campaigns across mainland China, many middle-class families and tycoons from Hong Kong sought safe heaven abroad, with Canada as their first choice. Their exodus came at a turning point in Canadian immigration reform with the introduction, also in 1967, of a merit point system that opened a much wider door to potential Hong Kong immigrants with skills or wealth, in addition to those qualified under the family reunion provisions. Between 1968 and 1976, some 90,118 Chinese immigrants were admitted into Canada, a threefold increase over the numbers entering before 1967 (Li 1998, p. 97). These immigrants infused new blood into the Canadian Chinese communities, which were still very largely "HongKongtowns" until very recently.

Since the 1980s Chinese from both the mainland and Taiwan have also begun to flood into Canada. This trans-Pacific diaspora was reinforced by a new influx from Hong Kong after the mid-1980s, following the signing by Britain and China in 1984 of the accord that provided for the retrocession of Hong Kong to China in 1997. This outbound traffic only intensified after the Tiananmen Incident of June 4, 1989, when the armed suppression of pro-democracy activists in Beijing triggered a serious crisis of confidence about Hong Kong's future under Chinese rule. Many Hong Kong families seeking safe haven abroad chose Canada over Australia or the United States (see Skeldon, ed. 1994 and Skeldon 1995). At the same time the United States became more engaged with Hong Kong and loosened its own historically tight immigration controls (Segal 1993, p. 112; see also Jencks 1990). The annual immigration quotas allocated to Hong Kong by the United States were raised from 600 in the 1960s and 1970s to 2,000 in 1983 and 20,000 from 1994 (Segal 1993, pp. 121–25 and 130–38, and Paau 2000, p. 205). Nevertheless, Canada remained Hong Kongers' first choice, and there were around 30,000 arrivals in Canada each year between 1991 and 1996. The British scholar Gerald Segal (1993) criticized Ottawa's poaching of Hong Kong's best as "immigration without responsibility," and a Canadian academic, Kim Nossal (1997, p. 87), called Canada's approach to Hong Kong during its problematic transition to 1997 the "most aggressive" as compared with the United States and Australia.

Behind the talk of "1997 blues" there were divergent personal and family factors, educational opportunities and career prospects, livelihood concerns and political calculations among the tens of thousands of Hong Kongers who decided to emigrate (see Skeldon 1994, Part III, and Salaff, Wong and Fung 1997, and Salaff, Wong and Greve, 2010). Yet it is clear that the two major waves of migration from Hong Kong to Canada, after 1967 and between 1984 and 1997, were propelled by political upheavals generated in mainland China, and can also be viewed as not untypical of the patterns of collective behaviour that have punctuated Hong Kong's record as a city with continuous inflows and circulation of migrants shaping its human landscape (see Siu and Ku, ed. 2008).

Hong Kong's more settled situation since 1997 and the revival of its economy have unleashed a reverse migratory cycle, with more Canadians of

Hong Kong origin heading toward Greater China than there are new arrivals from Hong Kong. Mainland China's impressive economic growth since 1978 has yielded business opportunities and career prospects for many transnational Chinese of Hong Kong origins with Canadian education and passports. The "brain drain" of the 1980s and 1990s, when there was a massive transplanting of Hong Kong talents and expertise to Canada, should not be regarded as a negative outflow, but rather as a long-term diversification and upgrading, an investment yielding enhanced global networks and Canada-educated talents capable of making greater positive contributions upon their return to Greater China (see Salaff 2009).

Official data show that immigration from Hong Kong has steadily declined since 1997, both in absolute numbers and as a proportion of total immigration (see Table 6.1).

In contrast, immigration from mainland China rose from 17,533 (7.8 per cent of the total) in 1996 to 29,336 (11.9 per cent) in 2008, yielding

Table 6.1   Immigration from Hong Kong to Canada, 1996 to 2005

	Numbers of immigrants from Hong Kong	Proportion of total immigrants to Canada, selected years (%)
1996	29,988	13.3
1997	22,250	
1998	8,087	4.6
1999	3,672	
2000	2,865	
2001	1,965	
2002	1,541	
2003	1,472	
2004	1,547	
2005	1,783	0.7
2006	1,489	
2007	1,131	
2008	1,324	0.5

Source: Statistics Canada, 2006.

a major demographic realignment within Canada's Chinese communities. The fact that mainland China is now, and likely will continue to be, the largest source of new Chinese immigrants to Canada has reshaped China-town politics. Chinese is now the third most widely spoken language in Canada, after English and French.

Even the SARS epidemic of spring 2003 testified to the intimacy of the relationship between Canada and Hong Kong. The return from Hong Kong of a single person infected with the SARS virus triggered a health crisis in Toronto, where 375 people were infected and forty-four died, while Hong Kong recorded a total SARS death toll of 299 in mid-2003 (see Mason 2007).

Education and Alumni Networks

A crucial dimension of this trans-Pacific bond is the two-way traffic in educa-tion and manpower development. Canadian schools and universities have long been Hong Kong students' prime choice for high-quality overseas edu-cation, while since the 1980s major Canadian cities have become havens of security and opportunity drawing in migratory Hong Kong families.

In the years following the Second World War Canadian degrees and qualifications, particularly in medicine and engineering, were recognized by Hong Kong's colonial officials as being of the same high standard as those from British universities. Many promising young Hong Kongers chose Canada for their university education, some with the hope of return-ing home after graduation. Canadian universities also represented a real bargain: during the 1960s and 1970s, two major prairie campuses, the Uni-versity of Saskatchewan and the University of Manitoba, drew many Hong Kong students, who paid only nominal tuitions as locals. Some 20,000 Hong Kong students are now studying in Canada. Data from Citizenship and Immigration Canada show that the annual inflow of those entering Canada on student permits from Hong Kong was 1,730 in 1996 (4.4 per cent of that year's total foreign student intake) and 1,297 (3.1 percent) in 1997, and fell still further to 1,148 in 2007 (1.6 percent) and 1,120 in 2008 (1.4 percent). This declining trend parallels the decrease in overall immigration from Hong Kong since 1997.

Nevertheless, a disproportionate enrolment of ethnic Chinese students, not only from Hong Kong, but also from mainland China, Taiwan and Southeast Asia, fills Canadian campuses from the University of Victoria on the Pacific to the Memorial University of Newfoundland on the Atlantic. At the University of Toronto, for example, the 1,736 students from China (including Hong Kong) constituted the single largest bloc (31 percent) of total international (non-Canadian) undergraduate enrolment in 2007, and the largest group (17 percent) among international postgraduates. These figures do not, of course, cover students who originated from Hong Kong and have become citizens or landed immigrants, or who were born in Canada to Hong Kong immigrant parents. It is fitting that the History Department at the University of Toronto offers a course on the history of Hong Kong, perhaps the only such regular course mounted at a leading university outside Asia.

Meanwhile, the Canadian presence in Hong Kong can be seen in the large number of organizations such as the Canadian Club, established in 1952, the Chinese Canadian Association, founded in 1989 and now with more than 3,000 members, and the Canadian University Association, which since 1961 has functioned as an umbrella body for more than twenty university alumni bodies active in Hong Kong, where an estimated 100,000 alumni of Canadian universities live and work. There are three schools in Hong Kong offering a Canadian curriculum: the Canadian International School of Hong Kong, the Delia School of Canada and the Christian Alliance P.C. Lau Memorial School. Hong Kong's various tertiary institutions currently employ some 200 Canadian faculty and staff members as well as more than 530 Canadian degree-holders.

Many Canada-trained Hong Kongers have returned home to become leading academics, professionals, captains of enterprises, tycoons or public officials. Today Canadian degree holders, many of them also Canadian landed immigrants or naturalized citizens, constitute the largest group of foreign-educated persons in Hong Kong. In fact, according to the Canadian Department of Foreign Affairs and International Trade, in 2008 the 320,000 Canadian citizens formed the largest single bloc of "foreigners" (strictly speaking, foreign passport-holders) in Hong Kong. Many of them are Hong Kong-born or Hong Kong-raised, but Canada-educated. These Canada-processed Hong Kong talents have penetrated into many layers of Hong Kong's social, cultural and economic fabric. For example, three graduates of Canadian universities serve in the Legislative Council of Hong Kong: Cyd Ho (University of Waterloo) and Albert Wai-yip Chan (who resided in Canada for ten years, from Grade 10 through two degrees, but later abandoned his Canadian citizenship to contest Hong Kong elections), both directly elected; and Patrick Lau (University of

Manitoba), who represents the functional constituency for architecture. Other prominent Hong Kongers with Canadian connections include the noted scientist Professor Lap-cheeTsui, Vice-Chancellor of the University of Hong Kong (see Huang 1992, pp. 146–53).

Hong Kongers and Canada's Asia–Pacific Outreach

Over the years persons of Hong Kong origin have contributed much to enrich Canada as a democratic, progressive and multicultural society.

Any list of Hong Kongers reaching the heights of the Canadian political establishment must begin with Adrienne Clarkson, who retired as Governor General in 2005 after almost six years in office (see Huang 1992, pp. 166–85). Three other Canadians with Hong Kong connections have been Lieutenant Governors of Canadian provinces. The late David Lam (1923–2010) arrived in Vancouver soon after the Second World War and served two terms as Lieutenant Governor of British Columbia, from 1988 to 1995 (see Huang 1992, pp. 58–69); Norman Kwong, born in Calgary of Cantonese parents who arrived via Hong Kong, became Lieutenant Governor of Alberta in 2005; and Philip S. Yee, who was born and raised in Hong Kong, has been Lieutenant Governor of Manitoba since 2009.

In 1998 Vivienne Poy, daughter of the prominent Hong Kong businessman and philanthropist Richard Charles Lee (see Poy 2006), became the first Asian Canadian to be appointed to the Senate. From 2003 to 2006, Senator Poy served as Chancellor of the University of Toronto, where she had obtained her history doctorate with a thesis entitled "Calling Canada Home: Canadian Law and Immigrant Chinese Women from South China and Hong Kong, 1860–1990." Senator Poy has founded the Richard Charles Lee Canada–Hong Kong Library at the university, where a Hong Kong property tycoon has also endowed the Cheng Yu Tong Library for East Asian Studies.

Raymond Chan, who arrived from Hong Kong in 1969, was elected Member of Parliament on the Liberal Party ticket in 1993 and served as Minister of State for the Asia–Pacific region in the Department of External Affairs from then until 2000. There are now five members of Hong Kong origin in the federal House of Commons, and quite a few Hong Kongers have been elected to provincial legislatures and municipal councils across Canada.

Paralleling the massive traffic in education and migration, trade, services and investment also flow across the Pacific, testimony to Hong

Kong's role as facilitator and bridgehead for Canada's economic, social and cultural links to East Asia, with particular effectiveness as a launch pad for Canadian business entering the China market. Canada attracted 130,100 visitors from Hong Kong in 2001 and 122,800 in 2002. The SARS epidemic caused a decline to 94,000 in 2003, but the total rose again to 121,000 in 2004, and reached 113,404 in 2007 and 128,139 in 2008, making Canada the twelfth most popular destination for Hong Kongers. Hong Kong saw growth of 17.7 percent in the number of visitors from Canada, which hit a record of 395,170 in 2007, then declined to 379,046 in 2008 because of the global recession, but still made Hong Kong Canadians' twelfth most popular destination. Air Canada and Cathay Pacific run seventy-one weekly passenger flights across the Pacific, forty-two servicing Vancouver and twenty-nine Toronto, including thirty-five non-stop direct flights, often at full capacity.

Hong Kong is consistently among Canada's top fifteen trading partners, and is Canada's fifth largest market for information technology and its third largest market for beef. Canada's total exports to Hong Kong reached a value of 1.59 billion Canadian dollars in 2006 and increased to 1.77 billion Canadian dollars in 2008. In 2005, Canada ranked twenty-second among suppliers of goods to Hong Kong, with merchandise imports from Canada valued at CA\$ 1.5 billion. The value of Hong Kong's exports to Canada totalled CA\$ 3.46 billion in 2008, while CA\$ 1.16 billion worth of Canada-made goods were re-exported by Hong Kong to the rest of the world. Cumulative investment from Hong Kong in Canada reached CA\$ 6.3 billion in 2006, while Canadian investment in Hong Kong totalled CA\$ 6 billion in 2008. These figures exclude extensive local assets owned by Hong Kongers who became Canadian passport-holders. Hong Kong is Canada's key spearhead into mainland China, which is Canada's second largest trading partner, with bilateral trade valued at more than CA\$ 50 billion in 2008.

According to official figures, as of August 2009 thirteen Canadian companies had located their regional headquarters in Hong Kong, while another thirty-two had regional offices there, amid a pool of more than 150 Canadian companies with offices in Hong Kong. Another 600 firms had representatives there. Twelve Canadian brokerage and investment advisory firms were active on the financial scene, and so too were eight Canadian insurance companies, including Manulife and Sun Life, and all of the big five Canadian banks (Canadian Imperial Bank of Commerce, Toronto Dominion, Bank of Nova Scotia, Bank of Montreal and Royal

Bank of Canada). The Canadian Chamber of Commerce–Hong Kong, which has more than 1,200 members, is the largest such body outside Canada. A Canadian Trade Commission was first established in Hong Kong in 1928, and now the Canadian Consulate General, with twenty-three Canada-based diplomats and 117 local staff, is among Canada's largest missions abroad. Reflecting Hong Kong's special importance, the Consulate General reports directly to the Department of Foreign Affairs and International Trade in Ottawa while Canada's other consulates in China, in Guangzhou, Shanghai and Chongqing, report to the Canadian Embassy in Beijing.

Being thus linked to Canada through extensive human ties, social and cultural exchanges, and substantial economic interests, Hong Kong has long been much more than a remote foreign policy item for Ottawa, which closely followed Hong Kong's retrocession to China and the establishment of the Hong Kong Special Autonomous Region. Even before the retrocession Ottawa hosted such benign undertakings as the Canada Festival in Hong Kong in spring 1992 and the Hong Kong Festival in Toronto that autumn. The growth of the Hong Kong immigrant communities has also enhanced Canada's search for opportunities in East Asia, especially mainland China. The maturing of the Hong Konger community in Canada, as second- and third-generation descendants come of age, has provided a new crop of Canada-educated professionals blessed with a special empathy for Chinese culture and deeply rooted Hong Kong sensitivity. As Canada's valuable Greater China assets, they function as powerful trans-Pacific human bridges.

Canadian Contributions to Hong Kong

It is to be expected that, as a mature democracy with high regard for civil liberties and the rule of law, Canada would wish to share with Hong Kong and the entire Chinese nation its vast knowledge and rich experience in the realms of human rights, social justice, constitutional reform, political pluralism and environmental protection, as well as advances in science, medicine and technology.

In 2002 and 2003, the authorities of the Hong Kong Special Administrative Region set out to pass a national security bill that would translate the provisions of Article 23 of Hong Kong's Basic Law into local legislation, and clamp down on "any act of treason, secession, sedition, subversion" against

Beijing, "prohibit foreign political organizations or bodies from conducting political activities" in Hong Kong, and "prohibit political organizations or bodies ... from establishing ties with foreign political organizations or bodies." Regina Ip, then Hong Kong's Secretary of Security, complained to this author on March 16, 2003, about vocal Canadian official criticisms of the draft bill, claiming that the Canadians were acting as if they were "surrogates of the departed British colonialists." By several estimates, around 50,000 Canadian passport-holders were among the 500,000 residents of Hong Kong who demonstrated against restrictions on civil liberties on July 1, 2003. Concerned parties in Hong Kong sought Canadian inputs into the drafting process, and the final version of the law as sent to the legislature by the regime (that was later forced to shelve it after the mass protests) did draw extensively, if not always accurately, on the Canadian Charter of Rights and Freedoms and other Canadian legal studies and precedents. (see Chan and Lo 2006, pp. 47-49).

Canada's society and economy have been enriched by inputs from Chinese who either hailed from Hong Kong or descended from Hong Kong immigrants. Likewise, many Hong Kongers have benefited from their Canadian upbringing, education, professional training and work experience, which have given them significant head starts in their lives and careers. In their hearts and minds, and through their lives and work, many have attempted in good faith and with deep conviction to transfer to Hong Kong some of Canada's finest attributes, institutions and processes, as well as its values and priorities. They naturally wish to share with their fellow Hong Kongers all the positive aspects of Canadian society that they hold dear.

Ottawa and the Canadian people are keen to see the successful realization of the "one country, two systems" formula in Hong Kong. The Toronto *Globe and Mail*, Canada's leading daily, devoted more coverage to political stories than to economic news concerning Hong Kong between 1997 and 2007 (see Salaff and Greve 2007). Canadians' vividly expressed concern for, and vocal public commentary on, Hong Kong matters should be regarded as friendly suggestions, to be received in good faith, as they mean no offence and harbour no ill will.

The levels of economic attainment in Canada and Hong Kong are converging fast: in 2006 GDP per capita in Canada was US$ 38,757 and in Hong Kong it was US$ 27,500, but in 2008 the figures were US$ 39,100 for Canada and US$ 43,700 for Hong Kong. Yet economic indicators are far less crucial than the realm of values and ideals that Canada embodies and is willing to share with Hong Kong and the entire Chinese nation. Canadian values of freedom, democracy, the rule of law, social and political pluralism,

and multiculturalism, as well as Canada's traditions of striving for concilia-
tion and accommodation of differences with mutual respect, and promoting
unity in diversity, should constitute the most magnificent gifts that Canada
could bestow on the students, immigrants and citizens of Hong Kong origin
who wish to share these with their homeland peers. Indeed, Hong Kong is
a potent transmitter of Canada's "soft power" toward Greater China. Perhaps enlightened Chinese may prefer China to evolve eventually into a more
Canada-like society, rather than becoming a replica of the United States as a
stressful global superpower.

Links between Canada and Macao

Canada and Macao have been interacting for more than 200 years, mainly
through trade and immigration. Canada's Consul General in Hong Kong
has served concurrently as Consul General to Macao since 1972. Enhanced
by its common membership of the World Trade Organization, and rid-
ing on a booming economy driven by gaming and tourism, Macao is a
promising market for Canadian products and services, and for cultural and
academic exchanges.

The enduring and dynamic links between Canada and Macao were little affected by Macao's relatively smooth retrocession to China on December 20, 1999, after nearly 450 years of Portuguese rule. Unlike in Hong
Kong, where the "1997 blues" triggered an exodus to Canada, Macao's
Chinese population adopted a calmer approach. A migratory trend did
emerge among the minority Macanese, mixed-race descendants of Portuguese and Chinese or other Eurasian families, with Canada as their most
popular destination after Portugal. Now there is a thriving network of
social and cultural associations among Macanese immigrants across Canada, including the Casa de Macao Vancouver, the Casa de Macao Toronto
and the Macao Cultural Association of Western Canada, which has been
based in Vancouver since 1989. These form parts of the international network of Casas de Macao, with sister organizations located in Lisbon, Rio
de Janeiro, Sao Paulo, Sydney, San Francisco and Hong Kong, though the
Vancouver *Boletim Macaense* is the only monthly newsletter issued by any
of the Casas de Macao.

In 2004 a Canadian Chamber of Commerce was set up to promote
the interests of Macao's burgeoning Canadian business community, as the
city moves toward becoming a hub for leisure tourism, conventions, and

exhibitions, attracting an annual inflow of more than twenty million tourists from Greater China and the rest of East Asia. In 2009, Canadian exports to Macao reached a value of CA$ 14,952,586, while Macao's exports to Canada totalled CA$ 22,271,035, and 73,384 Canadians visited Macao, less than in 2008, when 82,136 Canadians visited, due to the global recession.

Post-colonial Macao enjoyed double-digit economic growth and rapid transformation under the leadership of Edmund Ho, the first Chief Executive of the Macao Special Administrative Region, who was in office from 1999 to 2009. Ho attended high school in Ontario and graduated from York University in Toronto. Lawrence Ho, son of the casino tycoon Stanley Ho and founding President of the Canadian Chamber of Commerce in Macao, is a graduate of the University of Toronto, and runs his own Melco group of casino-hotel resorts. Another prominent community leader, Executive Councillor Vai Tac Leong, is a graduate of the University of Waterloo. Several dozen Canadian university graduates are faculty members at tertiary institutions in Macao, and the Macao Associated Canadian Alumni Union, operating since 1998, acts as a bridging organization by hosting business and social events that foster alumni relations and Canadian linkages. Canadians are increasingly visible and play active roles in Macanese society, notably through the establishment in 2002 of the only international school in Macao, which follows the Alberta curriculum. Cultural and arts exchanges include a permanent venue for Cirque du Soleil at the Venetian Macao, the city's largest casino, hotel and convention centre. Right next door, with a Maple Leaf flag flying at its entrance, is the Four Seasons Macao, managed by the Toronto-based hotel chain. Smaller than the US-owned and operated Las Vegas-style ultra-opulent Sands, Wynn and MGM casino-hotels in Macao, this elegantly refined hotel aptly symbolizes the low-key yet much appreciated Canadian presence in Macao.

Undersides of Hong Kongers' Canada Saga

Any nuanced overview of Hong Kong immigrant experience in Canada should include some account of the various undersides that have drawn public interest and media coverage. This section is informed by the insightful first-hand observations of a number of Canadian Chinese of Hong Kong origin with long professional and family experience in Canada.

Cross-border crimes, especially gang activities in major Canadian cities with large Chinese populations, have involved Hong Kong immigrants.

Some Hong Kong immigrants have also attracted resentment for their giant mansions, fancy cars and expensive tastes, and their speculative dealings that have driven up local property prices (see Matthews 1983, Cannon 1989 and DeMont and Fennell 1989). Some younger Hong Kong immigrants have shown an acute lack of interest in learning more about Canada, treating their Canada sojourn as a mere schooling interlude while obtaining Canadian passports as political insurance before returning to Hong Kong. There have also been some cases of broken marriages, due to prolonged spousal separation as husbands work in Hong Kong while wives stay in Canada with children in school, and problems among youth due to inadequate parental guidance, resulting from the parents' long absences from Canada.

The Hong Kong immigrant communities that sprouted in Canada in the 1980s and the 1990s have experienced stagnation or even shrinkage with the apparent success of the "one country, two systems" formula in Hong Kong since 1997. Many discontented immigrants have reverse-migrated back to Hong Kong to take part in the Greater China economic boom or to enjoy the Hong Kong lifestyle that they find difficult to forego. Most of the mid-career immigrants who landed in Canada during the 1980s and 1990s are now in their late fifties or sixties, approaching retirement. As their children come of age, it is less likely that one or both parents have to work in Hong Kong to support their decent living standards in Canada. Hence the problem of broken marriages and dysfunctional families due to prolonged spousal separation and parental absence is now less prevalent among Hong Kong immigrant families. Rather, a new trend has emerged: while their Canada-educated children work in Hong Kong, many parents living in Canada regularly visit their children back "home." Eventually, some of them move back to Hong Kong to join their children and grandchildren. Many immigrants who have returned to Hong Kong continue to collect Canadian social benefits, a windfall from their Canadian passport-holder status.

Reflecting the pulling effects of their Hong Kong roots and Greater China's career prospects, numerous immigrant children have returned to Hong Kong, probably permanently, to pursue their careers upon graduation from Canadian universities instead of working in Canada. As a result, the growth of the Hong Kong immigrant communities in Canada has peaked. Further growth will be much slower and will depend less on inflows from Hong Kong than on whether Hong Kongers' circles on both sides of the Pacific capitalize on the entrenched links between Canada and Hong Kong.

Some Hong Kong families have suffered uneasy adaptation and downward economic mobility in Canada, so their longing for the "good old days" in Hong Kong is understandable. Other Hong Kongers with Canadian degrees and work experience have sought work in Hong Kong rather than in Canada because they perceive the prospects of promotion in Canada to be less promising, due to their minority status. Nevertheless, Canada remains Hong Kongers' most favoured destination for migration and education. Among the professional bodies in Hong Kong there is a recent increase in membership of those with Canadian education, reflecting the intimate links that will shape a proportion of the next generation of Hong Kong elites.

Perhaps the expansion of the Hong Kong/mainland Chinese communities in major Canadian cities does not promote the inculcation of "Canadianness" among new immigrants. The concentration of Chinese immigrants and their descendants in a few major Canadian cities has resulted in almost cocoon-like communities, whose members have little need to interact with mainstream Canadian society. One Hong Kong immigrant banker in Vancouver admits that he has felt no pressure from the local "old timers," as Canada's government and society have embraced immigrants so well that many new immigrants do not bother to become "Canadianized."

Greater China immigrants today come from more diverse sources than Hong Kong and Guangdong, and have different reasons for immigrating to Canada. The recent upsurge of immigrants from mainland China and Taiwan has intensified the process of internal ethnic and cultural negotiation, making community politics among Chinese immigrants more layered and complicated. This influx of mainlanders has significantly reshaped facets of Canada's Chinese communities. The Canadian editions of *Sing Tao* and *Ming Pao* now publish sister newspapers in simplified Chinese characters for mainland immigrant readers. Staff in Chinese restaurants, shops and other businesses in Canada's Chinatowns and "Hong Kong Malls" now speak Mandarin to serve their mainlander clients, adding to internal Chinese diversities within Canada's multicultural mosaic.

An interesting recent phenomenon is the decline in criticisms of some Hong Kong immigrants' flamboyant lifestyles. This may be attributable to greater Canadian openness and tolerance, but it could also be due to the "political correctness" adopted by Canada's mainstream media after prolonged exposure to and interaction with Hong Kongers. The impact of Hong Kong immigrants has definitely altered the physical, social and cultural landscapes of major Canadian cities and the global outlook of many

Canadians. After more than twenty years of adjustment and adaptation, mainstream Canadians have come to appreciate their country's links with Hong Kong and Greater China. The saga of Hong Kongers in Canada should be studied in a contrasting perspective, not just as compared to their counterparts from mainland China and Taiwan, but through broader comparisons with other immigrants in Canada.

True Friends in Good Times and Bad

In a profound historical sense, the ties between the peoples of Canada and Hong Kong were cast in blood and tears when Hong Kongers and Canadians served together as comrades in arms. More than 550 men among the 1,975 Canadian soldiers of the Winnipeg Grenadiers and Quebec Royal Rifles sacrificed their lives defending Hong Kong against Japanese forces at the outbreak of the Pacific War in December 1941 (see Duff 1942, Ye 1984 and Greenhous 1997). These brave young Canadians have forever left their hearts and bodies in the Sai Wan Bay War Cemetery on Hong Kong Island. With a heroic and tragic twist of fate, these Canadians' unfulfilled dreams, aspirations and hopes for education, career, family and well-lived lives have been transferred to the Canadian youth of Hong Kong descent, who should contribute their best for the good of their Canadian homeland, and their ancestral homeland as well, as a token repayment of an historical debt.

The future of Hong Kong may depend on its evolution as a unique Chinese global city at the competitive cutting edge, contributing to China's social and economic advancement. If Hong Kong continues to flourish as an economically vibrant, politically open and socially free global hub, then, given Canada's open arms toward overseas students, professionals and other immigrants, the extensive linkages between Canada and Hong Kong will continue to thrive. The multiple networks, cosmopolitan outlook and international exposure that have developed through migration between Hong Kong and Canada, as experienced by many of Hong Kong's best and brightest, will be essential to Hong Kong's role in China's transformation. However, if economic opportunities available in Canada lag behind those in other parts of the Asia–Pacific region, it is possible that there will be a bigger wave of reverse migration among Canadian Hong Kong Chinese, leading to significant losses in the human capital that Canada has built up. It is imperative for Canada to retain the human resources that it has nurtured and benefited from.

The next chapter in relations between Canada and Hong Kong is unlikely to involve a repetition of the large-scale inflows of the 1980s and 1990s, but may well feature an intensifying of social, economic and cultural exchanges, reinforcing a mutually beneficial relationship whereby Hong Kong enjoys the positive influence of free, tolerant, compassionate, progressive and democratic Canadian values, while Canada benefits from having an edge in its trans-Pacific outreach. Many wish that Hong Kong and the entire Chinese nation could have more true friends like Canada, which has time and again extended its hands across the Pacific as a good partner.

It is to be hoped that Canadians of Hong Kong origin will leave positive imprints on Canada's society, politics, culture and economy, and become Canada's spearhead into Greater China, as human bridges across the Pacific. Their efforts will sustain the multiple connections between Canada and Hong Kong, which form an exceptionally enriching, fruitful and mutually beneficial North American outreach to Asia. By developing its vibrant bonds with Hong Kong, Canada exemplifies transnational partnership and cross-cultural collaboration. Indeed, endowed with unrivalled Hong Kong "assets," Canada enjoys uniquely privileged and highly effective access to Greater China. Through its potent Hong Kong bonds, Canada is well-positioned to engage and partner with a rising China, whose growing economic might and expanding strategic influence are of global significance. As Prime Minister Stephen Harper said during his visit to Hong Kong in 2009, Hong Kong is definitely Canada's most important Asian city, and in many ways is also a major Canadian city. Hence, Hong Kong's special role as a gateway and bridge must not be neglected in discussions of relations between Canada and China. Hong Kong will remain an essential hub through which Canada's links with mainland China and Greater China will continue to be fostered. The strengthening of the bonds between Canada and Hong Kong, as well as Greater China, will be a vital factor in the 21st century, which will be the Asia–Pacific century.

Perhaps one day the occupant of 24 Sussex Drive, Ottawa, will be someone of Hong Kong origin. Such a prospect is definitely not an impossible dream, and should constitute an uplifting aspiration for all Asians in Canada. Blessed with a deep reservoir of friendship, buttressed by an impressive repertoire of trans-Pacific bonds, and harbouring versatile talents, generous outreach capacities and noble ideals, Canada should shine as a trusted global partner and cherished old friend, contributing to Greater China's advancement in the years to come.

Acknowledgements

This chapter is a revised and expanded version of the keynote lecture for Asian Heritage Month delivered by the author at the Asian Institute of the University of Toronto on May 29, 2007, marking his thirtieth visit to Canada since December 1966. The author is grateful to Professor Joseph Wong, the Director of the Institute, for the invitation to deliver the lecture, and to Senator Vivienne Poy for her introduction. The author also appreciates the efforts of Prof. Simon Shen, Hong Kong Institute of Education, in providing sources for some reference notes in this essay's second draft revision in autumn 2009.

References

Bickers, Robert, and Ray Yip, ed. (2009). *May Days in Hong Kong: Emergency and Riots in 1967*. Hong Kong: Hong Kong University Press.

Cannon, Margaret. (1989). *China Tide: The Revealing Story of the Hong Kong Exodus to Canada*. Don Mills, ON: Harper & Collins.

Chan, Ming K., and Sonny S. H. Lo (2006). *Historical Dictionary of the Hong Kong SAR and the Macao SAR*. Langham: Scarecrow Press, 2006.

DeMont, John, and Thomas Fennell. (1989). *Hong Kong Money: How Chinese Families and Fortunes Are Changing Canada*. Toronto: Key Porter.

Duff, Lyman P. (1942). *Report on the Canadian Expeditionary Force to the Crown Colony of Hong Kong*. Ottawa: Edmond Cloutier, Printer to the King.

Greenhous, Brereton. (1997). *"C" Force to Hong Kong: A Canadian Catastrophe 1941–1945*. Toronto, Headington, and Buffalo, NY: Dundurn Press.

Hayhoe, Ruth. (2004). *Full Circle: A Life with Hong Kong and China*. Hong Kong: Comparative Education Research Centre, University of Hong Kong.

Huang, Evelyn. (1992). *Chinese Canadians: Voices from a Community*. Vancouver: Douglas & McIntyre.

Jencks, Harlan. (1990). "China's Evolving Interest in the Western Pacific: Korea, Taiwan, Hong Kong, and ASEAN," in Jurgen Domes, et al. *After Tiananmen Square: Challenges to the Chinese–American Relationship*. Washington, DC: Brassey's.

Lamb, W. Kaue. (1991). *Empress to the Orient*. Vancouver: Vancouver Maritime Museum.

Lazarus, Eve. (2003, March 3). "HSBC's National Dream." *Marketing Magazine*, 11.

Li, Peter S. (1998). *The Chinese in Canada*. 2nd ed. Toronto: Oxford University Press.

Liu Shiping. (2006). *HuifengJinrong Diguo-140 Nian de ZhongguoGushi* [HSBC's

Financial Empire: A Story of 140 Years in China]. Beijing: Zhongguo Fangzheng Chubanshe.

Mason, Christopher. (2007, January 10). "Poor Hospital Practices Blamed for 2003 SARS Epidemic in Toronto." *New York Times*, A7.

Matthews, Roy A. (1983). *Canada and the Little Dragons*. Montreal: Institute for Research on Public Policy.

Ng, Wing Chung. (1999). "Canada," in *The Encyclopedia of the Chinese Overseas*, ed. Lynn Pan. Cambridge, MA: Harvard University Press, 234–35.

Nossal, Kim. (1997). "Playing the International Card?: The View from Australia, Canada and the United States," in *Hong Kong's Reunion with China: Global Dimensions*, ed. Gerard Postiglione and James Tang. Armonk, NY: M. E. Sharpe.

Paau, Danny S. L. (2000). "Hong Kong, China, and the United States," in *Hong Kong the Super Paradox: Life after Return to China*, ed. James Hsiung. New York: St Martin's Press.

Poy, Vivienne. (2006). *Profit, Victory and Sharpness: The Lees of Hong Kong*. Toronto: York Centre for Asian Research.

Salaff, Janet. (2009). "Like Sons and Daughters of Hong Kong: The Return of the Young Generation," in *Hong Kong Mobile: Making a Global Population*, ed. Helen Siu and Agnes Ku. Hong Kong: Hong Kong University Press, 201–22.

Salaff, Janet, Wong Siu-Lun, and Fung Mei Ling. (1997). "Hong Kong Families' Views of 1997," in *The Challenge of Hong Kong's Reintegration with China*, ed. Ming Chan. Hong Kong: Hong Kong University Press, 149–75.

Salaff, Janet, and Arent Greve. (2007). "A Decade of Responses in North America to the Handover," in *The First Decade: The Hong Kong SAR in Retrospective and Introspective Perspectives*, ed. Yue-man Yeung. Hong Kong: Chinese University Press, 43–64.

Salaff, Janet, Siu-lun Wong, and Arent Greve. (2010). *Hong Kong Movers and Stayers: Narravtives of Family Migration*, Urbana: University of Illinois Press.

Segal, Gerald. (1993). *The Fate of Hong Kong*. New York and London: Simon & Schuster.

Siu, Helen, and Agnes Ku., ed. (2009). *Hong Kong Mobile: Making a Global Population*. Hong Kong: Hong Kong University Press.

Skeldon, Ronald, ed. (1994). *Reluctant Exiles: Migration from Hong Kong and the New Overseas Chinese*. Armonk, NY: M. E. Sharpe.

Skeldon, Ronald. (1995). *Emigration from Hong Kong: Tendencies and Impacts*. Hong Kong: Chinese University Press.

Statistics Canada. (2006). "2006 Census of Canada", Ottawa: Statistics Canada.

Ye Dewei. (1984). *Xianggang lunxianshi* [The History of the Fall of Hong Kong]. Hong Kong: Guangjiaojing Chubanshi.

Chapter 7

Canadian and Chinese Collaboration on Education: From Unilateral to Bilateral Exchanges

Qiang Zha

Collaboration on education started shortly after Canada and the People's Republic of China established diplomatic relations in 1970, although scattered exchanges of academic visits had occurred before that date. Collaboration after 1970 mostly took the form of Canadian development programmes, featuring a strong sense of "internationalism" but remaining largely unilateral until the late 1990s.

The Canada–China Scholars Exchange Program, starting in 1974, was operated and funded by the Canadian International Development Research Centre (IDRC) and the Social Sciences and Humanities Research Council (SSHRC). The Canada–China University Linkage Program (CCULP), launched in 1985, and operated and funded by the Canadian International Development Agency (CIDA), supported the linkage of thirty-one institutions, and included the highly successful Canada–China Management Education Program (CCMEP), which stimulated the renaissance of management and business education in Chinese universities. Following the success of CCULP, the Special University Linkage Consolidation Program (SULCP) was created by CIDA within its Country Development Policy Framework for China, adopted in 1994. SULCP supported eleven linkage projects involving twenty-five Canadian universities and more than two hundred Chinese universities, teaching hospitals, schools, other government agencies and non-government organizations (NGOs). As the Association of Universities and Colleges of Canada has noted (2001, p. 3), the combined span of CCULP and SULCP, from 1985 to 2001, "coincided with a period of pivotal change in Chinese society," and the two programmes, encompassing disciplines ranging from health to education, environmental studies, minority area development, engineering and agriculture, assisted Chinese universities to "improve their capacity to respond to China's development needs."

A little more needs to be said about CCMEP, given its significance to the resurgence of business education in China. Ten Canadian management schools were involved in Phase I of CCMEP, from 1983 to 1987, and the network was then expanded to twenty-four schools in Phase II, from 1987 to 1996. The federal government contributed nearly CA$ 38 million to CCMEP, which produced many graduates who went on to lead the transformation of business education in China. When the Chinese government created MBA programmes in nine universities in September 1991, they drew heavily from the experience gained through these CIDA-supported linkages, as did the seventeen additional MBA programmes created in 1993. Several of the Canadian universities that had been involved in CCMEP went on to develop other initiatives, mostly in Asia, based in part on their experience in China (see Anderson, Cooney and Langevin 2001).

Altogether CIDA has invested more than 250 million Canadian dollars in higher education for China since the early 1980s. Over the twenty-five years since CCULP began, more than one hundred institutional linkages and subprojects were created and funded. In addition, more than 37,000 Chinese scholars, researchers and students were educated in Canada and have since become leaders in their disciplines and institutions (see Klabunde 2009). Indeed, apart from the Soviet Union in the 1950s, it is hard to find any other country that has assisted development of China's higher education to a comparable level of generosity, particularly in view of the unique approach of pairing universities within an overall strategic perspective. It seems that Canada's contribution to higher education development in China is matched only by the World Bank's education projects of the 1980s, through which a total of US$ 1.2 billion in loans supported the building of infrastructure and the development of human resources at eighty-eight national and provincial universities throughout China (see Hayhoe 1996).

Education Collaboration in the 21st Century: Opportunities and Obstacles

With the shift of economic power to the East, China has emerged as the world's second largest economy and its principal international education market. Since the early 2000s, educational collaboration between Canada and China has become a bilateral process.

The Canadian federal government has continued to provide educational aid to China, but on a much smaller scale than before. For instance, an aid project implemented in 2003–2007 enhanced basic education in China's poverty-stricken western region, cost only CA$ 11.8 million, and in 2005 China was officially dropped from CIDA's list of "countries of focus." The Canada–China Scholars Exchange Program has continued, but has become more mutually beneficial, with both Chinese and Canadian scholars being assisted to carry out research in each other's countries. There are now twice as many Canadian scholars supported by the Chinese government through this programme than there are Chinese scholars supported by the Canadian government.

At the same time, Canadian colleges and universities have started to be increasingly active and to dominate educational collaboration with China. The University of Regina pioneered the signing of an international partnership agreement with Chinese institutions soon after China opened its doors to the outside world. The university signed its first international partnership agreement, with Shandong University, in 1981 and since then it has developed thirty-five such agreements with Chinese institutions, more than with any other country. Many other Canadian colleges and universities have been providing academic and professional development programmes of various kinds for Chinese partners and professionals. Unlike the previous development projects, these programmes are now mostly contracted and paid for by the Chinese side.

In my own institution, York University, there are ample examples to illustrate this changing pattern. The high-profile York University Asian Business Management Program (ABMP) was among the first in Canada to provide professional development and management training services to both the public and the private sectors in China, and it has maintained this focus ever since its establishment. York University's Faculty of Education is now contracted by the Department of Education of Jiangsu Province, which has been Ontario's Chinese "twin" for twenty-five years, to provide training for school teachers and administrators. In 2009 alone more than 900 teachers and administrators from Jiangsu came to York University for training for periods ranging from a number of weeks to three months.

These examples amount to a tiny proportion of the collaborative activities taking place between educational institutions in Canada and their counterparts in China, but they may give a sense of how Canadian institutions are benefiting from an increasingly mutual process. They disseminate Canada-based knowledge to China, and make some profit out of the knowledge transfer. What still remain to be developed more fully are the collaborative research opportunities. China is now ambitious enough to lift a few dozen of its universities to world standing by pouring research funds in and intensifying research activities. The research budgets of these universities, on average, are now approaching the average among the member institutions of the Association of American Universities (AAU) and, backed up by China's foreign exchange reserves of US$ 3 trillion which are by far the world's largest, and desperately looking for meaningful and significant spending opportunities, there should be future possibilities for joint research projects between Chinese and Canadian universities.

Institutional Opportunities for Canada

Canada has become both provider and beneficiary in the process of educational collaboration with China. This change promises numerous opportunities for Canada, and is in Canada's long-term interest.

First of all, educational collaboration with China serves Canada's geopolitical interest in China and the Asia–Pacific region. Educational collaboration facilitates the flow and communication of people and ideas. Once the channels and mechanisms are in place, cultural and political barriers to mutual understanding are much easier to overcome. This is particularly true in the case of Canada and China, since the two countries have never been geopolitical rivals and in fact often have complementary interests, so that the rise of China can benefit Canada as well. Specifically, Canada needs China, now perhaps the world's largest market and manufacturer, to secure its ambitious Asia–Pacific Gateway and Corridor Initiative and to expand its export-oriented economy. For its part, China seeks not only Canada's energy and natural resources to maintain its manufacturing capacity, but also an overall strategic partnership with Canada as an endorsement of its peaceful rise. Globally, Canada has the image of a well-liked country. International opinion surveys conducted on behalf of the BBC World Service since 2005 indicate that Canada has consistently been among the most popular countries in the world (see BBC World Service 2010). With the world's highest per-capita immigration rates and a firmly upheld ideology of multiculturalism, Canada may be taken as a model for the future of the planet in many ways. When the leaders of China and Canada met in June

2010, a clear message was sent out that they would seek a strategic partnership. On his tour of Canada the Chinese President, Hu Jintao, extended invitations to one hundred local educational officers and school principals to visit China in 2010, and to one hundred middle school students to attend summer camp in China in 2011, explicitly attaching political significance to educational collaboration. In this sense, educational collaboration serves to underpin the strategic partnership between Canada and China.

Almost as a footnote to this point, both the US and Chinese governments have recently endeavored to strengthen educational and cultural exchanges in order to boost the relations between the two countries. On May 25, 2010, the US and China signed an agreement to establish the High-Level Consultation on People-to-People Exchange (CPE), and to launch the "100,000 Strong" Initiative. The purpose of the CPE is to promote people-to-people engagement between the US and China in education and culture as well as other related fields by providing a high-level annual forum for government and private-sector representatives to discuss cooperation in a broad, strategic manner. The "100,000 Strong: US Students in China" Initiative, which was announced by the US President Barack Obama during his November 2009 visit to China, promotes mutual understanding through encouraging private-sector student exchanges and aspires to have 100,000 American students study in China over the next four years (US Department of State 2010). The US Secretary of State Hillary Clinton hailed the importance of people-to-people engagement by saying: "tens of thousands of Chinese and American young people study in each other's country each year. We want to see those numbers rise." "What we call people-to-people diplomacy has taken on greater significance, as our world has grown more interdependent, and our challenges more complex. Government alone cannot solve the problems that we face…we have to tap in to the challenge of our people, their creative[ness] and innovation, and their ability to forge lasting relationships that build trust and understanding." (Clinton 2010).

Second, Canada also benefits economically from educational collaboration with China. Of course, economic interests are associated with the political interests elaborated above. Education, and higher education in particular, has moved to centre stage in the geopolitical contest for increasing shares of the global economic market, and China has emerged as the largest single market for international education and training, being expected to have reached a value of US\$ 200 billion in 2010 (see JLJ Group 2009). From 1978 to 2009, China sent a total of 1.6 million students of all kinds to undergo education or training in other countries. Ever since China opened its doors to the outside world, the number of Chinese students going abroad has been increasing at an annual rate of 25.8 percent, and it is expected to have reached 300,000 in 2010 alone. Educational collaboration is crucial to enlarging Canada's share of this market. In addition, due to demographic changes an increasing number of Canadian colleges and universities might have to attract international students to sustain their enrolments (see Hango and de Broucker 2007). Thus, for example, the government of Canada's most populous province, Ontario, has recently pledged to make it a major destination for international students. In its five-year *Open Ontario Plan*, unveiled in the Speech from the Throne in 2010, a goal was set to "aggressively promote Ontario post-secondary institutions abroad, and increase international enrolment by 50 percent," on the understanding that an increase in international student enrolment would bring about an increase in revenues: "These dollars could be reinvested to improve and expand our schools, and create more Ontario jobs" (see Ontario 2010).

Now that Canada and China have pledged to double their bilateral trade by 2015, Canadian colleges and universities will be part of the effort to balance Canada's trade deficit with China. In 2009 Canada exported slightly over CA\$ 11 billion worth of goods and services to China, while importing close to CA\$ 40 billion worth of goods and services from China. Indeed, apart from energy and natural resources, Canada has few other options to offset the flow of Chinese products into Canada. In particular, the export of educational services fits quite well with existing initiatives such as the *Open Ontario Plan*.

Third, academic and cultural internationalization is a catalyst for improving the diversity and quality of higher education. As Philip Steenkamp, then Deputy Minister of Training, Colleges and Universities for Ontario, nicely put it in 2008:

> [i]nternational students bring valuable diversity to the classroom, the campus, and the larger community, enhancing the academic experience for all students. Diversity in the classroom enriches all students' understanding of the world by allowing them to share different perspectives, approach problems from different angles, and discover different cultural experiences.

A strong presence of Chinese scholars and students on Canadian campuses would enhance the possibility of integrating ideas and perspectives from the very different Chinese epistemological tradition, and thus bringing greater diversity to academic thought and discourse in Canada. Chinese scholars are also likely to add to Canada's brain stock of doctorate-holders. China has been a major source of foreign-born PhDs in Canada since the late 1990s, replacing the United States and the United Kingdom, which were historically the dominant sources: China's share of Canadian PhDs reached twenty-five percent in 2000, having increased rapidly from just two percent in the early 1990s (see Gluszynski and Peters 2005). There could be more room for growth if benchmarked with what is happening in the United States, where, between 2004 and 2006, two Chinese universities, Tsinghua and Peking, overtook the University of California, Berkeley, as the "most fertile feeder schools" for American PhDs (see Mervis 2008). Since the Chinese government started in 2006 to select 5,000 doctoral students each year from the country's leading universities and sponsor them to study in Western universities for up to four years, there seem to be plenty of opportunities for Canadian universities to attract a group of students of high quality.

Obstacles on the Canadian Side

Canada became among the first countries in the West to recognize the People's Republic of China when Pierre Trudeau's government established diplomatic relations with China in 1970, nine years ahead of the United States and almost three years before the United Kingdom and Australia. Ever since the early 1970s, successive Canadian governments have invested enormous efforts and resources in educational collaboration with China, which has led to hundreds of institutional linkages, as well as a positive attitude to Canada among the Chinese. Against this backdrop, it seems logical and natural that Canada should have gained a harvest from the plantings of these earlier years, now that China is emerging as a major international education market. However, this is not really the case, and Canada substantially lags behind its competitors—the United States, Australia, the United Kingdom and New Zealand—in this market. There are at least two identifiable reasons that may have contributed to this unfortunate situation.

First, there is no permanent agency at the federal level to trace the effects and outcomes of past educational collaboration programmes and projects, even though these have mostly been funded at the federal level. Over the years, different federal agencies seem to have taken turns playing the leading role in educational aid to China, but none of them has been given a permanent mandate to follow up their initiatives. When programmes and projects end, their effects and influences start to fade away, and the resources accumulated during the process, in particular the networking resources, have gradually been lost. This approach was not particularly problematic in the era when educational collaboration chiefly meant supplying development aid, but it has become dysfunctional in face of the neoliberal current of internationalization of education, which requires networking and niche determination. For Canadian–Chinese educational collaboration to thrive, it is urgent to step out of the aid mentality, and shift to an approach based on marketing and service. Efforts should be made to develop a good understanding of what is happening in China and what is in demand in the Chinese market, above all by creating and maintaining permanent links with Chinese scholars and their institutions.

I may use my personal experience to highlight this point. At a conference at Harvard University in 2009 I encountered a leading Chinese scholar in management studies, who now works at the frontier of internationalization of higher education as the executive president of a joint campus operated in China by one Chinese university and one British university, each ranked high in their respective systems. He used to be a vice president of the Chinese university and, in order to qualify him for his current position, he was later appointed a pro-vice chancellor of the British university. Then I assumed that he was a shining product of the British education system, but, unexpectedly, I discovered that he had actually started his academic pursuits at a Canadian university, through CCMEP, back in the 1980s. He unveiled this part of his story in a "by the way" manner. Over the years, he had never been contacted by any Canadian institution, and his memories of his Canadian experience had been covered with thick dust until I showed up as a sort of reminder. In contrast, having been sponsored by the British Chevening Scholarship Programme to study at the University of London in the mid-1990s, I have been kept connected to the network created, maintained and updated by the British Council to facilitate contact and communication between former scholarship holders and their British sponsors. The rationale is evident and effective, when examined against the facts that, according to the British Council, "in 2009 over 85,000 Chinese students engaged in learning experiences in the UK," increased by 40% from 2008 (see British Council 2010). Chinese students are now the largest single group of overseas students in the UK, even compared with those from other member states of the European Union.

Meanwhile, there are almost no efforts devoted to branding Canadian education. As Carin Holroyd wrote nearly five years ago, "While the Government of Canada is constrained by its lack of constitutional authority in the delivery of educational services at home, it has been generally absent from the promotion of Canadian education overseas" (see Holroyd 2006). The "Pan-Canadian Education Brand," launched in 2008 and jointly managed by the federal Department of Foreign Affairs and International Trade (DFAIT) and the Secretariat of the Council of Ministers of Education, Canada (CMEC), is evidence that both the federal government and the provincial governments have started to make an effort in this realm, although the branding of specifically *Canadian* higher education is still in its infancy. Consequently, many Chinese students regard Canadian higher education as largely a derivative enterprise of the US system, and a second choice when they have no opportunity to go to a university in the United States.

The United Kingdom and Australia, in contrast, do benefit from and take advantage of strong promotional efforts. The British Council manages a strong "Education UK" brand, which distinguishes the British system from its major competitors. In 1999, the government of Tony Blair declared international education a cornerstone of its plan for the "New Economy" and committed a huge amount of resources to international recruitment. The British Council now has 250 offices in 110 countries, among which thirty have a particular focus on student recruitment. Part of the Council's annual budget of around US$ 900 million, one third of which is a direct grant from the government, is for international education, and an additional US$ 13 million was earmarked specifically for marketing, promotion and branding of British education over three years in the early 2000s (see Holroyd 2006). Advertisements encouraging study in the United Kingdom can even be seen on buses in Beijing, and the British Council has built a strong relationship with the Chinese media to ensure that "Education UK" activities gain the maximum possible coverage. Australian International Education, primarily funded through the federal government, runs ten overseas offices, while IDP Education Australia, a university-owned non-profit organization, operates an additional sixty-eight offices in thirty-eight countries. The Australian federal government committed US$ 114 million between 2004 and 2009 to market Australian post-secondary institutions internationally (see Holroyd 2006). It is thus not surprising that education has become an export industry for Australia, worth US$ 14 billion, half of that in post-secondary education, and is essentially the third largest Australian export after coal and iron ore (see Hazelkorn 2008).

Canada does not have a national coordinating body for national marketing or any sustained federal investment in marketing Canada as a destination for international education. Education is a provincial responsibility under the Canadian Constitution, yet the provinces do not necessarily view its marketing as a major concern. As a result, Canada has been struggling and even suffering over recent years in the international education market. In 2007, the Canadian Bureau for International Education (CBIE) reported Canada had dropped out of the top five destinations for international students (see Tibbetts 2008), to seventh place, with a share of less than three percent of the international market (as shown in Figure 7.2). Without renewed efforts Canada will not be able to compete with the United Kingdom and Australia for a sufficient share, whether in China or elsewhere. Canada's Chinese students recruitment has been declining relative to these competitors and the number of Chinese students in Canada is also small in comparison. In 2004, Canada received slightly more than half of the number of Chinese students attracted to Australia, and around three quarters of the numbers of Chinese students enrolled in New Zealand and the United Kingdom (as shown in Table 7.1). As China is now the largest single source country for international student mobility (as shown in Figure 7.1), Canada needs to attract more Chinese students in order to recover its position as a major destination of international education. Canada's share of international students stagnated between 1999 and 2007 (as shown in Figure 7.2). Now, as Canada is pledging to increase its share and rise to become, once again, one of the leading destinations for international students, it would have a better chance of success if its performance in the Chinese market could be improved.

Table 7.1   Numbers of Chinese Students in Selected Countries, with Annual Rankings, 2002–2004

	2002	2003	2004
United States	64,757 (1st)	61,765 (1st)	62,523 (2nd)
Australia	47,904 (2nd)	58,574 (2nd)	68,857 (1st)
Canada	26,312 (3rd)	33,188 (5th)	36,747 (5th)
New Zealand	n/a	51,965 (3rd)	48,630 (3rd)
United Kingdom	20,710 (4th)	35,155 (4th)	47,740 (4th)

Source: Adapted from Holroyd 2006, p. 7.

Figure 7.1 Main Source Countries of Internationally Mobile Students, 2007

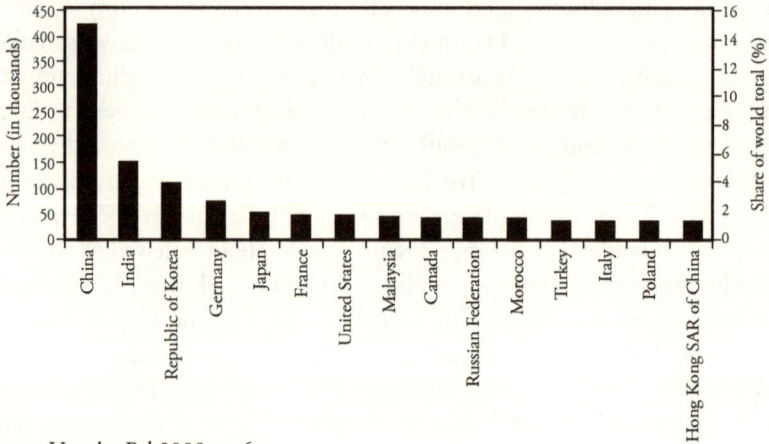

Source: Van der Pol 2009, p. 6.

Figure 7.2   Main Destination Countries of Internationally Mobile Students, 1999 and 2007

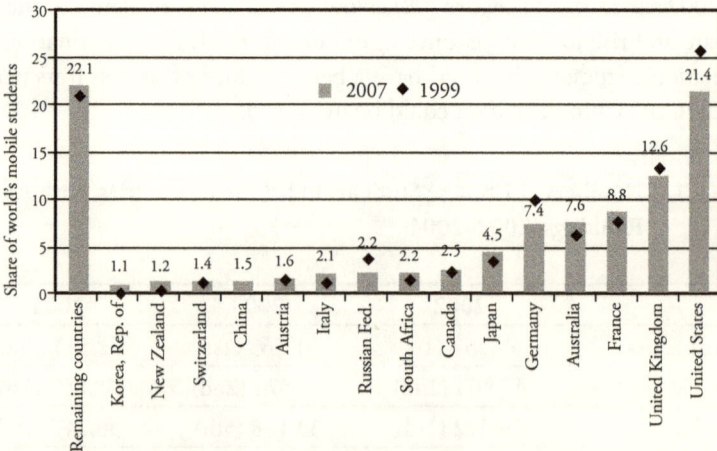

Source: Van der Pol 2009, p. 8.

Suggested Policy and Strategy Framework

Despite the obstacles discussed above, it is not realistic to alter the Canadian constitutional arrangement that places educational affairs under provincial jurisdiction, or to create a special federal agency, on the model of the British Council, in order to promote and brand Canadian education around the world. What Canadians can and should do is to become more practical and creative.

In this respect, the "glonacal" agency heuristic, a paradigm developed by two distinguished scholars, Simon Marginson and Gary Rhoades (2002), appears to be both suggestive and inspiring (see Figure 7.3). Though originally suggested for use in studying globalization and higher education, their paradigm is applicable and useful in the domain of international education policy and strategy in the Canadian context. The "glonacal" agency heuristic emphasizes the intersections, interactions and mutual determinations of all levels (global, national and local), as well as domains (organizational agencies and the agency of collectivities). Rather than a linear flow from the global to the local, it sees a simultaneity of flows. In other words, local entities and collective efforts can undermine, challenge and define alternatives to national and global patterns, and "they can also shape the configuration of global flows" (Marginson and Rhoades 2002, p. 289). When it is applied to policies and strategies for international

Figure 7.3   A "Glonacal" Agency Heuristic

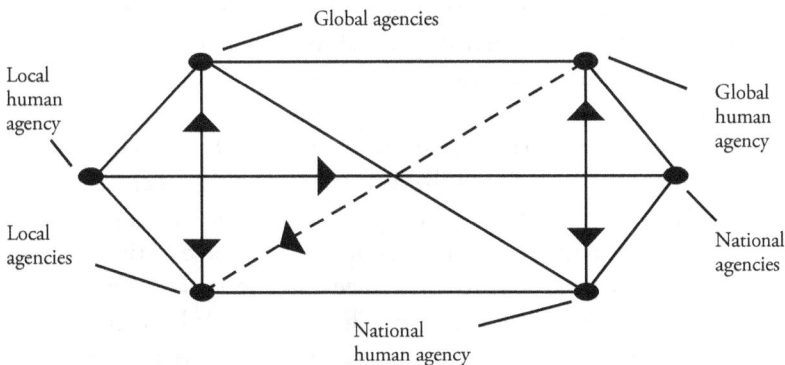

Source: Marginson and Rhoades 2002, p. 291.

educational collaboration, a "glonacal" agency approach can lead us to work from the local level and reach the national and global level.

This paradigm also suggests local adaptation as well as resistance. Traditionally, Canadians have had a tendency and strong potential to work from a local level. This is evident in the unique approach taken to executing CCULP and SULCP through the pairing of Canadian and Chinese universities. Such an approach made it possible to acquire good knowledge of partners and of the target community's conditions and needs, to ensure that the planned intervention would be appropriate and that the benefits of the project would effectively reach the intended beneficiaries. Indeed, the CCULP and SULCP partnerships were effective in providing venues to adapt Canada-based knowledge and expertise to the Chinese context. In this sense, this paradigm may inspire us to transform the apparent policy and strategy disadvantage determined by the Canadian context into a sort of practical model with a Canadian flavour or Canadian characteristics.

This notion is closely linked to ways in which the meaning of "agency" is incorporated into this paradigm. Two meanings of the word "agency" are used here. First, the paradigm uses agency "in the sense of an entity or organization that could exist at the global, national or local level," with examples being the World Bank, the European Union, national ministries of education, national legislatures and individual education institutions (Marginson and Rhoades 2002, p. 289). In this sense, the initiatives and practices of individual colleges or universities may have an impact and influence across an entire nation. Canada's lack of a central policy or a central coordinating agency means that international outreach has been left to the provinces, and even more to individual institutions. Therefore, it is useful and indeed imperative to take the alternative approach of identifying, demonstrating and disseminating good and successful local initiatives, strategies and practices, as models for others.

For instance, the China focus approach adopted by the University of Regina, as discussed above, may be an experience that other institutions could emulate. Similarly, Seneca College in Toronto has been particularly involved in the development of partnerships with Chinese institutions. The college has arrangements with twenty-three Chinese academic institutions involving forty-one programmes, and it has spearheaded the effort to set up joint diploma and degree programmes with Chinese partners. Typically, students spend a year or two in China and then finish their studies in Toronto. Seneca also offers a complete training programme for flight attendants at the Guangzhou Civil Aviation College in China. It is now taking the lead in building an offshore campus in China, which looks like a wise move, given the huge potential and demand in the Chinese market. Following this lead, Simon Fraser University launched an innovative dual-degree programme in computer science with Zhejiang University in Hangzhou in 2007, in which students study at both institutions, providing an excellent opportunity for collaboration across cultural boundaries. More recently, York University partnered with Fudan University in Shanghai and began in 2009 to offer dual-degree programmes in history, financial mathematics, computer science and design. Students spend two years at Fudan University, followed by two years at York University, and receive a joint degree from both institutions. This move marked York University's first such broad-based agreement with any university in the world.

These few examples show the rich resources of good and successful local initiatives, strategies and practices that others may draw upon. A benefit of this bottom-up approach may be the promise it embodies for institutional adaptation. While the central policy approach may result in greater efficiency and more power, it may also lead to institutions reacting homogeneously, engaging in blind competition at the cost of precious resources, or even resisting change. The framework suggested here may warrant some sort of retention of institutional individuality and capacity for niche determination. In the same sense, the concept of glocalization that is modeled on Japanese word *dochakuka* and adopted much earlier, first by business professionals and then by sociologists, may better help to overcome the conceptual difficulties of global-local relationship, and therefore better capture this Canadian flavor. "The problem of simultaneous globalization of the local and the localization of globality can be expressed as the twin processes of macro-localization and micro-globalization. Macro-localization involves expanding the boundaries locality as well as making some local ideas, practices, institutions global…While in this view local is the provider of the response to the forces that are global, we argue that local itself is constituted globally" (Khondker 2004, p. 4).

There is a second meaning of agency in the "glonacal" agency perspective, which "refers to the ability of people individually and collectively to take action at the global, national, and local levels" (Marginson and Rhoades 2002, p. 289). For example, there are international professional groups that extend across national boundaries, and help to shape national policies and local practices. There are also national groups that work to influence those policies and practices. Further, "there are local collectivities, such as professors and administrators in a department or institution, that influence local practice and undertake initiatives for their units to compete in international education markets" (Marginson and Rhoades 2002, p. 289). In short, at each level, global, national and local, there are collective human actions that are central to understanding, planning and undertaking international educational collaboration. It is the notion of human agency that appears to be most interesting and appealing in this paradigm. Once human agency is mobilized and motivated, it is possible that local entities can effectively influence, define and challenge alternatives to national and global patterns, which is particularly true in Canada's decentralized context. Ultimately, it is people who can carry ideas and experiences around, and make them available nationally and internationally. As a matter of fact, individual faculty have been reported most influential in terms of setting international linkages, among all the internal and external stakeholders of Canadian universities (Metcalfe et al. 2010). Given the absence of a national coordinating agency, it is crucial to bring human agency into full play, in order to push forward the frontiers of Canadian–Chinese educational collaboration and broaden the horizon of policy initiatives and strategy choices.

The most significant example along this line might come from University of Alberta. Its China Opportunity Funds was created in 2005, and supports University of Alberta's Joint Research Laboratories (JRL) program with China's State Key Laboratories (SKLs) and National Laboratories (NLs). Initially the idea came from a community-based group, Association of Chinese Canadian Professors (ACCP) at University of Alberta, and was piloted by some of its members. Then it was adopted as a university initiative, and further supported by Alberta provincial government through Alberta Advanced Education and Technology, and then the Chinese government via the Ministry of Science & Technology (MOST), which funds State Key Laboratories (SKLs) and National Laboratories (NLs). So, the University of Alberta case illustrates a typical alternative approach advocated by the "glonacal" agency heuristic: a good initiative started with the local human agency, and then helped to mould policy and practice of the local organizational agency. When it was proven successful, it further influenced and impacted the policy at the provincial and national level across the countries. Now University of Alberta's China Opportunity Fund gives priority to research areas of energy, environment, nanotechnology, and life sciences, and supports 3 types of collaboration between its researchers and SKLs/NLs: to initiate contact with SKLs/NLs; to nurture an existing research partnership with SKLs/NLs; to support technology commercialization.

It is in this sense that Canada must give priority to, and make full use of, the longstanding but often ignored advantages it has already acquired, in terms of the rich legacies of educational collaboration with China, and in particular the people associated with these legacies, as well as the large Chinese communities in Canada. There are nearly 1.6 million Canadian Chinese, who have made Chinese the third language in the country, after English and French, and who hold promise of endless possibilities for Canadian–Chinese educational collaboration.

Reflections and Recommendations

There is a broad consensus in Canada that the rise of China is generally positive, that engagement has been useful and sustainable, and that "China's role in the development of Asian-centred international institutions is likely to be of value to Canada and the world order, rather than a threat to them" (Evans 2006, p. 292). Given this consensus, it is important to further Canadian–Chinese collaboration, and educational collaboration certainly has a big role to play. To this end, I would like to make a number of concrete recommendations.

First, it is necessary to reopen the old files concerning Canadian–Chinese educational collaboration in the 1980s and 1990s, in particular those concerning university partnerships, and to conduct follow-up studies to trace both the legacy and the efficacy of these programmes. By design, CCULP and SULCP provided venues to adapt Canadian expertise and approaches to the Chinese context in areas where Canada is a world leader, such as minority education, bilingual education, agriculture, energy, health and environmental assessment. Ten years after they were all closed, it is important to find out what long-term effects these Canadian programmes had on the transition of Chinese society, which has gone through dramatic changes in recent years. This work would also, to a large extent, to re-establish the network among Canadian and Chinese universities as a sort of extension from the past. From there, diligent work must be done to explore opportunities for collaborative research in the new context. Canadian universities have contributed a great deal to China's development through CIDA and other linking institutions, and have long played a unique role in connecting Canada and China. With this significant shift in patterns of Canadian–Chinese educational collaboration, Canadian universities should take advantage of the historical linkage with Chinese partners, as well as the increasing capacity on the Chinese side, and see this shift as an opportunity to collaborate with their Chinese partners in joint projects that seek innovative science- and technology-based solutions to some of the 21st century's biggest challenges, including clean energy and climate change, food security and agriculture, and public health. The complementary skills and strengths of Canada and China in research in these fields would create a "synergy" benefiting both countries.

Second, as an emerging economy, China has been dropped from CIDA's list of "countries of focus" for development aid, yet it is essential to continue to provide projects in the domains of social and cultural development in China. These domains have been suffering tremendously under the impact of the "GDPism" prevailing in China, which gives by far the highest priority to economic development. Governments at all levels have aggressively pursued rapid economic development, as measured by GDP growth rates, disregarding the social, cultural and environmental effects resulting from such rapid economic growth. Related to this, the Canadian government should consciously support collaborative research and development work with China in the social sciences and the humanities. These efforts, in turn, would effectively help to exert Canadian influence on Chinese society, and ultimately contribute to China's peaceful rise as a responsible global power. For instance, the Chinese government's programme of sponsoring doctoral students to study abroad provides a potential opportunity. Canadian universities may seize such an opportunity to work out some sort of exchange programme with selected Chinese universities, ideally those with historical connections, and host a certain number of Chinese doctoral students in the social sciences and the humanities. Such a move could create a "win–win" situation, attracting a group of students with great potential, on the one hand, and creating opportunities for Canadian students to study in China, on the other. In this regard, it is noteworthy that the recent US–China Consultation on People-to-People Exchange has a strong focus on the social sciences and humanities, and that the US government supports more students studying abroad in China than in any other country, the majority of them in the social sciences and the humanities. Universities are places of teaching and learning where new generations form their knowledge base and values. Universities also draw on extensive networks of alumni and benefactors, including personnel in government agencies, private enterprises and NGOs. Through these networks and links, study programmes can often disseminate their results and influence far more broadly than may have been originally planned, and thus help to forge lasting relationships, exchange and cooperation between peoples. Indeed, universities are highly effective agents of change and innovation.

Last but not least, given the absence of a federal agency to facilitate and coordinate policies and strategies, it is imperative to use NGOs and private think tanks to identify good policy initiatives and practices in educational collaboration with China, as well as the unique aspects and overall strength of Canadian higher education. Notably, Canadian universities are exclusively public, and Canadian policies emphasize developing a network of comprehensive post-secondary institutions of approximately comparable standards, rather than specialized institutions or stratified systems. Canadian higher education has a reputation for "providing a wide range of opportunities to its diverse and geographically dispersed population" (Skolnik 1991, p. 1079), and even "[I]f Canada has fewer Harvards and Chicagos than the U.S., it also has fewer institutions of dubious standards" (Skolnik 1986, p. 21). From the perspective of securing equality of access and experience, this seems to be a better solution than a set of highly dispersed and diverse institutions. In general, Canadian higher education is excellent in quality and very affordable, and can also be a catalyst for social justice. Indeed, some NGOs, such as the Asia Pacific Foundation of Canada, have begun to promote Canadian education, and a Montreal-based private branding company, Bang Marketing, is behind the "Pan-Canadian Education Brand" mentioned above. More such groups should be brought in to make the effort truly successful. Even more importantly, educational collaboration between Canada and China should seek to encourage greater involvement by the private sector, which would not only broaden the horizon of policy initiatives and strategy choices, but also enlarge the pool of resources and opportunities available for people-to-people engagement.

References

Anderson, Gary, Geraldine Cooney, and John Langevin. (2001). "Canadian Support for Management Education Internationally: Lessons Learned." *Canadian and International Education* 30:2, 1–34.

Association of Universities and Colleges of Canada. (2001). *Executive Summary: Final Report of the Special University Linkage Consolidation Program (1996–2001)*. Ottawa: Association of Universities and Colleges of Canada.

BBC World Service. (2010, April 18). "Global Views of United States Improve While Other Countries Decline." London: BBC World Service. Online at http://www.globescan.com/news_archives/bbc2010_countries [consulted January 14, 2011].

British Council. (2010, July). "China Market Introduction." London: British Council. Online at http://www.britishcouncil.org/eumd-information-background-china.htm [consulted January 14, 2011].

Clinton, Hillary Rodham. (2010, May 25). "Remarks at a Signing Ceremony Launching the U.S.-China Consultation on People-to-People Exchange." Online as http://www.state.gov/secretary/rm/2010/05/142181.htm [consulted July 26, 2010].

Evans, Paul. (2006). "Canada, Meet Global China." *International Journal* 61:2, 283–97.

Gluszynski, Tomasz, and Valerie Peters. (2005, July). "Survey of Earned Doctorates: A Profile of Doctoral Degree Recipients." Ottawa: Statistics Canada and Human Resources and Skills Development Canada. Online as http://dsp-psd.pwgsc.gc.ca/Collection/Statcan/81-595-MIE/81-595-MIE2005032.pdf [consulted January 14, 2011].

Hango, Darcy, and Patrice de Broucker (2007). *Postsecondary Enrolment Trends to 2031: Three Scenarios.* Ottawa, Ontario, Canada: Statistics Canada.

Hayhoe, Ruth. (1996). *China's Universities, 1895–1995: A Century of Cultural Conflict.* New York: Garland.

Hazelkorn, Ellen. (2008, Fall). "Globalization, Internationalization, and Rankings." *Journal of International Higher Education* 53, 6–8.

Holroyd, Carin. (2006, January 26). "Canada Missing Opportunity in the Booming China Education Market." *Canada–Asia Agenda.* Vancouver: Asia Pacific Foundation of Canada. Online at http://www.asiapacific.ca/canada-asia-agenda/canada-missing-opportunity-booming-china-education-market [consulted January 14, 2011].

JLJ Group. (2009). *China's Training and Education Market.* Shanghai, Beijing, and Boston, MA: The JLJ Group. Online as http://www.jljgroup.com/uploads/Press_Room/China_Education_Training_Market.pdf [consulted January 14, 2011].

Khondker, Habibul Haque. (2004). "Glocalization as Globalization: Evolution of a Sociological Concept." *Bangladesh e-Journal of Sociology* 1: 2: 1-9.

Klabunde, Niels. (2009). *Translating the Olympic Spirit into a Canadian–Chinese Year of Education and Sciences.* Ottawa: Canadian Bureau for International Education.

Marginson, Simon, and Gary Rhoades. (2002). "Beyond National States, Markets, and Systems of Higher Education: A Glonacal Agency Heuristic." *Higher Education* 43:3, 281–309. Online as http://www.springerlink.com/content/j1n-wk4r8a120dqpq/fulltext.pdf [consulted January 14, 2011].

Mervis, Jeffrey. (2008, July 11). "U.S. Graduate Training: Top PhD Feeder Schools Are Now Chinese." *Science* 321: 5886, 185.

Metcalfe, A. S., D. Fisher, Y. Gingras, G. A. Jones, K. Rubenson, and I. Snee. (2010). "How influential are faculty today? Responses from the Canadian professoriate." *Academic Matters*, October-November 2010: 16-20.

Ontario. Office of the Premier. (2010). "Investing in Post-Secondary Education: Increasing Spaces and Connecting Online," in *Open Ontario: A Five-Year Plan for Our Economy*. Toronto; Queen's Printer for Ontario. Online at http://www.premier.gov.on.ca/openOntario/#Postsecondary [consulted January 14, 2011].

Skolnik, Michael L. (1986). "Diversity in Higher Education: The Canadian Case." *Higher Education in Europe* 11, 19–32.

Skolnik, Michael L. (1991). "Canada," in *International Higher Education: An Encyclopedia*, ed. Philip G. Altbach. Vol. 2. New York: Garland.

Steenkamp, Philip. (2008, September). "The Development of Ontario's Internationalization Strategy." *e-MAGINED: Canadian e-Magazine of International Education* 1:3. Online at http://emagined.apps01.yorku.ca/internationalization-policy-and-strategy/the-development-of-ontarios-internationalization-strategy [consulted August 8, 2010].

Tibbetts, Janice. (2008, March 2). "Come to Canada, Invent the Next Blackberry." CanWest News Service. Online as http://www.cbie.ca/data/media/news/20080302_CanWestComeToCanada.pdf [consulted January 14, 2011].

US, Department of State. (2010, May 25). "U.S., China Celebrate People-to-People Engagement in Beijing. Outline of new U.S.-China Consultation on People-to-People Exchange." Online as http://www.america.gov/st/texttrans-english/2010/May/20100525132821ptellivremos0.9987757.html#ixzz0uuQ0QU3v [consulted July 26, 2010].

Van der Pol, Hendrik. (2009)."New Trends in International Student Mobility." Press conference presentation. Montreal: UNESCO Institute for Statistics. Online as http://www.unescobkk.org/fileadmin/user_upload/efa/Publications/UIS_press_conference_presentation.pdf [consulted January 14, 2011].

CANADA-CHINA:

THE GROWING

INTERDEPENDENCE

Chapter 8

Canada and China after the Global Financial Crisis

A Speech to the Canada–China Business Forum at the Fairmont Royal York Hotel, Toronto, September 15, 2009

Yuen Pau Woo

This week marks the first anniversary of the collapse of Lehman Brothers, the unofficial starting date of a global financial crisis unlike any we have seen in a generation. As we welcome the prospect of the Canadian economy emerging from recession, perhaps sooner than expected, the biggest danger we face is to assume that the world will be more or less the same as it was before the economic downturn. The temptation to be complacent is exacerbated by self-congratulatory pronouncements about Canada's relatively strong performance compared to other G8 members and the fact that our financial institutions were well supervised and therefore did not face the kind of meltdown that was seen south of the border. It is in some respects inconceivable that Canadians could believe that the world has not changed. But habit, wishful thinking, narrow-mindedness and vested interests have a powerful way of combining to resist change. The unwillingness of our political and business elites to show leadership further compounds the problem.

I am, of course, referring to the shift in global economic and political power that is taking place as a result of the US financial crisis. We should be clear that this power shift did not begin with the collapse of Lehman Brothers. The rise of so-called emerging markets has been discussed for many years. The economic crisis did, however, expose some fundamental weaknesses in the US economy and it has, I believe, accelerated the shift in global economic weight away from North America and Europe to Asia, and to China and India in particular.

I remember that when the crisis first erupted a parade of commentators and analysts in North America confidently predicted that China would not be immune from the downturn, that "decoupling" was a fantasy and that the recession would in fact be the undoing of China's export-led economy. One columnist in the *Globe and Mail* even mused on the prospect of widespread social unrest in China, leading to the collapse of the Chinese government. What these analysts failed to understand was that there is a huge difference between an economic downturn due to a financial sector crisis and a downturn caused by weak external demand. Crudely speaking, the US problem is one of excessive spending, whereas the Chinese problem is one of excessive saving. You don't need a PhD in economics to understand that, interdependence notwithstanding, the Chinese problem is preferable to the US one. The solution to what are euphemistically called "global imbalances" is for the United States to spend a lot less and for China to spend a lot more. It is no wonder, therefore, that the Chinese stimulus package unveiled in November 2008 was the largest of any major economy's as a share of total output. The fact that there is enormous pent-up demand in China for infrastructure, capital equipment and, above all, consumer goods has simply made the stimulus package more effective.

But all is not rosy in China. The collapse in US and EU demand has meant sharp declines in Chinese exports and massive layoffs. Despite the attractive headline GDP growth numbers, Beijing faces a very serious unemployment problem in the rural areas and the attendant risk of social unrest. There is no triumphalism, therefore, among the Chinese political, business and intellectual elites about the relative rise of China's influence in the world economy. On the contrary, what I am hearing over and over again from Chinese colleagues is the need to rebalance the economy towards a greater emphasis on domestic demand. They are convinced that the US economy is headed for a period of sub-par growth because of the huge debt overhang, with all its implications for interest rates and inflation. This sentiment is shared across much of East Asia, which has also relied on exports to industrialized countries as a principal source of economic growth. There is a palpable anxiety across the region about how to generate growth if not by exporting to the United States.

What astonishes me is how much less this anxiety seems to have taken root in Canada, which is overwhelmingly more dependent on exports to the United States, and which does not have the option of turning to domestic demand as an alternative engine of growth. It has, of course, become popular again to talk about diversifying our export markets so that we are less reliant on the US market. Diversification is important, but selling more to China or India is only part of the story. The point about a fundamental power shift in the world economy is not simply about rapidly growing markets in Asia and other developing regions, it is about the impact of the Chinese economy and Chinese enterprises on every link in the supply chain, about upward pressure on the prices of raw materials and downward pressure on the prices of finished goods, about the global competition for talent, about research and innovation, and, above all, about the deployment of capital globally.

In recent years we have seen Chinese companies and sovereign wealth funds spend billions of dollars to secure access to natural resources around the world, through a combination of equity investment, loans for oil and long-term contracts. The pace seems to have picked up recently with major deals announced in Latin America, Russia and Australia. For a while, Canada was conspicuously missing from the list of destination countries. That changed last month with a succession of megadeals, including a $1.7 billion investment by China Investment Corporation (CIC) in Teck Resources, followed by a $1.9 billion bid by PetroChina for a majority share of two Athabasca Oil Sands Corporation projects. Anyone wondering if Petro-China has used up its financial war chest should wonder no more: China Development Bank announced last week that it had agreed to provide a loan of $30 billion to PetroChina, at a discounted interest rate, to fund the oil and gas company's "going global" strategy.

Recent Chinese investments in Canadian companies are a very good sign that we are on the Chinese outward investment radar, and that Chinese companies perceive Canada to be open to investment from the People's Republic. But we can do more to encourage and facilitate investment from China. An important test ahead will be the Government of Canada's review of PetroChina's bid for the oil sands projects. Mr. [Jim] Flaherty was in Beijing recently, where he was widely quoted as saying that Canada welcomes Chinese investment. His words are currently being put to the test, and the results will be watched very closely by the global investment community.

The Asia Pacific Foundation of Canada is releasing today the results of a major survey of Chinese outward investment intentions. Working with the China Council for the Promotion of International Trade, the co-organizer of this Forum, we asked 1,100 Chinese companies about their existing overseas investments and their plans for future spending abroad. While I do not have time to go into the detailed findings, I can leave you with this overall message: Chinese outward investment is on the rise, not just in energy and mining, but also in the manufacturing, agrifood and services sectors. While Canada hitherto has not ranked highly as a destination for Chinese investment, respondents rated Canada very well as a potential destination for outward investment. The most promising sectors for investment in Canada were identified as agrifood, information and communications technology, energy, and natural resources. I invite you to have a look at the full report, which is available at www.asiapacific.ca. There are also a limited number of copies at our display table outside the conference hall.

Allow me to conclude on a note of optimism. Canada's relative resilience during the economic crisis has not gone unnoticed in China. For a change, we are seen by the Chinese as a bastion of financial stability and not just as a vast source of natural resources. The ease with which the CIC investment in Teck sailed through the review process stands in stark contrast to Chinalco's failed bid for Rio Tinto of Australia and Sinopec's aborted attempt to purchase Unocal of California a few years earlier. Relations between Ottawa and Beijing are improving, and it appears that Messrs. Harper and Ignatieff are in a race of sorts to visit Beijing, if not before an election, then likely soon after. This warming of relations could not come at a better time, since Canada and China celebrate forty years of diplomatic relations in 2010. There is much to celebrate about the past forty years, but the best way to get ready for the coming anniversary is to think about the role that China will play in the world economy over the next forty years, and to prepare for it.

Chapter 9

Post-Colonial Transformations in China's Hong Kong and Macau: Implications for Cross-Taiwan-Strait and Canada–PRC Links

The Keynote Address to the Conference of the Same Title at the University of Waterloo, June 27, 2009

Vivienne Poy

Many Canadians believe that we are regarded as friends of China because of Pierre Trudeau, and because of the sacrifices of Norman Bethune, and, of course, Dashan is our best cultural ambassador to China. So why is it that, when Canadians travel to China today, we are asked by ordinary people, such as taxi drivers, why we hate them? This morning I will present an overview of the relationship between our two countries since the establishment of the People's Republic of China, within the ever-changing economic and political dynamics of Greater China. You will notice that I will not be mentioning Macau, and that is purely because of my ignorance of that Special Administrative Region.

Canada was the leading Western country in building a relationship with China in the early days. Despite the lack of formal economic or political ties, Canada started to sell wheat to China in 1958. Sales grew from $9 million in 1960 to $147 million two years later. Until the end of the 1960s the total exports from Canada varied from $100 million to $185 million annually, and they almost entirely consisted of wheat.

In October 1970, China and Canada established formal diplomatic relations, and in 1973 the two countries signed the Canada–China Trade

Agreement, which allowed for the mutual extension of "most favoured nation" status. By 1973, Canadian exports to China had doubled. After the death of Chairman Mao in 1976, the Open Door Policy was introduced, and it led to further improvements in Canadian access to Chinese markets. In 1978, the Canada–China Trade Council was established: it was later renamed the Canada China Business Council. In 1980, Canada granted preferential trade status to China, reducing tariffs on imports from China by over one third from the regular "most-favoured nation" tariff rate. However, many products were excluded from this agreement. Between 1978 and 1988, Chinese exports to Canada grew, averaging an increase of twenty-six percent a year, while Canadian exports grew only by an average of eighteen percent a year.

As early as the 1960s, Britain began to differentiate passports carried by Hong Kong residents. This was a prelude to the negotiations between Margaret Thatcher's government and Beijing on the return of sovereignty over Hong Kong to China, which subsequently led to an exodus of Hong Kong residents, many of whom came to Canada. Emigration from Hong Kong was on many people's minds. I remember hearing of the fear of change whenever we visited Hong Kong. Many were sure that it would be for the worse. On the other hand, Canada, like many other immigrant-receiving countries, opened its doors to attract wealthy immigrants by making it easier for businesspeople, entrepreneurs and investors to immigrate to Canada.

The influx of immigrants from Hong Kong was due to fear of political change, but the movement of people also coincided with changes in the economic situation in Canada and Hong Kong. This, we will see, in subsequent years, was the reason why so many returned from Canada to Hong Kong or mainland China. During those years I watched with great interest as many members of my extended family immigrated to Canada. The only person who said he would never leave Hong Kong was my father. He passed away before the final agreement was signed between Britain and China.

The return of sovereignty at the end of the 1990s had far-reaching consequences for Canadian relations with that part of Asia. The number of Canadians of Chinese heritage suddenly swelled, and Chinese became the third most spoken language in Canada. In the mid-1990s the economy boomed in Hong Kong, which seemed to overshadow the fear of Communism. Many immigrant heads of households returned to Hong Kong to work while leaving their families in Canada, and the children attended school here. These children grew up being bicultural, with one foot in Canada and one in Asia. As Greater China flourished economically, many Canadians of Chinese heritage born or raised in Canada were drawn by the opportunities there. Now, about 250,000 Canadians live in Greater China and 1.3 million Canadians in Canada claim Chinese heritage. As a result Canada's relations with Greater China have grown closer, largely through the movements of people who feel equally at home in both worlds.

Ideally, this should mean that Canada has increased its ties with and influence over Greater China, but this is not the case. Ironically, just as Greater China has grown in importance as a global economic power, Canada has decreased its influence and presence. Relations between our two countries, like that of China with other western nations, were strained after the Tiananmen Square massacre in 1989, even though trade continued to grow. By 1994, the two-way trade exceeded $6 billion. In the same year, Canada established its "four pillar" policy on China, comprising economic partnership, peace and security, sustainable development, human rights, good governance and the rule of law.

In 2001, China joined the World Trade Organization, and in the following six years Chinese exports worldwide quadrupled, rising twenty-nine percent a year. By 2007, globally, China accounted for more than eight percent of exports and almost seven percent of imports. Over the past ten years, China has expanded its international trade dramatically and transformed many of its cities into vibrant financial and manufacturing centres. The Chinese growth rate averaged about nine percent over the past two decades, and was often in double digits. As a result of this astonishing growth, many millions have climbed out of poverty and joined the middle class. Despite all the problems China still has to overcome, this phenomenon cannot be ignored by the rest of the world.

Appearing before the Senate's Standing Committee on Foreign Affairs on April 29 this spring, China's Ambassador to Canada, His Excellency Lan Lijun, said, "Over the past few years, we have seen a downturn in our relationship. There has been no active exchange of high-level visits. The approach taken on certain issues is not conducive to developing a sound, better relationship." So what happened? Successive Canadian governments, and many companies, have failed to understand the extent of China's transformation. Canada's dependence on trade with the United States has paid dividends in the past, but, as we can see, we are dragged under when there is an economic crisis in the United States. Some individuals in the current government still seemed fixated on the Cold War dichotomy, fearing Communism in any form. This is ironic because, when I am in Hong Kong or on the mainland, I recognize how socialistic we are in Canada. Some in our government feel that closer economic ties would mean condoning

China's labour conditions and its poor record on human rights. There are also national security and other concerns that state-owned Chinese companies, using sovereign wealth funds (pools of government-owned financial assets), should be limited in their ability to acquire foreign assets. Much of the tone from the present government has been judgmental and negative, and we all know that this approach does not work, whether between people or between governments.

With the recent economic crisis, the dramatic changes in Greater China over the past decade are now being recognized more widely. China surpassed Germany as the third largest economy in the world at the beginning of this year. As America's banker, with huge savings among its many citizens, and as a global trader, it is roughly five times more involved in the global economy than other emerging economies such as India, Russia or Brazil. The recent Chinese contribution of US$ 40 billion to replenish the International Monetary Fund was an international triumph for China. It is, therefore, not surprising that Hillary Clinton said, "some believe that China on the rise is by definition an adversary. To the contrary, the US and China benefit from, and contribute to, each other's successes." This certainly offers China's leaders strategic opportunities. It was no surprise when in April, at the G20 summit in London, many were musing about a "G2," a China–US duopoly to guide world affairs. This came as a wake-up call to Prime Minister Harper.

Nationalism is on the rise in China. The Beijing Olympics in 2008 were a huge source of pride for both China and the Chinese diaspora around the world. The next big international event is the Shanghai Expo. Criticism of China at these international events will only serve to spur on this nationalism.

Many have overcome poverty in China, but many more have yet to be swept up by the wave of progress. Despite its economic miracle, there is huge disparity between the coastal regions and the vast hinterland. With the recent economic crisis, millions of university graduates are joining the tens of millions of migrant workers among the unemployed. Economic decline of this magnitude could lead to the destabilization of Chinese society. China faces huge environmental issues as well, which will affect us all if climate change continues unabated. As a global citizen, despite its economic power, China has a long way to go in assuming a leadership role because of its human rights record. It can, however, be an arbiter of conflicts, such as that with North Korea.

On the positive side, despite early fears of repression, citizens of Hong Kong were able to mark the twentieth anniversary of the Tiananmen Square

Massacre without incident. It is also not surprising that, in the Fraser Institute's annual report of 2008, Hong Kong retained its status as having the greatest degree of economic freedom in the world. Recently, Shanghai hosted its first gay pride festival, which would have been unthinkable a mere decade ago.

With respect to Taiwan, since the election of Ma Ying-jeou as President, China's cross-Strait relationship has improved dramatically. In late April China Mobile announced that it would acquire twelve percent of the third largest provider in Taiwan, Far EasTone, in the amount of US$ 525 million, which is the first-ever investment from China in Taiwan. Another significant development this May was when Beijing agreed to let Taiwan have observer status at the World Health Assembly in Geneva, using the name "Chinese Taipei."

In 2006, when the Harper government discontinued Canada's dialogue with China on human rights, citing ongoing concern over China's lack of progress, President Hu Jintao snubbed Prime Minister Harper at an economic summit in Vietnam. So why, with Colombia's dismal record on human rights and its violent past as a narco-state, did the government conclude a free trade deal with that country this March? I don't want to suggest that the previous Liberal government had sufficient foresight to move from its dependence on US trade to recognize the economic importance of China. There was dialogue, and there were a few Team Canada missions, but it is only recently that the Liberals have recognized Canada's need to look towards the emerging economies in Asia. The Harper government has taken pains to criticize China's human rights record publicly at every opportunity, meeting with the Dalai Lama at the Prime Minister's Parliament Hill office. The Prime Minister also refused to attend the Beijing Olympic Games. There has been little contact at senior political and diplomatic levels. This is a major impediment to engagement, since Chinese culture places great importance on long-term personal relationships.

Members of our present government seem to be ignorant of the fact that, while we need China, China does not need us. China has a global reach and has also negotiated a free trade pact with ASEAN countries. China is Canada's second largest trading partner overall, and our third largest market for Canadian merchandise exports, just behind the United States and the United Kingdom, and yet eighty percent of our merchandise exports still go to the United States, with only about two percent going to China. Despite the tremendous commercial potential of China, Canada lags behind in foreign direct investment there, which is less than one percent, and China's investment in Canada is at a similar level.

Canada is also failing to take advantage of its biggest long-term asset, the 250,000 Canadians, many of whom are young professionals, who live in Greater China. Particularly regressive is the new citizenship law that took effect this April, and created a two-tiered citizenship that will affect the Canadian diaspora. The Asia Pacific Foundation of Canada urges Ottawa to update its understanding of the global knowledge-based economy and to "embrace Chinese transnationalism." Chinese civilization has been around for thousands of years and we have long memories, so I am very puzzled by the government's recent about-face regarding restarting dialogue with China. The visits of Ministers Stockwell Day and Lawrence Cannon to China, with an upcoming visit planned for Prime Minister Harper, seem like a good start, but not nearly enough to build any kind of permanent relationship.

The Harper government has done some things right. The significant appointment of David Mulroney as Ambassador to China will, I hope, enable a more sustained approach involving high-level officials in the Department of Foreign Affairs and International Trade. Another positive recent appointment was that of Dashan as the Canadian Commissioner General for the Shanghai Expo.

Canada has finally identified China as one of the priority countries in its Global Commerce Strategy and has stated that it wants to double the level of bilateral trade by next year. As of 2008 we suffered from a substantial trade imbalance with China, with imports surpassing exports by a ratio of four to one. Given the diminishing opportunities for exports to the United States, it is important that Canada revitalizes our relationship with China. However, it will take more than stated goals on paper. Canada is not spending very much on the Global Commerce Strategy, just $50 million, an amount that many of our competitors would direct towards one single country.

Unlike Australia, Canada has failed to have a "whole government" strategy toward China. Australia has had this approach since the 1980s, involving immigration, post-secondary education and trade with an Australian brand. Australia's approach emphasizes a constant flow of positive visits between senior-level officials. For example, in 2008 the Prime Minister of Australia visited China twice, the Governor General went to China, the Minister for Trade visited China three times, and no less than five other ministers with various portfolios went to China. Australia also maintains a number of ongoing bilateral dialogues with China on trade, resources, aid, defence, human rights, climate change and regional security, and is working actively towards a free trade deal with China. On human rights, Australia's policy revolves around dialogue, technical assistance and an incremental approach. Its Department of Foreign Affairs and Trade notes that, "though progress is slow, this approach is preferable to the alternative—public condemnation of China—which is often counterproductive." The policy notes that while differences on human rights exist, substantial progress has been made by China over the past thirty years. Australia's overall two-way trade was more than AU$ 67 billion in 2008, an increase of 28.3 percent year on year, and more than fourteen percent of Australia's merchandise exports go to China. Needless to say, our government has much to learn.

Given Canada's status as an exporter of natural resources, our leadership in scientific research and environmental technology, and our role as the Asia–Pacific gateway, China should be our natural ally. For Canadian corporations, Hong Kong, and now increasingly, Taiwan can be our gateways into China. China's Foreign Minister, Yang Jiechi, was in Ottawa this Tuesday, taking the initiative to turn the page on the rocky relationship that exists between the Harper government and China. I am sure that all of us will be watching to see what follows.

As is often the case, the Canadian public is ahead of the government. A poll by the Asia Pacific Foundation of Canada, taken three years ago, found that most Canadians identified China as the export market with the greatest potential, way ahead of the United States, and sixty percent of Canadians believed that the rise of China was more of an economic opportunity than a threat. The Canadian government needs to make China a priority, so that other countries will not continue to realize substantial gains at our expense, and Canada will not become irrelevant on the world stage.

Chapter 10

Hong Kong: Canada's Partner in Prosperity

A Speech to the Hong Kong–Canada
Business Association's Parliamentary Breakfast
in Ottawa, May 18, 2006

Perrin Beatty

I am very grateful for the invitation to join you for this meeting of the Hong Kong Canadian Business Association. Hong Kong is a true symbol of the new global economy and the key location where East meets West. It boasts an impressive resume: the world's eleventh largest trading economy, the world's sixth largest foreign exchange market, the world's thirteenth largest banking centre, and Asia's second biggest stock market. Hong Kong is one of the world's top exporters of garments, watches and clocks, toys, games, electronic products and certain light industrial products. Hong Kong was the world's tenth largest exporter of services in 2004. Civil aviation, shipping, travel and tourism, trade-related services and financial and banking services are the main components of its trade in services. The prices of many services are among the lowest in the world. More than 3,800 international corporations have established regional headquarters or offices in Hong Kong. The major types of business include the wholesale/retail and import/export trades, other business services such as accounting, advertising and legal services, finance and banking, manufacturing and transport and related services.

Hong Kong advocates and practises free trade—a free and liberal investment regime, the absence of trade barriers, no discrimination against overseas investors, freedom of capital movements, a well-established rule of law, transparent regulations, and low and predictable taxation. In 2002, it was ranked the world's freest economy in the Heritage Foundation's Index of Economic Freedom as well as the Cato Institute's Annual Report on Economic Freedom of the World.

My first trip there was twenty years ago, when I was the first minister in the newly elected Mulroney government to visit Hong Kong. I saw many things during my short visit, but the impression that lasted was of millions of people living in an area not much larger than my constituency whose only resources were geography and ingenuity, but who had become world leaders in a wide range of areas. It left me feeling that, if Canadians could combine the advantages that come from our natural bounty and diverse population with the creativity and work ethic that typify Hong Kong, the result would be a world-beater. Fast forward to 2006, and still, for many of us, the fourteen-hour flight makes it seem that Canada and Hong Kong are worlds apart, when in fact, the exact opposite is true. Canadians are well aware that many of our citizens have come from Hong Kong, but we are less conscious of the fact that there are about 250,000 Canadians living and working there today, and more than 150 Canadian companies operating in Hong Kong, ranging from Canada's big banks and insurance companies to locally incorporated service companies. Direct investment from Canada reached CA$ 2.9 billion last year.

Hong Kong offers excellent commercial opportunities to Canadian firms. Last year Canada exported almost CA$ 2 billion in goods to Hong Kong, making it our fourteenth largest export destination for goods and likely higher in terms of services. Hong Kong companies have cumulative investments in Canada of CA$ 5 billion. The Canadian presence can be felt almost everywhere. As you drive in from the airport, you cross the magnificent Tsing Ma Bridge. That state-of-the-art engineering marvel was built with the help of Canadian expertise. Similarly, it is impressive to walk into the Hong Kong Convention and Exhibition Centre where last December's WTO meetings were held, and see where the University of Western Ontario's Richard Ivey School of Business became the first business school in North America to establish a campus in Asia, the Cheng Yu Tung Management Institute. When you look at the windows and glasswork in the magnificent Convention Centre, you should know that much of it was done by Fulton Windows, an SME and CME member from Mississauga.

I believe that the Canada–Hong Kong relationship today symbolizes business around the globe in the 21st century. Geography is no longer a barrier. Technology, much of it Canadian, like the BlackBerry in my pocket, has bridged that gap. It is great to see that made-in-Canada technology for sale in the shops there. Technology has created a 21st-century reality with a world of new opportunities at your fingertips, where your customer can be found with just the click of a mouse.

However, this new opportunity has also spawned a host of new challenges. For my organization, Canada's largest trade and industry organization, we live it every day. No other sector has weathered as many storms over the past few years as Canada's manufacturing and exporting sector, and it does not look as if it is going to get any easier in the future. Industry is changing at a relentless pace in Canada, in North America and around the industrialized world. Business practices employed only five years ago will not work today. New, emerging Asian economic and industrial powerhouses like China and India are fuelling this "next-generation industrial revolution" and rewriting the rules of the game. Simply put, business as usual is not an option.

China is fast becoming the world's manufacturing and exporting giant. China's gross domestic product now exceeds US$ 1.3 trillion, about forty percent more than Canada's. After discounting for price changes, it is thirteen times larger today than it was thirty years ago. China's official economic growth rate last year was nine percent and economic growth has exceeded seven percent annual rates since 1999. The growth in actual economic activity is probably much higher than that. In 2003, China accounted for sixteen percent of the growth in the world economy, second only to the United States. The Asian giant's exports are now eight times larger than they were only ten years ago. They amounted to US$ 380 billion in 2003, giving China six percent of the global export market as compared to 3.9 percent only three years before. But China is also a key source of demand for goods and services from around the world. China is now Canada's third largest trading partner and Canada is China's tenth. Two-way trade totalled more than $8 billion last year, fifty times higher than it was in 1970.

Many Canadian businesses see China as a huge challenge, the land of outsourced Canadian production, but with a population of more than 1.3 billion, the Asian giant represents a potentially colossal market for Canadian companies. It all depends on whether you consider the glass half-full or half empty. CME believes that it is half-full and, with some imagination and hard work on our part, we can fill it the rest of the way. China is a land of opportunity for Canadian companies, and Hong Kong is positioned as the gateway to this emerging economic powerhouse. We speak the same language, have a better appreciation for the Western-influenced culture and share similar values.

The Asian tiger has a voracious appetite for almost everything. China absorbed more than two fifths of the world's cement output last year and overtook Japan as the world's second largest importer of oil after the United States, partly due to a boom in car sales. Additionally, in 2003 it bought over eight percent of global oil supplies. In 2004 there was an eighty-seven percent surge in commodity prices. Foreign direct investment in China totalled US$ 65 billion, while outward investment in China topped US$ 85 billion. One of China's largest trading partners is not a country, but a company, Wal-Mart, which accounted for fourteen percent of all exports in 2004. China now has a whopping thirty-eight percent of the world's electronics production and chances are that the refrigerator in your home has a "Made in China" sticker on it.

China's nine percent *per annum* compounding growth over the past two decades has already had a profound effect on Hong Kong, where people now talk not about goods being "made in Hong Kong," but about goods being "made *for* Hong Kong." While the actual production of goods may be taking place across the border, in the Pearl River Delta or beyond, Hong Kong manufacturers have focused on high-value-added elements of their business, such as design, distribution, promotion, sales, financing, service and brand management. Hong Kong's manufacturing community, which once saw China's growth as a threat, now sees it as the key to prosperity.

Here in North America businesspeople and policy-makers are less certain of the impact. For many, the threat of China obscures the opportunities the country presents. It would be foolish to pretend that China is not already a powerful competitor, one that will become even more formidable in the future. But forward-looking manufacturers believe that it is possible to see China as a competitor, as a partner *and* as a customer. Here is how Jim Owens, the CEO of Caterpillar, recently described what American businesses need to do:

> We have work to do to compete with the world's best. There are steps we must take to get our own house in order. For starters, American manufacturers must focus on designing and producing the highest-quality products, incorporating the most up-to-date technology. We have to stay aggressive with our product development programmes, and ensure that the goods we manufacture are desired the world over.
>
> Second, we must continue to embrace lean manufacturing principles, increase the use of robotics and automation, and focus on just-in-time delivery. These tools will enable us to keep costs low and productivity high.
>
> Third, we must invest in our people, providing the education and workforce development training they need to help us succeed. Over time, our international competitors will work to produce better products and adopt world-class processes, but they cannot replicate our market size and proximity. The ideas and competitive spirit that our people bring to the workplace must be nurtured.

Fourth, we must believe that we can compete on the world stage. We must look at globalization and international competition as an opportunity to make ourselves stronger and more efficient, and not, as some are proposing, as a reason to turn inward, and put up barriers to trade and investment.

The formula for success is no different for Canadian manufacturers. During our Manufacturing 20/20 initiative, the largest public consultation in history on the future of Canadian industry, more than 3,000 Canadian manufacturers told us that today their industry is heavily dependent on technological knowledge and skills, ever more customized and service-oriented, and increasingly integrated into international markets and global supply chains. The future for manufacturers is one of global customers, global supply chains and business networks, and the potential to source from the best companies, the best technologies, and the best skills, not just from across the continent, but from around the world.

Our customer base must be global. As a result, our trade agreements must reflect the changing needs of Canadian companies in this new international reality, and ensure that Canadian industrial and services companies can enjoy more secure and open access to major global markets. As a parent who worries about the society our children will inherit, it is clear that their standard of living will depend on how well we perform in the global economy.

Future prosperity hinges on our business strategies and public policies moving beyond a model in which Canadian companies are simply exporting to, importing from, or investing in other countries. They must focus instead on the requirements of the global enterprise, on businesses, supply chains or business networks in which all aspects of commercial activity take place concurrently in a number of countries around the world, and on what is necessary to capture the highest economic benefits of that activity for Canadians. More markets, better access, freer trade: when you have a well-educated and highly motivated public, those are the key ingredients in the recipe for future success.

Canada is the world's fifth largest exporter and importer. It is the most trade-dependent nation in the developed world, with exports of goods and services representing about forty percent of gross domestic product, about four times as much, in percentage terms, as the United States or Japan. In that regard, the greatest difference between Canada and most other countries in the world is that we are even more trade-dependent. We are not a superpower that can dictate the terms on which the rest of the world must do business with us. That is why the rule of law is critical. Canadian prosperity hinges on the existence of an international regulatory framework that facilitates access to expanding world markets, and that can adapt to changes in technology, trade practices and social systems. The World Trade Organization provides the cornerstone of our nation's trade policy and the foundation for Canada's relations with its trading partners, including emerging markets and developing countries.

In this uncertain and tumultuous economic era we must enhance our relationship with Hong Kong. For well over a century, Hong Kong has served as the gateway to mainland China. Obviously, there is nowhere better to obtain the expertise, information and facilities needed to tap into the Chinese market, especially as economic expansion is fuelled through trade due to its entry into the WTO.

One project that CME has been championing has been the Pacific Gateway Initiative, which will have immense economic benefits and spin-offs for the whole of Canada. Many of you probably know that we like to boast that we are Hong Kong's closest neighbour in North America in terms of nautical miles. Prince Rupert is approximately 5,286 miles across the Pacific, while Seattle and Los Angeles are 5,768 and 6,380 miles respectively. Constructing not only a state-of-the-art superport, but a high-tech intermodal logistics network that includes ships, trains and trucks, begins in Western Canada and unfolds all over North America, will benefit not only North America and China, but the entire global supply chain system as well.

Looking to the future, it is a safe bet to say that Canada and Hong Kong will enhance their relationship as more and more of our businesses develop new business partnerships. Remember RIM? The company—a CME member, I may add—that revolutionized communication in the West has now headed East. Just yesterday China Mobile Communications Corporation began offering BlackBerry mobile e-mail service to some of its existing corporate clients in Asia. China is the world's biggest mobile communications market, with more than 400 million cellphone users, most of whom are China Mobile customers. Hong Kong has a few thousand BlackBerry subscribers registered since the service was started in 2002. When I was in Hong Kong last December, my BlackBerry functioned as seamlessly as if I were in Ottawa. Some analysts are predicting that in three years' time more than 3.9 million Chinese will be using the BlackBerry as the preferred mode of communication. Currently RIM has five million subscribers. That type of creativity, innovation, leadership and vision must stand as a model for success for all Canadian companies moving forward.

We may be thousands of miles apart geographically, but Canada and China are just a mouse-click away, and Hong Kong remains the gateway to the opportunities that wait for us in the world's fastest-growing economy.

Chapter 11

The Transformative Effects of the Global Economic Crisis: Implications for the World and Shanghai's Aspirations

The Keynote Address to the International
Business Leaders' Advisory Council for the
Mayor of Shanghai, November 1, 2009

Thomas d'Aquino

It is a special privilege for me to deliver this address in the great city of Shanghai on the occasion of the 2009 meeting of the International Business Leaders' Advisory Council. I am pleased that among the very talented group of Advisory Council business leaders is my colleague and friend Laurent Beaudoin, whose company, Bombardier, is a global leader in rail equipment and civil aviation manufacturing, a company that exemplifies the commitment of Canadian business to China.

Mayor Han, you have vividly demonstrated to us in your address this morning and in the events you graciously included us in yesterday that you are no ordinary Mayor and that Shanghai is no ordinary city. We were all moved, I am sure, by the drama of the new Yangtze River tunnel and bridge, by the tenderness in the release of birds at Dongtan Wetland Park, and by the beauty of last night's performance in the splendid architecture of the Oriental Art Center.

As we meet in Shanghai, the impact of the most severe global economic crisis since the Great Depression of the 1930s continues to reverberate. One of the notable aspects of the crisis is its global reach. People, businesses and governments in every part of the world have felt its sting. This surprised some observers, who argued that parts of the world could somehow be isolated from one another, that the crisis could in effect be quarantined. This turned out to be impossible. Regardless of where we live, we are all actors on a global stage.

I am a believer in the benefits of globalization, as I know you are, Mayor Han, and as I know are the outward-looking people of this dynamic city. It is a plain fact that globalization has accelerated economic progress, lifted hundreds of millions of people out of poverty, spurred innovation and scientific advancement, and brought people, cities and countries closer together, ensuring that we are better able to confront challenges that touch us all, whether the challenge be a financial crisis, a devastating earthquake, a killer tsunami or a raging pandemic. Understandably, not everyone is convinced of the virtues of globalization, especially in difficult economic times. Looking around the world, we know that the benefits of rapid globalization are not equitably shared. This takes time, to be sure, but the forces that are propelling globalization, spurred on by ground-breaking networking technologies, are stronger than ever. United Nations Secretary General Kofi Annan once offered a telling perspective: "Arguing against globalization," he said, "is like arguing against the laws of gravity."

There are signs of hope that the worst of the economic crisis has passed. Output has stopped shrinking in the world's largest economies, stock markets have rallied, company inventories are being replenished, financial markets are beginning to thaw, and confidence is re-emerging. It is heartening, for example, that the International Monetary Fund is now predicting that global GDP will expand by 3.1 percent next year. However, we cannot ignore that in most parts of the world unemployment is still on the rise, business continues to face tough conditions, a large amount of global manufacturing capacity remains idle, many financial institutions are still shaky, and governments are saddled with huge and growing fiscal obligations. As our Chinese hosts know firsthand, China has not been immune. The global nature of the recession, the pullback of consumers in the United States and elsewhere, and the precipitous fall of international trade volumes, the worst since the Great Depression, have meant job losses and industrial contraction even in this country, where growth continues to be impressive.

Looking ahead five years, even ten years, what will the global economic landscape look like? I believe that the answer, in large measure, will depend on how the major developed and emerging economies face up to a number of critical challenges. I am going to mention five of them.

In dealing with these challenges, China is destined to play a key role. This country's remarkable transformation of the past three decades in political, economic, trade and financial power continues without significant interruption. GDP over this period has multiplied more than eighty times and, according to the People's Bank of China, China's foreign exchange reserves now are approaching US$ 2.3 trillion. Forecasts point to China achieving 8.1 percent growth in 2009, a more than respectable showing against a backdrop of global recession. Data released in recent days point to momentum in China that could very well lead to even higher growth this year. However bright China's prospects are, Chinese leaders have rightly identified the need to achieve a recovery from the effects of the crisis that is sustainable. Last month, in a speech to the World Economic Forum in Dalian, Premier Wen Jiabao acknowledged that China's economic recovery "is not yet steady, solid and balanced." The Premier's frank assertion underscores a growing consensus among thought leaders in China that urgent priorities need attention. Key among them are the need to accelerate unfulfilled economic reforms, to deal with widespread poverty and widening income disparity, to respond to serious environmental problems, and to foster expanded domestic consumption.

As China and the world look beyond the economic crisis, what are the most urgent challenges that need to be addressed? The first is to gain a proper perspective on the crisis itself. While it is true that the direct causes of the crisis—the combustible mixture of excess leverage in both consumer and financial markets, the bank failures, the credit collapse and the contagion to the broader economy—have led to painful consequences, it would be folly to conclude that the foundations of market economics have been irreparably damaged. A serious failure in the conduct of global finance should not result in the wholesale condemnation of a market system that in large measure functions responsibly, a market based on the rule of law and ethical principles, a market that promotes competition and innovation. As has been amply demonstrated in recent decades, a market that functions responsibly offers the best hope to people who seek a better and more secure life, wherever in the world they may live. This is absolutely fundamental.

A second challenge facing the global community is how to deal intelligently with the huge fiscal challenges ahead. The robust response of central banks and governments to the economic crisis may very well have averted a global catastrophe. Their actions certainly stemmed public panic, helped to restore the conditions for an eventual return to stability and confidence, and launched a healthy debate about a wide range of possible financial reforms. At the same time, however, governments have assumed massive fiscal obligations that will take many years to unwind. The IMF points out that, in the G20 as a whole, deficits have grown from 1.1 percent of collective GDP in 2007 to 8.1 percent in 2009. The Fund further predicts that government debt in the advanced G20 countries will rise from a pre-crisis average of seventy-nine percent of GDP to 120 percent in 2014. These are staggering numbers. As governments face up to this fiscal challenge, two risks must be carefully balanced. On the one hand, it is vital that fiscal stimulus measures not be withdrawn too quickly, for fear that the slowly emerging recovery will be snuffed out. On the other hand, fiscal stimulus that is sustained for too long will fuel already abundant fears of a massive spike in inflation, and the emergence of new and ever more dangerous asset bubbles. Countries with looming demographic pressures and unaffordable entitlement programmes face additional risks. What is needed is for countries to develop and execute smart "exit" strategies. This requires a determined pullback in government spending as the private sector returns to growth. Not an easy task: as we all know, the politics of unwinding government programmes can be daunting. Here political courage and good public policy go hand in hand. Given the interdependence of the global economy, close coordination on this front by the G20 nations is crucial.

A third challenge that must be addressed if the global economy is to return to stable growth is protectionism. Despite exhortations by G8 and G20 leaders to stop growing protectionism in its tracks, examples abound throughout the world as political authorities offer preferences to home-based businesses and seek ways to cushion rising unemployment. The severity of the problem was underscored recently by the Geneva-based World Trade Alliance. It claims that, on average, a G20 country has violated the "no new protectionism" pledge once every three days since it was made last November.

Last week's report of the authoritative Netherlands Bureau for Economic Policy suggests that the dramatic contraction in global trade, estimated at close to twelve percent this year, may not be reversing itself as quickly as hoped. In the face of these gloomy statistics there is much that should concern us. Trade rules are being flouted regularly in developed and emerging countries alike. Again and again, short-term political expediency is trumping the rule of law and common sense. The world continues to spin away from the goal of a single, credible and effective set of multilateral trade rules. The Doha Round is paralyzed and its prospects are dim. In its place, a patchwork of bilateral and regional trade agreements is growing in size and complexity. The time for action is long overdue. Here it would be apt to reflect on the teachings of Confucius, who said, "Looking at small advantages prevents great affairs from being accomplished."

Let me turn now to a fourth challenge that deserves urgent attention. In Pittsburgh this past September G20 leaders acknowledged that the global economy is out of balance and that this is one of the reasons for the financial crisis. Excessive reliance on external demand carries with it real consequences, as does excessive reliance on foreign investors to finance consumption and deficits for long periods of time. As we have found, such imbalances can cause serious and long-lasting economic damage. Over the past year these imbalances have started to unwind. For example, the current account deficit of the United States has dropped from about five percent of GDP in 2008 to less than three percent in the second quarter of 2009. Meanwhile, China's current account surplus has declined from about ten percent of GDP in the first half of 2008 to 6.5 percent in the first half of 2009. With these trends moving in the right direction, I would argue that a return to ever-increasing imbalances in global trade and capital markets must be avoided at all costs. Otherwise, we risk precipitating yet another crisis, with even greater negative consequences for the global economy.

So what should we do? Put simply, Americans in particular are going to have to save more of their income and consume less, and Asian economies will have to foster greater domestic demand. In both cases, this is far easier said than done. There is no magic set of policy prescriptions to motivate individuals to change their habits so as to dramatically increase savings on the one hand and consumption on the other. In the case of the United States, with recovery, the federal government must put in place a credible exit strategy. This means achieving balanced budgets over an economic cycle. This goal will be out of reach unless health care costs are contained, taxes on consumption are raised, social security reforms are implemented and "pay as you go" spending is embraced. In the case of the Asian economies, and especially China, the shift towards expanded consumption should focus on strengthened pension schemes, and increased government spending on health care and education. Earlier this year, McKinsey & Company reported that the development of service industries and easier access to consumer products and credit could increase domestic demand in China by more than US$ 2 trillion by 2025.

In my view, China, in addition, will have to come to terms with the issue of exchange rate flexibility. With the global recovery, China's exports are growing once again and more capital is flowing back into the country, raising expectations for currency appreciation. The alternative is future price inflation in certain asset classes. Chinese central bank Vice Governor Ma Delun recently highlighted the risk that asset bubbles could begin to build within China as the economy roars back to life. There needs to be an outlet, and that outlet should be to allow the currency to appreciate.

There is also the challenge, or opportunity, of what to do with China's immense foreign exchange reserves. A Chinese think tank has come up with an intriguing idea: that the reserves could be put to good use through the development of a "Marshall Plan" for Africa, Asia and Latin America. Such a development fund, or loan facility, would increase living standards in the targeted countries. These funds would ignite new engines of global growth and recovery to offset lower American and European consumption. Perhaps China's leadership will consider such a bold move. Indeed, President Hu Jintao has acknowledged the role of global imbalances as a key contributor to the financial crisis and to negative impacts on "global wealth distribution, resource availability and consumption, and the international monetary system." Putting the enormous supply of China's foreign reserves towards greater development would go some way to answering the challenge of imbalances in the global economy.

Let me turn now to a fifth enormously complex challenge that deserves attention. In a few weeks the world's eyes will turn to Copenhagen, as some 190 governments attempt to negotiate a more robust global plan to tackle climate change. I sometimes feel that we have loaded so many expectations onto the climate change agenda, and the Copenhagen summit in particular, that it cannot help but fail. To listen to the rhetoric, you would think that tackling this issue will give us vast new sources of cleaner energy, spawn whole new industries of clean technology, almost single-handedly cure unemployment through the growth of millions of "green" jobs, and allow for the transfer of massive amounts of financial and technological aid to emerging economies. I have always believed that we should have lofty aspirations and continually challenge ourselves to do better, but in the politically charged and confusing debate around climate change it is easy to forget fundamental realities. For example, that climate change affects every man, woman and child on Earth, and therefore we must find new ways for *all* nations to contribute, according to their capabilities and strengths, to a lower carbon future. I know that some of you will say that the developed world has had 200 years of industrial activity and wealth accumulation, and therefore must act first. This is undoubtedly true, but the simple fact is that, going forward, the developing world will account for significantly more than half of annual global emissions. Unless the rapidly emerging economies become key players, there can be no solution.

China's leadership is pivotal. Having recently overtaken the United States as the world's largest producer of greenhouse gases, your country has a vital stake in achieving a global consensus on tackling climate change. Your leaders have acknowledged the primacy of improving environmental quality at home. The simple fact is that the health of China's citizenry, the liveability of China's cities, and the competitiveness of China's workforce and industries will depend heavily on embracing advanced environmental standards and green technologies.

This leads me to some relatively simple propositions about the role of business going forward. First, we must encourage our political leaders to work harder to forge an international climate change plan that is fair, effective, affordable and sustainable. In each of our countries we can do more to foster policy that integrates economic development, energy and the environment. We must push our governments to adopt policies that incent new technologies, rather than encouraging them to hide behind green protectionism or the false hope of weakened intellectual property rights. Whatever the outcome in Copenhagen, we need a framework that will unleash the creativity of the market, whether it be in renewable energy, advanced materials with a much lower environmental impact, or leading-edge technologies such as clean coal or carbon sequestration. Businesses themselves, throughout the world, have to step up to the plate. Even in challenging times, we need to greatly enhance our investment in research and development and commercialization of lower-carbon energy, products and services. We need to build direct business-to-business engagement, and foreign investment and technology partnerships. As we already see happening here in China, such partnerships create innovative capacity in both the developers and the adopters of new technologies. The centrality of these new technologies to long-term prosperity cannot be overemphasized. This is a point that President Obama made last week in an address to the Massachusetts Institute of Technology when he said: "From China to India, from Japan to Germany, nations everywhere are racing to develop newer ways to produce and use energy. The nation that wins this competition will be the nation that leads the global economy."

Mayor Han, responding decisively to the five challenges I have outlined this morning, I believe, is essential if we are to build a prosperous and peaceful world. Success will require a degree of cooperation among countries and peoples unprecedented in our lifetimes. The global economic crisis has been a powerful catalyst and, in one respect at least, it has been beneficial. In shaking our confidence and our institutions, it has compelled us all to think about how we can create a better world. This indeed is a crisis that must not be wasted.

The response to the crisis is taking many forms. It has given prominence and momentum to the G20, signalling a seismic shift in the architecture of global governance. While the G20 may lack the cohesion of the G8, its greatest virtue is that it brings to the table the most important global players. The hard truth is that the challenges I have outlined—restoring faith in the market, balancing growth and fiscal responsibility, defeating protectionism, bringing balance to world finances and achieving a cleaner, more sustainable environment—cannot be realized without a new consensus among the global heavyweights. In recent public debate, some have argued that the task of building such a consensus should fall primarily on China and the United States, the so-called G2. This, in my view, would be a mistake. While cooperation between China and the United States is essential in dealing with a host of political, economic and security issues, I believe that the interests of China, the United States and the global community as a whole would be better served in a multipolar world guided by effective multilateral institutions.

In such a world, one in which the ideas and vitality of many countries and peoples interact, the role of cities is central. We are here today as your guests, Mayor Han, because we share your view that Shanghai is destined to be among the greatest of cities in the 21st century. Shortly, we will hear the views of various business leaders from around the world on what it takes to aspire to the front ranks of urban achievement and excellence. In my view, "quality of life" should be the ultimate determinant of rank.

In June the *Economist* Intelligence Unit released its Liveability Ranking of 140 cities around the world. It rates more than thirty factors across five categories: stability, health care, culture and environment, education and infrastructure. We Canadians are pleased to find that Vancouver once again was ranked first, and two other Canadian cities, Toronto and Calgary, were among the top ten. Shanghai is making progress on these fronts. With an international trade volume of some US$ 600 billion in 2008, its financial strength and its strategic position in the Yangtze River delta, it has staggering potential. The city government's plan to build four centres for international economics, finance, shipping, and trade and services by 2020 signals a wise selection of priorities for moving forward. This plan and your speech this morning, Mayor Han, signal a continuing shift from labour-intensive to capital- and knowledge-based industries. This entails the need to attract diverse and world-class skilled workers at the same time as devoting more resources to education and training. It implies improvements in infrastructure. It implies "going green" in a massive way, embracing the most advanced sustainable technologies. It makes clear the need for a sound legal system and best practices in accounting, regulation and governance. Most fundamentally, it implies an open economy, where capital, goods, services and people move freely. In the pursuit of all these objectives the citizens of Shanghai and the people of China will be greatly inspired by World Expo 2010. So will the approximately 70 million visitors who are expected to witness firsthand the meaning of the Expo motto, "Better city, better life."

Mayor Han, I wish you, and the hard-working and creative people of Shanghai, every success as you continue your impressive efforts to make your city a 21st-century leader. I have no doubt that you will succeed. China and the world will be a better place for it.

Chapter 12

The Canadian Constitution and the Charter of Rights and Freedoms: A Global Template for Minority Rights with Relevance to China?

Errol P. Mendes

The rights of minorities are an arena that is becoming perhaps the principal battle ground for human rights in the 21st century. Recent history seems to offer the stunning paradox that federal states may not be the best form of human governance for societies with multiethnic populations. The former Soviet Bloc had nine states, six of which were unitary states, while three were federal in structure. With the unification of Germany, the six unitary states are now five, but the three federal states—Yugoslavia, the Soviet Union and Czechoslovakia—are now twenty-three independent states (see Stepan 1999 and Malesevic 2000). Most of these newly independent states were forged by minorities who did not feel that their rights were sufficiently protected by the federal structures they previously existed within. I suggest that ethnic identities are not predetermined to be in conflict with those of other groups and that the causes of ethnic conflict are influenced not only by history, but also by the ways in which such groups are treated. As one Bosnian Muslim teacher is reported to have said (by Jentleson 2007, p. 19): "We were Yugoslavs, but when we began to be murdered because we are Muslims, things changed. The definition of who we are today has been determined by our killing."

At first sight, this does not bode well for federations being particularly good structures for the protection of minority rights. Yet the orthodox thesis is that it is federations, rather than unitary states, that can best protect minorities across diverse populations or across large territories. Perhaps this view is outdated and should be replaced with the thesis that it is only multiethnic societies, whether federations or not, that develop the appropriate constitutional and legal frameworks for the substantive equality rights of their minorities, together with an appropriate method of balancing individual and collective rights, that can hope to remain united and avoid the human rights catastrophes that we see today in so many multiethnic societies.

More controversially, I suggest that the protection of such minority rights is even more important than instituting the procedural elements of democracy in a multiethnic society, as the tragedy unfolding in Iraq arguably demonstrates. In another tragic example, Sri Lanka, a democratic multiethnic state, has stood accused of violating the human rights and equality rights of its Tamil and other minorities, and found itself in a devastating civil war that has left more than 70,000 dead and with no resolution of the underlying causes of the conflict, even though the Sri Lankan army defeated the rebels in May 2009 and took over all the areas previously held by them (Tiruchelvam 2000, p. 198; it is worth noting that Neelan Tiruchelvam, a friend and colleague, was a moderate Tamil scholar and jurist who was killed by a suicide bomber on July 29, 1999, paying with his life for his belief that constitutional reform in the direction of regional autonomy could resolve Sri Lanka's ethnic conflict). Similarly, other formally democratic multiethnic states, such as the Russian Federation, are still being condemned in the annual reports of Amnesty International and Human Rights Watch for gross violations of human rights and lack of effective democratic institutions, and are, in practice, refusing to go down the road of an effective constitutional and legal framework that respects the substantive equality of its minorities—with similar disastrous consequences. The future for authoritarian non-democratic multiethnic states is even bleaker. We only have to look at the genocidal carnage in Sudan to understand this horrible future.

Substantive Equality in the Context of Minority Rights

I suggest that at the core of what substantive equality means for minority groups is the acceptance that treating minorities identically in all respects with the dominant population can lead to a sense of oppression that can fuel civil conflict (for a discussion of equality, and the accommodation of differences between minority groups and majorities, see Kymlicka 1995a, pp. 108–16). Substantive equality, I suggest, would promote treating all groups in a multiethnic society with equal concern and respect, which often requires differential treatment to respect their human dignity, while formal equality would promote identical treatment of all minorities, regions and citizens (for further discussion of this hotly contested view, see Milne 1991, pp. 285–307). Indeed, in some cases equal treatment can often result in discrimination, even for those disadvantaged groups that may not belong to national minorities. For example, it would be rampant discrimination to treat the disabled equally with everyone else as regards access to public transportation.

Canada could provide a global template, albeit one that is not perfect, of appropriate striving to attain the foundational value of substantive equality for its minorities and indigenous populations within a multiethnic federation. That being said, it must also be accepted that we have been far from perfect in treating our minorities and indigenous populations with substantive equality during the course of our history. Canada is both a very new country, less than 200 years old, and also a very old country, since its first inhabitants, the Aboriginal peoples, have lived here from time immemorial. We have, in comparison to many European nations, a very diverse population. Over one third of Canadians can trace their origins from France and are concentrated in the province of Quebec, where they form a powerful majority. However, more than one million francophones live outside Quebec in minority linguistic communities spread across the country. Increasingly, Canadian society is becoming a mirror of the global society as we welcome immigration from all over the world. In the near future our major cities of Toronto, Montreal and Vancouver will have majority populations that are non-European in origin (see Statistics Canada 2005), creating calls by racial and ethnic minorities for collective rights to non-discrimination and equality. Eventually demands for equality by these groups may lead to a push for representation in elected bodies, as an extension of the principle of federalism that regions should be represented in national institutions (see Kymlicka 1995a, p. 137).

The Chinese Canadian diaspora has had a long and important history in the development of Canada, including being an indispensable part of the labour force that built the Canadian Pacific Railway and thus set the stage for the creation of the country itself. It is important to regard the Chinese Canadian population as being comprised not only of recent immigrants but also of the many early settlers who helped to establish the country, along with their descendants (see Innis 1971).

The Recognition of Collective Rights in the Canadian Constitution

The founding document of the Canadian state, the British North America Act 1867 (retitled the Constitution Act from 1982), is replete with provisions related to diversity. However, what is particularly interesting about the evolution of the Canadian constitution is that it contains critical provisions that sometimes allow differential (or "asymmetrical") treatment and sometimes mandate identical (or "symmetrical") treatment for national, linguistic and some religious minorities, which allows differences to flourish. Examples include:

- the guarantee of seventy-five seats for Quebec in the Canadian House of Commons in Section 37, a critical asymmetrical provision;
- the entrenchment of the provinces' jurisdiction over property and civil rights in Section 92(13), a critical symmetrical provision that allows differences between the provinces to flourish;
- the asymmetrical protection of denominational schools in Ontario and Quebec under Section 93; and
- the official use of English and French in the Canadian and Quebec legislatures under Section 133, another important asymmetrical provision.

The maintenance of the civil law system in Quebec is another example of asymmetrical federalism entrenched in the constitutional history of the country. The genius of the founding architects of Canadian nationhood was to entrench asymmetry up to the limits of the politically possible, but then to permit differences to flourish under other symmetrical provisions (see Beaudoin 1990).

Leading US theorists of federalism, such as the late William H. Riker (1975), have argued that it is only symmetrical federalism that is truly compatible with democratic federalism. However, where multiethnic nations have large and historically settled national ethnic, linguistic or religious minorities, an insistence on symmetrical federalism or constitutional frameworks would be a denial of the substantial equality of these minorities. Absolute symmetrical federalism and formal equality can often lead to the assumption of uniformity where it does not exist, and could lead to the coercive institutions of the federal state attempting to impose uniformity and assimilation that national minorities will resist. The result can be disastrous, as we have seen in the case of the former Yugoslavia.

Asymmetrical constitutional provisions in multiethnic federations are especially important to promote the essential features of cultural self-determination of such minorities in areas such as language, education, culture, religion and, as in the case of Canada, the legal traditions and systems. Effective participation in decision-making at the central level and at the highest levels of political decision-making, which may be asymmetrical to the proportions of the minorities within the federation's population, is essential to protect against the "nationalizing" tendencies of the dominant population in a multiethnic federation (see Kymlicka, ed., 1995b). This is the chief rationale for providing the guarantee of seventy-five seats to Quebec, regardless of what proportion of the total Canadian population the population of that province may comprise. It also accounts for the fact that three of the judges of the Supreme Court of Canada must be from Quebec, and the tradition of ensuring regional and national minority representation in the governing party's federal cabinet.

To reiterate, substantive equality differs from formal equality in that it recognizes that identical treatment can lead to discriminatory treatment of minorities, and impose uniformity and coercive assimilation that would threaten the existence of such minorities (Kymlicka 1995a, pp. 10–130). Democratic multiethnic federal states such as India and Canada (some would add Spain) have learned that asymmetrical federalism has been critical to the survival of their countries (see Stepan 1999, p. 53).

The dilemma of how to fit minority rights within a constitutional framework that respects both individual and collective rights is being addressed in theory and practice by Canadians within the Canadian constitutional framework. Will Kymlicka argues that "group-specific" rights are compatible with liberal fundamental tenets that uphold the supremacy of individual rights. The fundamental premise of these theorists (and I include myself in this group) is that it is because the rights and liberties of individual citizens include the right to associate that most such rights have a group-related or group-specific dimension. Thus, belonging to a minority based on common cultural, linguistic or religious heritage is an important factor of identity and indeed of human dignity for most members of such minorities. Where individuals thus freely associate, no central or state government or majority, however large, may deny the right of such groups to cultural self-determination within the limits of the supremacy of individual and universal rights, and the rule of law (Kymlicka 1995a, pp. 75–106).

Some of the collective rights within the growing diversity of Canadian society have been guaranteed in the Canadian Charter of Rights and Freedoms, which was entrenched as Part 1 of the Constitution Act, 1982 (through Schedule B of the Canada Act, 1982 (UK); see Beaudoin and Mendes, ed. 2005). In the Constitution we recognize the collective rights of Aboriginal peoples. Through provisions of the original Constitution and the Charter, and court decisions, we recognize the collective rights of linguistic minorities and, in the case of Quebec, a linguistic majority that wishes to preserve its language within a predominantly English-speaking continent.

Protection of minorities has been confirmed as one of four foundational principles of Canadian federalism by the Supreme Court in its landmark ruling on the right of Quebec unilaterally to secede from Canada (in Reference re Secession of Quebec [1998] 2 S.C.R. 217). However, the Charter and Canadian society also recognize the equal value of civil and political rights based on the dignity of the individual human being. I suggest that through Section 1 of the Charter a mandate was given by the Parliament of Canada to the judiciary, in particular the Supreme Court of Canada, to work out a legal framework for adjudication between collective and individual rights. Section 1 of the Charter allows governments in Canada to infringe rights if they can demonstrate that such infringements are "reasonable limits prescribed by law," and "can be demonstrably justified in a free and democratic society." In the rather complex interpretations of Section 1, it should never be forgotten that one of the most pre-eminent jurists in Canadian history, the late Chief Justice Brian Dickson, focused (in R. v. Oakes [1986] 1 S.C.R. 103) on the final words of Section 1, just quoted, as they formed "the ultimate standard against which a limit on a right or freedom must be shown, despite its effect." Chief Justice Dickson argued that, because Canada is a free and democratic society, the courts must be guided in interpreting Section 1 by the values inherent in concepts such as

> respect for the inherent dignity of the human person, commitment to social justice and equality, accommodation of a wide variety of beliefs, respect for cultural and group identity, and faith in social and political institutions which enhance the participation of individuals and groups in society.

There can be no better statement of the fundamental values that must underpin multiethnic states if minority rights are to be protected.

What China Could Learn from This Canadian Experience

While minorities amount to only around nine percent of the total population of China, that figure represents more than 110 million individuals, and their numbers are growing. The territories where most minorities live contain most of China's natural resources. While official China often talks of the grim struggle with separatist or "splittist" forces, in the long run the strength of China's territorial integrity will, in my view, in large measure depend on how the government enhances ethnic relations and minority rights. While many in China would argue that the constitutional and legal structures for minority rights in China—with the provisions for limited autonomy and ethnic self-rule, and the proliferation of preferential policies—already do benefit minorities, some experts, both within and outside China, point out three critical weaknesses (see Sautman 1997).

First, the law and the Constitution of China have yet to provide unquestionable genuine autonomy to minority areas. Such autonomy involves fewer powers than are minimally required to ensure cultural self-determination. Article 4 of the Constitution refers to regional autonomy for minorities living in compact communities who are free to "preserve or reform their own ways and customs." The Law on Regional Autonomy both sets out and also restricts that autonomy, which must be "under unified state leadership" and under the principle of "democratic centralism," in other words, under the discipline of the Chinese Communist Party. In addition, under Article 4 all self-governing organs of minorities must implement the laws and policies of the state. Under Article 118 of the Constitution and Article 19 of the Law on Regional Autonomy, laws and regulations made by autonomous areas that govern the exercise of autonomy must be approved by higher bodies. The laws and regulations of the five autonomous regions—Xinjiang, Inner Mongolia, Guangxi, Ningxia and Tibet—must be approved by the Standing Committee of the National People's Congress (Sautman 1997, pp. 22–23).

Second, policies and laws are not sufficient to allow for the degree of economic autonomy that would help minority areas to meet the challenge of bridging the gap between the Han majority and the various minorities. There is a large and growing income disparity between minorities and the Han majority population. There is a wealth gap, estimated at twenty to one, between the rapidly developing coastal areas and the minority northwestern provinces, and within the minority areas there is a wage gap between the minority peasants and the majority Han peasants. Some call this an "ethnic psychological imbalance," which can threaten the unity of the country (Sautman 1997, p. 5).

Third, there is insufficient protection against the encroachment of cultural self-determination by the Han majority. In particular, minority leaders accepted by the Chinese government as legitimate representatives, such as Adbulahat Abdurixit, Governor of Xinjiang, or Tomur Dawarnat, a Vice-Chair of the National People's Congress, have argued strenuously against unlimited migration by members of the Han majority into minority areas. These leaders voiced opposition, for example, to the plan to move 100,000 people, mostly from the Han majority, from the site of the Three Gorges Dam to Xinjiang, and accurately predicted that interethnic tensions would result. Such cultural encroachment is also worsened by what some leading Chinese scholars call the affront to the dignity of minority peoples posed by the discriminatory attitudes of the Han majority, and of Han minorities in autonomous areas, which regard many minorities as backward and uncivilized in culture and education (see Sautman 1997, pp. 6 and 15–21).

In conclusion, both Canada and China have struggled with the evolution of minority rights in their multiethnic societies. In Canada our constitutional, legal and societal evolution has led us to recognize that minority rights constitute a central part of Canadian identity, unity, and competitive advantage in a globalized economy. In China, I suggest, much of the constitutional, legal and societal evolution of minority rights that occurred in the 1980s was premised on a planned economy, where minority rights and preferences were regarded as part of the centrally organized development of the state. Today, with globalization making non-minority areas of China, such as the Special Economic Zones, more autonomous than the autonomous regions, with all the attendant benefits of economic and social development, some have suggested that it may be time to contemplate offering the minority autonomous regions the status of "special cultural zones," in which there could be sufficient enlarged economic and cultural autonomy for China's national minorities to feel that their very existence is not threatened (Sautman 1997, p. 39). This could, in time, become not only the solution to the problem of separatist movements, but also a competitive advantage for China in the global economy, as the Canadian model has demonstrated.

References

Beaudoin, Gérald-A. (1990). *La Constitution du Canada: institutions, partage des pouvoirs, droits et libertés*. Montreal: Wilson & Lafleur.

Beaudoin, Gérald-A., and Errol Mendes, ed. (2005). *The Canadian Charter of Rights and Freedoms*. 4th ed. Markham, ON: LexisNexis–Butterworth.

Innis, Harold A. (1971). *A History of the Canadian Pacific Railway*. Toronto, Buffalo, NY, and London: University of Toronto Press.

Jentleson, B. W. (2007, Winter). "A Responsibility to Protect: The Defining Challenge for the Global Community." *Harvard International Review* 28:4.

Kymlicka, Will. (1995a). *Multicultural Citizenship: A Liberal Theory of Minority Rights*. Oxford: Oxford University Press.

Kymlicka, Will, ed. (1995b). *The Rights of Minority Cultures*. Oxford: Oxford University Press.

Malesevic, Sinisa. (2000). "Ethnicity and Federalism in Communist Yugoslavia and its Sucessor States," in *Autonomy and Ethnicity: Negotiating Competing Claims in Multiethnic States*, ed. Yash Ghai. Cambridge: Cambridge University Press.

Milne, David. (1991). "Equality or Asymmetry: Why Choose?" in *Options for a New Canada*, ed. Ronald L. Watts and Douglas M. Brown. Toronto, Buffalo, NY, and London: University of Toronto Press.

Riker, William H. (1975). "Federalism," in *Handbook of Political Science*, ed. F. Greenstein and N. W. Posby, Vol. 5. Boston, MA: Addison–Wesley.

Sautman, Barry. (1997, May 9). "Legal Reform and Minority Rights in China." Hong Kong University of Science and Technology Working Paper in the Social Sciences no. 11.

Statistics Canada. (2005, March 22). "Study: Canada's Visible Minority Population in 2017." *The Daily*. Ottawa: Statistics Canada. Online at http://www.statcan.ca/Daily/English/050322/d050322b.htm [consulted January 14, 2011].

Stepan, Alfred. (1999, October). "Federalism and Democracy: Beyond the U.S. Model." *Journal of Democracy* 10:4.

Tiruchelvam, Neelan. (2000). "The Politics of Federalism and Diversity in Sri Lanka," in *Autonomy and Ethnicity: Negotiating Competing Claims in Multiethnic States*, ed. Yash Ghai. Cambridge: Cambridge University Press.

THE CHINESE DIASPORA

AND IMMIGRATION IN

CANADA

Chapter 13

Chinese in Canada and Canadians in China: The Human Platform for Relationships between China and Canada

Kenny Zhang

The movement of people across international borders has significant implications for international relations. Today the flow of people between Canada and China has become varied and complex, reflecting changing economic and social circumstances in the two economies, and the evolving relationship between Canada and China.

China is a major source country for immigrants to Canada. The concentration of Chinese immigrants in Toronto, Vancouver, Montreal and other major cities has implications not only for their settlement and integration but also for the shaping of foreign policy. Diaspora politics and transnational business networks have the potential to affect relations between Canada and China in ways that are generally not well understood. Further, a sizeable community of Canadian citizens has moved to live in Greater China (comprising mainland China, Hong Kong, Macau and Taiwan). The push and pull factors of Canadians abroad, who number around 600,000 in Asia and around 2.8 million globally (see Zhang and Woo 2006 and DeVoretz 2009), are also not well understood, but have profound implications for citizenship, consular services, public finance, health care, border security, international business, research and innovation, and more.

Rather than following the tradition of analyzing the economic performance of Chinese immigrants in Canada, this paper is aimed to addressing how Chinese communities in Canada and Canadians in China are shaping a human platform for stronger relations between Canada and China, and the policy challenges associated with this human platform.

Redefining Canada's Chinese Communities

The Canadian Census of 2006 reported that more than 1.3 million people in Canada claimed that their ethnic origin was Chinese. (This figure does not include those who self-reported mixed ethnicity, having been born of interethnic marriages, nor does it include the 17,705 who self-identified as Taiwanese or the 4,275 who self-identified as Tibetan.) This made the Chinese community the eighth largest ethnic group in Canada and the largest of Asian origin (see Figure 13.1). Chinese languages, including Cantonese and Mandarin, formed the third largest mother tongue group in the country after English and French, and three percent of the population reported that their mother tongue was one of the Chinese languages.

The Chinese community in Canada has changed, is changing, and will continue to change in many ways (see Li 2005 and 2010, Wang and Lo 2005 and Guo and DeVoretz 2006), which will ultimately have an impact on relations with China (see Woo and Wang 2009 and Zhang 2010a). There is no longer a homogenous Chinese community in Canada: the community has become very heterogeneous despite common places of birth, mother tongues, educational background, citizenship, and so on.

Figure 13.1 Canada's Top Ten Communities by Ethnic Origin, 2006

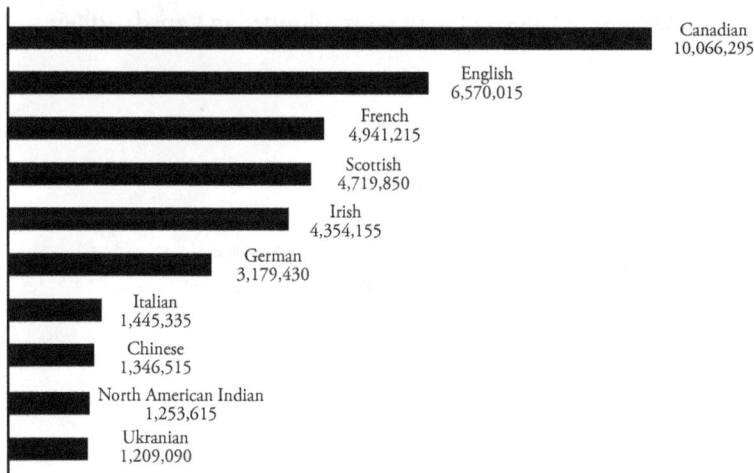

Canadian 10,066,295
English 6,570,015
French 4,941,215
Scottish 4,719,850
Irish 4,354,155
German 3,179,430
Italian 1,445,335
Chinese 1,346,515
North American Indian 1,253,615
Ukranian 1,209,090

Source: Statistics Canada, 2008.

People of Chinese ethnic origin are not necessarily newcomers to Canada. Some of them were born in Canada and their families may have lived in Canada for more than two generations. The Canadian-born Chinese has become a significant phenomenon within the Chinese community. The Census of 2006 reported that 27.4 percent of respondents who claimed they were ethnic Chinese had been born in Canada. The Census also reported that 14.3 percent were second-generation and 2.3 percent were third-generation or more. However, 83.4 percent were first-generation Canadians.

According to the Census, forty-nine percent of the Chinese immigrants had arrived in Canada from the People's Republic of China, twenty-three percent came from Hong Kong, and others came from the Caribbean and Bermuda, the Philippines, India and other countries in Asia (see Figure 13.2).

Members of ethnic Chinese groups have achieved different skill levels in Canada's two official languages. The Census found that nearly eighty-six percent had some knowledge of English, French or both, and only fourteen percent claimed they had no knowledge of English or French. They may also speak different dialects. Nearly one in five ethnic Chinese reported English or French as their mother tongue. Seventy-nine percent indicated that neither English nor French was their mother tongue. One third reported that they spoke English or French most often at home, with about sixty percent saying that they spoke other languages most often at home.

Figure 13.2 Origins of Chinese Immigrants Admitted to Canada, 2006

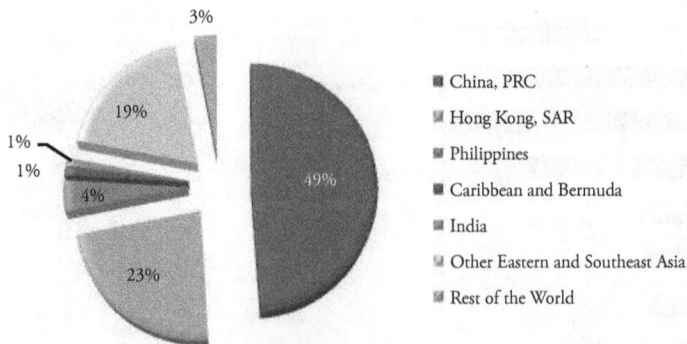

Source: Statistics Canada, 2008.

Among those whose mother tongues were non-official languages, the number of respondents with a Chinese language as their mother tongue grew from fewer than 100,000 in 1971 to nearly 900,000 in 2001 and more than one million in 2006 (see Table 13.1). However, respondents who reported a Chinese language as their mother tongue may actually have spoken different dialects. In the Census of 2006 "Chinese languages" were broken down into seven major languages—Mandarin, Cantonese, Hakka, Taiwanese, Chaochow (Teochow), Fukien and Shanghainese—as well as a residual category, "Chinese languages not otherwise specified."

Chinese immigrants have been admitted to Canada under different entry categories. Canada's Immigration and Refugee Protection Act establishes three categories of permanent residents, which correspond to the major objectives of reuniting families, contributing to economic development and protecting refugees. Around two thirds of all immigrants to Canada from mainland China are admitted as economic immigrants, including skilled workers, professionals, investors and entrepreneurs. Nearly a quarter of immigrants from mainland China gain entry as relatives of persons already living in Canada. Only a small number are admitted to Canada on humanitarian grounds. This pattern contrasts with thirty years ago, when around two thirds of immigrants from the mainland were relatives of people resident in Canada, around a quarter were in the humanitarian category, and only seven percent were economic immigrants (see Figure 13.3).

Figure 13.3 Immigrants from Mainland China to Canada by Entry Category, 1980–2008

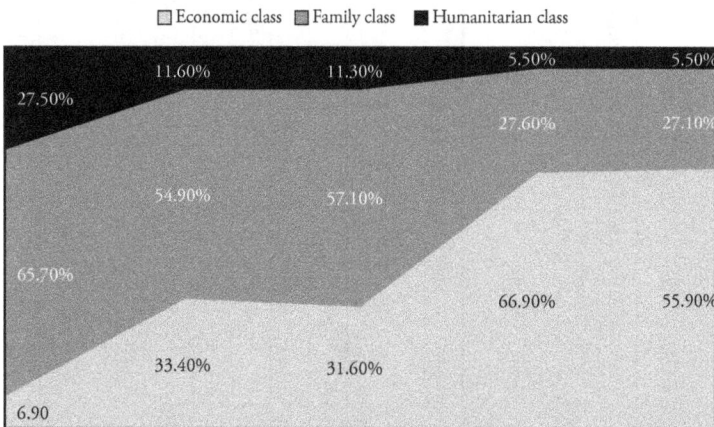

Sources: Guo and DeVoretz 2006; Citizenship and Immigration Canada.

Table 13.1 Speakers of Non-Official Mother Tongues in Canada, 1971, 2001 and 2006

	1971			2001			2006		
	Number of speakers	Proportion of non-official mother tongues (%)	Proportion of all mother tongues (%)	Number of speakers	Proportion of non-official mother tongues (%)	Proportion of all mother tongues (%)	Number of speakers	Proportion of non-official mother tongues (%)	Proportion of all mother tongues (%)
Chinese	95,915	3.4	0.4	872,400	16.4	2.9	1,034,090	16.4	3.3
Italian	538,765	19.2	2.5	493,985	9.3	1.7	476,905	7.6	1.5
German	558,965	19.9	2.6	455,540	8.5	1.5	466,650	7.4	1.5
Punjabi	..	..	..	284,750	5.3	1.0	382,585	6.1	1.2
Spanish	23,950	0.9	0.1	260,785	4.9	0.9	362,120	5.8	1.2
Arabic	28,520	1.0	0.1	220,535	4.1	0.7	286,785	4.6	0.9
Tagalog	..	..	..	199,770	3.7	0.7	266,440	4.2	0.9
Portuguese	85,845	3.1	0.4	222,855	4.2	0.8	229,280	3.6	0.7
Polish	136,540	4.9	0.6	215,010	4.0	0.7	217,605	3.5	0.7
Urdu	..	..	..	86,810	1.6	0.3	156,415	2.5	0.5
Ukrainian	309,890	11.0	1.4	157,385	3.0	0.5	141,805	2.3	0.5

Sources: Statistics Canada, 2006a.

Differences in educational background and citizenship status have also contributed to the diversity of Canada's Chinese community. The Census of 2006
reported that fifty-five percent of the ethnic Chinese population fifteen years
of age and over had a post-secondary certificate, diploma or degree, compared
to fifty-one percent of all Canadians in the same age group; more significantly,
nearly half of all Chinese, compared to only sixteen percent of all Canadians, had received post-secondary education outside Canada (see Table 13.2).
In addition, seventy-seven percent of the Chinese population held Canadian
citizenship only, while five percent possessed both Canadian and at least one
other citizenship, and another eighteen percent had not yet become Canadian
citizens (see Table 13.3).

The Wide-ranging Visibility of Chinese Canadians

As one of the largest visible minority groups in Canada, the visibility of the
Chinese community varies considerably from province to province, from
city to city, and from federal election district to federal election district. In
2006 ethnic Chinese were most visible in the provinces of British Columbia
(ten percent), Ontario (five percent) and Alberta (four percent), while in
other parts of Canada the odds of seeing a Chinese person were close to or
less than one in a hundred (see Figure 13.4). Chinese were concentrated
in Toronto, Vancouver, Montreal and, more recently, Calgary, and their
visibility varied from nearly one in five in the Census metropolitan area
(CMA) of Vancouver, to one in ten in the Toronto CMA, one in twenty in
the Calgary CMA and one in fifty in the Montreal CMA (see Figure 13.5).
     The ethnic Chinese vote is important in some ridings, but overall it has had
little impact on the Canadian House of Commons. In 2006, the proportion of
ethnic Chinese in federal election districts varied considerably, from as high as
fifty percent in Richmond, British Columbia, to four percent in Calgary and
just 0.2 percent in parts of Prince Edward Island (see Statistics Canada 2006b).
     The visibility of ethnic Chinese also varies in schools and job markets. Like
other Canadians, Chinese Canadians typically select four areas as their major
fields of study in post-secondary education: business, management and public administration; architecture, engineering and related technologies; health,
parks, recreation and fitness; and social and behavioural sciences and law. However, Chinese students are more visible than average Canadians in three areas
of applied science and business-related studies: mathematics, computer science
and information sciences; business, management and public administration;
and physical and life sciences and technologies (see Table 13.4).

Table 13.2 Population of Canada Aged 15 and Over by Educational Attainment, 2006

	All ethnic groups	%	Chinese	%	Non-Chinese	%
No postsecondary certificate, diploma or degree	12,651,750	49	495,740	45	12,156,010	49
Postsecondary certificate, diploma or degree	13,012,475	51	603,370	55	12,409,105	51
Inside Canada	10,948,475	84	326,255	54	10,622,220	86
Outside Canada	2,064,000	16	277,115	46	1,786,885	14
China	142,885	1	140,545	23	2,340	0
Philippines	160,555	1	19,700	3	140,855	1
United States	291,115	2	19,475	3	271,640	2
United Kingdom	235,465	2	11,030	2	224,435	2
Other	1,134,675	9	86,365	14	1,048,310	8
Totals	25,664,225		1,099,110		24,565,115	

Source: Census, Statistics Canada, 2008.

Table 13.3 Population of Canada by Citizenship, 2006

	All ethnic groups		Chinese		Non-Chinese	
		%		%		%
Canadian citizens	29,480,165	94	1,104,430	82	28,375,735	95
Citizens of Canada only	28,617,055	92	1,042,765	77	27,574,290	92
Citizens of Canada and at least one other country	863,110	3	61,660	5	801,450	3
Not Canadian citizens	1,760,865	6	242,080	18	1,518,785	5
Totals	31,241,030		1,346,510		29,894,520	

Source: Census, Statistics Canada, 2008.

Figure 13.4 Visibility of Chinese Canadians in Populations of Canada, Provinces and Territories, 2006

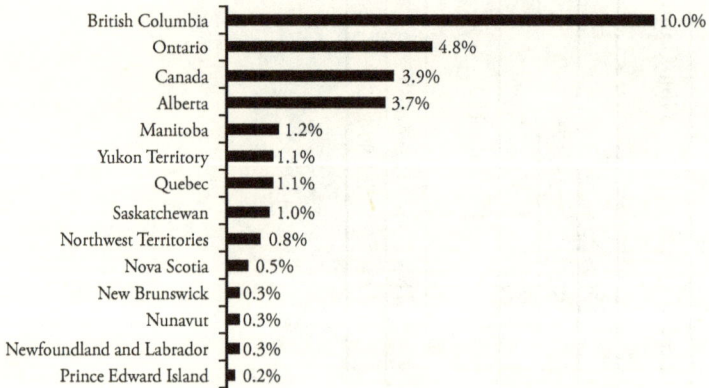

Region	Percentage
British Columbia	10.0%
Ontario	4.8%
Canada	3.9%
Alberta	3.7%
Manitoba	1.2%
Yukon Territory	1.1%
Quebec	1.1%
Saskatchewan	1.0%
Northwest Territories	0.8%
Nova Scotia	0.5%
New Brunswick	0.3%
Nunavut	0.3%
Newfoundland and Labrador	0.3%
Prince Edward Island	0.2%

Source: Statistics Canada, 2008.

Figure 13.5 Visibility of Chinese Canadians in Populations of Four Major Cities, 2006

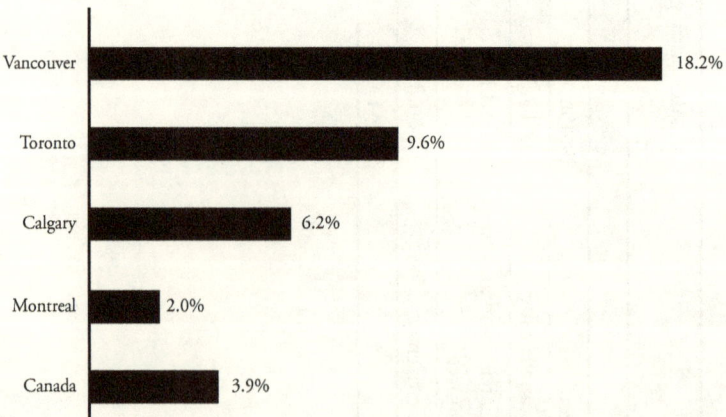

City	Percentage
Vancouver	18.2%
Toronto	9.6%
Calgary	6.2%
Montreal	2.0%
Canada	3.9%

Source: Statistics Canada, 2008.

Table 13.4 Population of Canada Aged 15 and Over by Major Field of Study, 2006

	All ethnic groups		Chinese		Non-Chinese	
		%		%		%
Education	994,665	8	24,030	4	970,635	8
Visual and performing arts, and communications technologies	481,190	4	22,200	4	458,990	4
Humanities	717,125	6	29,215	5	687,910	6
Social and behavioural sciences and law	1,275,105	10	56,335	9	1,218,770	10
Business, management and public administration	2,801,720	22	157,870	26	2,643,850	21
Physical and life sciences and technologies	451,960	3	38,040	6	413,920	3
Mathematics, computer and information sciences	568,755	4	58,155	10	510,600	4
Architecture, engineering and related technologies	2,922,085	22	136,770	23	2,785,315	22
Agriculture, natural resources and conservation	291,510	2	6,685	1	284,825	2
Health, parks, recreation and fitness	1,728,890	13	59,450	10	1,669,440	13
Personal, protective and transportation services	777,370	6	14,575	2	762,795	6
Other fields of study	2,105		50		2,055	

Source: Statistics Canada, 2008.

Chinese Canadians are more likely to work in occupations related to applied sciences and business, such as natural and applied sciences, and related occupations; processing, manufacturing and utilities; business, finance and administrative occupations; and sales and services. However, Chinese Canadians are underrepresented in certain fields, including equipment operation and related occupations, primary industry, education and government services (see Table 13.5).

Perhaps not surprisingly, Chinese Canadians are more visible than average Canadians in accommodation and food services (restaurant jobs), professional, scientific and technical services (accountants and lawyers), finance and insurance (jobs in banking), manufacturing (general labour) and wholesale trade (import and export). However, Chinese are less likely than average Canadians to work in construction, agriculture, forestry, fishing and hunting; health care and social assistance; or public administration (see Table 13.6).

The image of Chinese Canadians today is vastly different than it was for much of the past 200 years, when Chinese immigrants were stereotyped as railway coolies, laundrymen or waiters. Hollywood exaggerated the stereotype with movies about opium dens, "celestials" in pigtails with knives hidden up their silk sleeves, or slant-eyed beauties with bound feet and ancient love potions (Lee 1984, p. 178). What the Chinese Canadian community looks like today is as diversified as Canadian society is as a whole.

Emerging Canadians in China

Canadians historically have travelled widely, and today an estimated 2.8 million Canadians live and work abroad (see DeVoretz 2009). There have always been large numbers of Canadians living outside the country for extended periods, especially but not only in the United States. One of the prominent Canadian pioneers in China, for example, was Dr. Norman Bethune (1890–1939), whose spirit of service, courage and innovation continues to inspire innovative partnerships between Canada and China today.

The Asia Pacific Foundation of Canada has classified Canadians living in China into the following groups (see Guo 2009 and Zhang 2010b): (1) owners or employees of Canadian or multinational businesses; (2) Chinese Canadian returnees, including members of the first, second and later generations; (3) teachers of English as a second language (ESL); and (4) students and others.

Table 13.5 Visibility of Chinese Canadians by Occupation, 2006

	All ethnic groups	%	Chinese	%	Non-Chinese	%
Total labour force aged 15 years and over	17,146,135		695,515		16,450,620	
Occupation – Not applicable	284,950	2	19,460	3	265,490	2
All occupations	16,861,180	98	676,050	97	16,185,130	98
Management	1,631,730	10	67,425	10	1,564,305	10
Business, finance and administration	3,025,425	18	138,255	20	2,887,170	18
Natural and applied sciences and related	1,108,045	6	91,275	13	1,016,770	6
Health	950,360	6	34,480	5	915,880	6
Social science, education, government service and religion	1,414,320	8	44,250	6	1,370,070	8
Art, culture, recreation and sport	502,195	3	18,365	3	483,830	3
Sales and services	4,037,725	24	173,045	25	3,864,680	23
Trades, transport, equipment operators and related	2,550,295	15	45,005	6	2,505,290	15
Occupations unique to primary industry	648,315	4	4,975	1	643,340	4
Occupations unique to processing, manufacturing and utilities	992,760	6	58,970	8	933,790	6

Source: Statistics Canada, 2008.

Table 13.6 Visibility of Chinese Canadians by Industry, 2006

	All ethnic groups	%	Chinese	%	Non-Chinese	%
Total labour force 15 years and over	5,453,550		695,515		4,758,035	
Industry - Not applicable	80,040	1	19,465	3	60,575	1
All industries	5,373,510	99	676,055	97	4,697,455	99
Agriculture, forestry, fishing and hunting	177,635	3	3,895	1	173,740	4
Mining and oil and gas extraction	69,285	1	4,695	1	64,590	1
Utilities	46,270	1	3,500	1	42,770	1
Construction	358,325	7	16,700	2	341,625	7
Manufacturing	684,780	13	98,955	14	585,825	12
Wholesale trade	222,300	4	42,385	6	179,915	4
Retail trade	662,720	12	73,870	11	588,850	12
Transportation and warehousing	265,530	5	19,210	3	246,320	5
Information and cultural industries	118,320	2	22,045	3	96,275	2
Finance and insurance	193,790	4	48,170	7	145,620	3
Real estate and rental and leasing	79,305	1	16,115	2	63,190	1
Professional, scientific and technical services	290,310	5	74,035	11	216,275	5

Management of companies and enterprises	5,035	<1	1,120	<1	3,915	<1
Administration and support, waste management and remediation services	211,200	4	21,210	3	189,990	4
Educational services	342,680	6	38,550	6	304,130	6
Health care and social assistance	571,045	10	51,840	7	519,205	11
Arts, entertainment and recreation	111,635	2	10,550	2	101,085	2
Accommodation and food services	354,945	7	78,595	11	276,350	6
Other services (except public administration)	262,630	5	28,315	4	234,315	5
Public administration	345,790	6	22,310	3	323,480	7

Source: Statistics Canada, 2008.

First, as China increasingly becomes a global economic powerhouse and the biggest recipient of foreign direct investment, more than ninety percent of the top 500 multinationals have set up in China, and thirty percent of those have established regional headquarters there (see China Radio International 2008). Canadian businesses are among those active in China, and there are increasing numbers of native-born and naturalized Canadian executives, engineers and other professionals and specialists working in China.

Second, in 2008 a study by the Organization for Economic Cooperation and Development found that, depending on the country of destination and the time frame, twenty percent to fifty percent of immigrants return home or move to a third country within five years of their arrival (see Migration Policy Institute 2008). A recent report from Statistics Canada demonstrated that a significant number of male immigrants to Canada of working age, especially skilled workers and entrepreneurs, are highly mobile, suggesting that a substantial part of migration to Canada is temporary. The estimated out-migration rate twenty years after arrival is around thirty-five percent among young working-age male immigrants. About six out of ten of those who leave do so within the first year of arrival, which suggests that many immigrants make their decisions within a relatively short period after arriving in Canada. Controlling for other characteristics, out-migration rates are higher among immigrants from source countries such as the United States and Hong Kong (see Aydemir and Robinson 2006). Despite these general conclusions, the return of Chinese Canadians to China remains underdocumented. What we do know is that many are not actually returning to China forever, but are what we may call "transnational," often moving back and forth between two countries at different periods in their lives.

Transnational parenting is not uncommon among young Chinese Canadian families. High child care costs, the lack of family support in Canada and a volatile job market have led some families to send their children back to China, so that grandparents or other relatives can look after them. A study in 2002 of Chinese immigrants in five prenatal programmes discovered that seventy percent of the female respondents said they planned to send their children back to China to be raised by relatives (see Ng 2007). Transnational schooling is also quite common. Many Chinese Canadian families who want their children to be bilingual and well-schooled in mathematics send their children back to China for certain years of their education.

Transnational entrepreneurship also plays a key role in connecting Canada and China. A report commissioned by the Asia Pacific Foundation of Canada in 2008 revealed that foreign-educated Chinese transnational entrepreneurs make up a distinct segment of the immigrant community (see Lin, Guan, and Nicholson 2008). Key characteristics distinguish them from classic middlemen traders, returnee entrepreneurs, or those who have returned to their home countries permanently. Instead, the characteristics of Canada-based Chinese transnational entrepreneurs include a greater likelihood of multinational experience, a higher level of establishment within their professions, a deeper degree of entrenchment in Canada, and a stronger desire to engage Canada in cross-border entrepreneurial endeavours. The same report also identified a variety of mechanisms used by transnational entrepreneurs to link Canada and China through innovation.

Transnational retirement allows senior Chinese Canadians to enjoy the pleasure of two homes. Like many Canadian "snowbirds" migrating into the United States, these senior citizens move across the Pacific as the season changes.

Third, Canadian ESL teachers are another significant group of Canadians in China. They are in high demand, not only because of the importance of learning English as a second language, but also because some Chinese students seem to prefer "Canadian" English. One contemporary Canadian, Mark Rowswell, known in China as Dashan, has even been described as "the most famous foreigner in China," where he has worked as a performer, television host and cultural ambassador for more twenty years (see Rowswell 2010). Although he is relatively unknown in the West, it is hard to find anyone in China who does not know of Dashan, and his success story has also helped to raise the profile of Canadian English in China.

The growing body of Canadians, whether Canadian-born or naturalized, living and working in mainland China and Hong Kong suggests that there is an emerging Canadian diaspora. What policy areas does the Canadian government need to develop to recognize this diaspora, maintain and enhance Canada's international ties, and maximize the benefits of those ties to Canada? The size and importance of Canada's diaspora in China suggests that Canada should revisit its foreign policy toward China.

Understanding China as a Source and a Destination

When Stephen Harper's Conservative government came into office in 2006 many people in Canada expected a new China policy that would take Sino-Canadian relations to a new level, although some China watchers in Canada suggested that Ottawa actually does not have a China policy (see, for example, *Ottawa Citizen* 2008). So far Canada has emphasized four foreign policy goals or "pillars" in relations with China (see Government of Canada 2009): (1) to work with Beijing towards China's greater adherence to internationally accepted standards on human rights and the rule of law; (2) to ensure that China's economic rise benefits Canada by increasing two-way trade and investment in goods and services; (3) to work with China to advance shared interests in areas such as health, the environment and regional peace and security; and (4) to position Canada as a preferred destination for Chinese immigrants, students and visitors. This four-pillar China policy appropriately reflects a multifaceted relationship between the two countries and recognizes the importance of cooperation with China. However, it overlooks some of the complex trends that have emerged in the flow of people between the two countries. As a result Canada's China policy faces a number of challenges.

The first of these challenges is understanding China as both a source and a destination. It is easy for Canadians to see that China is a major source country for immigrants, students, and visitors to Canada. While Canada is still in a position to promote itself as a preferred destination, the magnitude of China as a source country also needs to be better understood. China has become the leading source of newcomers to Canada since 1998, particularly for economic migrants, such as skilled workers and investors. China has become the second largest source country for annual arrivals of international students in Canada since 2000, and is currently the largest source of total student stock studying in Canada. China is currently the ninth major source country for overnight travellers to Canada, with the highest average spending per trip in Canada among all international travellers (see Citizenship and Immigration Canada 2009).

In addition to the importance of China as a source of inflows to Canada, it is equally important to realize that China is becoming an economic magnet for human capital. Although China is not a country of immigration, it is increasingly being seen as one of the few economies in the world with brighter job prospects. China has issued increasing numbers of work permits to foreign workers. In Shanghai alone the number of work permits issued has increased thirteen times over the past thirteen years, and Canada is the seventh largest source country for foreign workers in Shanghai (see *LaowaiZaiZhongguo* 2007 and *Oriental Morning Post* 2008).

Tourism and education are also increasingly important transnational activities. According to Statistics Canada (2005), China was the tenth most visited international destination for Canadians. By 2008, China had surpassed Canada as the sixth major destination for international students at the post-secondary level, and it is likely to attract more Canadian students in the future (see Institute of International Education 2010).

Looking ahead, it is unrealistic to predict that the immigration flow from China to Canada will remain the same as it has been over the past ten to fifteen years. This should not be regarded as making these flows less important for Canada, however, even if China is no longer the top source country of immigration. In fact, many Chinese may still consider emigrating to Canada for lifestyle reasons rather than purely economic reasons (see Anderssen 2009). Canada has to be prepared to leverage this new trend for Canada's economic and social benefit, rather than just for the benefit of its labour market. With the conclusion of an agreement on "approved destination status," more Chinese visitors are likely to come to Canada as tourists.

Further, Canada is not only competing for international students with the United States, the United Kingdom, France, Germany and Australia, but also has to compete with emerging education markets, including China itself. While China retains its importance as one of the major source countries for many types of human flows to Canada, perhaps more significant is that Beijing is increasingly seen as a destination for international human flows, including those from Canada. With efforts by Beijing to attract global talent and to promote Chinese culture and language globally, interest in learning Chinese, visiting China and working and living there is on the rise among Canadians with or without Chinese heritage.

Only if more Canadians understand the importance of China as both a source and a destination of flows of people will policy be changed to reflect the importance of these two-way flows. Canada needs to position itself as a preferred destination for Chinese immigrants, students, and visitors. It is equally if not more important that Canada also prepares more Canadians to "go East" to study and work. A broadened China policy could ensure that China's economic rise benefits Canada by increasing two-way trade and investment in goods and services, as well as by increasing two-way flows of people.

Understanding Chinese Communities in Canada

The second major policy challenge is to understand the importance of Chinese communities in Canada, which has been underestimated for a long time. As a country of immigrants, Canada has been accustomed to looking at immigrants almost exclusively from an economic perspective. Chinese immigrants, like all immigrants, have traditionally been seen primarily as suppliers of needed manpower. All too often, when people try to measure the contribution of Chinese communities to Canada they refer to their higher unemployment numbers and lower earnings due to insufficient English-language skills or the fact that their foreign credentials are not recognized here. They also tend to focus on the concentration of Chinese communities in Vancouver or Toronto, or the fact that they may not integrate fully into Canadian society.

In 2008, when Beijing was gearing up for the 29th Summer Olympic Games, the first Olympic Games ever to be held in China, the loyalty of Chinese communities to Canada was brought into question by some commentators, for example by Joanne Lee-Young (2008) writing in the *Vancouver Sun*: "Members of Vancouver's large overseas Chinese community will face a complex set of dual loyalties during the Beijing Summer Games, rooted in a simple quandary: whether to cheer for Chinese or Canadian athletes, or both." Questioning the loyalty of Chinese Canadians during a major international sporting event was unjustified, for a number of reasons. First, as the Census of 2006 showed, about 27.4 percent of all ethnic Chinese in Canada were actually born in Canada and 16.6 percent were of the second or earlier generations. Their education and experience, and the degree to which they are Canadian, is likely no different than any other citizens born in Canada. Second, seventy-seven percent of all ethnic Chinese in Canada as of 2006 held Canadian citizenship only. In other words, nearly half of all ethnic Chinese in Canada were naturalized citizens, with Canadian identity and values created and shaped during the process of immigration and naturalization. For these individuals Canadian citizenship is a formal recognition that Canada has accepted them as Canadians. Naturalized Chinese Canadians should be treated equally with other naturalized citizens. Third, more than half of all Chinese immigrants in Canada come from countries other than the People's Republic. In other words, nearly half of all Chinese immigrants in Canada are likely to have nothing to do with mainland China. Finally, cheering for Chinese or Canadian athletes has nothing to do with one's political loyalty. When a Chinese team led by a Canadian coach, Dan Raphael, defeated its opponents, including a Canadian team, and claimed the gold at the World's Women's Curling Championships in 2009, should Canadians have questioned Raphael's loyalty to Canada? When Raphael brought this Chinese team to the Vancouver Winter Olympics in 2010, should this still have been an issue?

Statistical evidence provides more meaningful measures with which to judge the loyalty of Chinese communities to Canada (see Lindsay 2007). According to the Ethnic Diversity Survey conducted by Statistics Canada, in partnership with the Department of Canadian Heritage, in 2002 seventy-six percent of Canadians of Chinese origin felt a strong sense of belonging to Canada, and fifty-eight percent said that at the same time they had a strong sense of belonging to their ethnic or cultural group. The survey also showed that Canadians of Chinese origin are active in Canadian society. For example, sixty-four percent of those who were eligible to vote reported doing so in the federal general election in 2000, while sixty percent said that they had voted in the most recent provincial election. In addition, about thirty-five percent reported that they had participated in an organization such as a sports team or a community association in the twelve months preceding the taking of the survey. However, 34 percent of Canadians of Chinese origin reported that they had experienced discrimination or unfair treatment based on their ethnicity, race, religion, language or accent in the past five years or since their arrival in Canada. Of those who had experienced discrimination, sixty-three percent said that they felt it was based on their race or skin colour, while forty-two percent said that the discrimination had taken place at work or when applying for a job or promotion.

Victor Odlum (1880–1971), who spent most of his life in Vancouver and, in the course of a long career in public service, was Canada's Ambassador to China from 1942 to 1946, once looked forward to the day when Chinese Canadians would "not be distinguished from other Canadians" (Lee 1984, p. 169). That wish remains as relevant today as it was during Odlum's lifetime.

Understanding Canadian Communities in China

The remaining policy challenge is to understand Canadian communities in China, which have been growing for many reasons. Although the exact number remains unknown, the best estimate puts the number of Canadians in mainland China and Hong Kong at between 250,000 and 300,000, and thus significantly larger than the population of a medium-sized Canadian city such as Saskatoon or Windsor, Ontario (see Zhang 2009 and Guo 2009). Canada cannot afford to ignore the fact that so many Canadians live in China. How Canada can turn its diaspora in China into an advantage is at the core of this huge challenge.

First, how should Canadians living in China or other parts of the world be recognized as part of Canada, rather than as foreigners who happen to hold Canadian passports? Canadians have to change their mindset to accept the fact that the flow of people moves in two directions. Canada must learn to respect the fact that Canadians, native-born or naturalized, are more internationally mobile than ever before and that many wish to live abroad. When they settle down in Beijing or in another city, Canada must learn to treat them the same as any other Canadians in terms of their rights and obligations.

Second, how should Canada encourage the political and civic participation of its citizens abroad? For one thing, Ottawa should consider changing the current rules that do not allow overseas citizens to vote in Canadian elections after they have lived abroad for five years. Canada should also consider creating political mechanisms that would represent overseas citizens at the federal and provincial levels. This would significantly encourage political and civic participation by all Canadians, including citizens residing abroad. The views of Canadian communities in China should also be taken into account in Sino-Canadian policy-making.

Third, how can Canada better communicate with its overseas communities? Canada must develop a consultation and communication process with Canadians living overseas, to keep them involved and informed of any changes in citizenship laws or rules regulating their movement across borders, and listen to their needs, including their need for consular protection and other services. This would also ensure that any risks associated with Canadians abroad are properly assessed and addressed.

Fourth, how should Canada better leverage its expatriate communities in China to enhance opportunities for trade, investment and business between the two countries? Traditionally, diaspora communities have contributed significantly to their home countries through remittances (India, Mexico and the Philippines), trade and investment (China and South Korea), and technology transfers (Taiwan, South Korea and China). This is a new task for Canadian policy-makers and members of the business community.

Finally, in pursuing such policy agendas and addressing the new challenges, a major effort must be made to bring together interests from across a range of government departments and organizations, including those at the provincial level.

Conclusion

The turn of the 21st century witnessed growing flows of people from China to Canada. Greater freedom of movement in and out of China, and the growing affluence of Chinese citizens, are combining to bring about rapid changes in the pattern of these flows, broadening them to include tourists, students and professional workers. The flows of people between the two countries have also become two-way flows. The same economic forces that have transformed China's place in global production, trade and finance have also affected human resources. China is no longer an exporter of labour, but has become a magnet attracting foreign talent. The popular perception that immigrants to Canada who return to their native countries have "failed" or are "opportunistic" is outdated.

The Chinese community in Canada has changed, is changing and will continue to change in many aspects that will ultimately have profound impacts on relations between Canada and China. Chinese Canadians are as diversified within their groups as Canadian society is overall, though Chinese Canadians remain more visible in certain locations, schools, occupations and industries. This poses new challenges for Canada and all Canadians as they come to an understanding of Chinese Canadians, not as a distinctive or homogeneous group, but as an integral part of Canada's multicultural society. Nor can Canada afford to ignore the growing body of Canadians, native-born or naturalized, who choose to live in China, an emerging global powerhouse. More fundamentally, Canadian communities in China can play an important role and potentially be of great benefit to Canada.

People flows between Canada and China will increasingly be characterized by two-way movements and by transnational citizens with personal, business and emotional attachments on both sides of the Pacific. While there are many challenges that arise from the growth of such diaspora-like populations at home and abroad, the phenomenon of international labour mobility, especially of the most talented (and, sometimes, the most notorious), is here to stay. The challenge for policy-makers is to take a holistic and multi-generational view of transnational citizens, rather than to treat international mobility as a problem.

Of all the reasons for Canada to have a robust and forward-looking China policy, people-to-people linkage is arguably the most fundamental. Currently the flow of people between Canada and China is unmatched by that between China and any other member state of the Organization for

Economic Cooperation and Development. Seen in this light, the human capital nexus is a unique focal point for relations between Ottawa and Beijing. While other countries are lining up to sign trade and investment deals with China, Canada can go a step further and investigate the possibility of an agreement in the arena based on this human platform. Such an agreement could encompass issues such as citizenship, visas, education and training, professional accreditation, social security, taxation and even extradition. Given the large number of Canadians and Chinese with deep connections across the Pacific, it is a certainty that these bilateral issues will become bigger policy challenges for both Beijing and Ottawa in the years ahead. There is an opportunity now to address these issues in a comprehensive fashion and to turn potential problems into competitive advantages for the bilateral relationship.

References

Anderssen, Erin. (2009, October 3) "PEI's Big Immigration Boom," *Globe and Mail.*

Aydemir, Abdurrahman, and Chris Robinson. (2006, March). "Return and Onward Migration among Working-Age Men." Analytical Studies Branch Research Paper Series, Ottawa: Statistics Canada. Online as http://www.statcan.gc.ca/pub/11f0019m/11f0019m2006273-eng.pdf [consulted January 14, 2011].

China Radio International. (2008, September 28). "Multinational Corporations Make China Home." Online at http://english1.cri.cn/4026/2007/09/28/1361@278675.htm [consulted January 14, 2011].

Citizenship and Immigration Canada. (2009). *Facts and Figures 2008: Immigration Overview.* Ottawa: Citizenship and Immigration Canada. Online at http://www.cic.gc.ca/english/resources/statistics/menu-fact.asp [consulted January 14, 2011].

DeVoretz, Don J. (2009, October 29). "Canada's Secret Province: 2.8 Million Canadians Abroad." Canadians Abroad Project Research Report. Vancouver: Asia Pacific Foundation of Canada. Online as http://www.asiapacific.ca/sites/default/files/filefield/PP_09_5_DD_estimate_0.pdf [consulted January 14, 2011].

Government of Canada. (2009, December). "Canada–China." Ottawa: Department of Foreign Affairs and International Trade. Online at http://www.canadainternational.gc.ca/china-chine/bilateral_relations_bilaterales/china_canada_chine.aspx?lang=eng&menu_id=14&menu=L [consulted January 14, 2011].

Guo, Shibao. (2009, September). "Portrait of Canadians Abroad: Beijing." Canadians Abroad Project Portrait Report. Vancouver: Asia Pacific Foundation of Canada. Online as http://www.asiapacific.ca/sites/default/files/filefield/ Portrait_Report_Beijing.pdf [consulted January 14, 2011].

Guo, Shibao, and Don J. DeVoretz. (2006, June). "The Changing Face of Chinese Immigrants in Canada." *Journal of International Migration and Integration* 7:3.

Institute of International Education. (2010). "Global Destinations for International Students at the Post-Secondary (Tertiary) Level, 2001 and 2008." *Atlas of Student Mobility*. New York: Institute of International Education. Online at http://www. atlas.iienetwork.org/page/48027/ [consulted January 14, 2011].

LaowaiZaiZhongguo. (2007). 老外在中国 [Foreigners in China]. Online at http:// view.news.qq.com/zt/2007/laowai/index.htm [consulted January 14, 2011].

Lee, Wai-man. (1984). *Portraits of a Challenge: An Illustrated History of the Chinese Canadians*. Toronto: Council of Chinese Canadians in Ontario.

Lee-Young, Joanne. (2008, August 6). "Chinese Canadians Face a Test of Patriotism." *Vancouver Sun*. Online at http://www.canada.com/vancouversun/news/west-coastnews/story.html?id=4b676251-297f-4212-9c3c-9dcbda94ca3a&p=2 [consulted January 14, 2011].

Li, Peter. (2005, August). "The Rise and Fall of Chinese Immigration to Canada: Newcomers from Hong Kong Special Administrative Region of China and Mainland China, 1980–2000." *International Migration* 43:3, 9–32.

Li, Peter. (2010, January). "Immigrants from China to Canada: Issues of Supply and Demand of Human Capital." *China Papers* no. 2. Toronto: Canadian International Council.

Lin, Xiaohua, Jian Guan, and Mary Jo Nicholson. (2008, December 19). "Transnational Entrepreneurs as Agents of International Innovation Linkages." Research Report. Vancouver: Asia Pacific Foundation of Canada. Online as http://www.asiapacific.ca/sites/default/files/filefield/ImmigEntrepreneurs.pdf [consulted January 14, 2011].

Lindsay, Colin. (2007, March). "The Chinese Community in Canada 2001." Ottawa: Statistics Canada. Online as http://www.statcan.gc.ca/pub/89-621-x/89-621-x2006001-eng.pdf [consulted January 14, 2011].

Migration Policy Institute. (2008, December). "Top 10 Migration Issues of 2008. Issue No. 6: Return Migration: Changing Directions?" Online at http://www.migrationinformation.org/Feature/display.cfm?id=707 [consulted January 14, 2011].

Ng, Susanna. (2007, January 2). "'Transnational Parenting' Separates Chinese Immigrants, Kids." Blog post online at http://www.chineseinvancouver. ca/2007/01/transnational-parenting-separates-chinese-immigrants-kids/ [consulted January 14, 2011].

Oriental Morning Post. (2008, December 31. 最新字表明：在上海就业外国人13年已增加13倍 [Foreign Workers in Shanghai Increased Thirteen Times in Thirteen Years]. Online at http://www.lm.gov.cn/gb/employment/2008-12/30/content_271511.htm [consulted January 14, 2011].

Ottawa Citizen. (2008, August 26). "Canada's China Policy." Online at http://www.canada.com/topics/news/national/story.html?id=ae0a032b-7a10-484a-a839-440680e52617 [consulted January 14, 2011].

Rowswell, Mark. (2010). "Who Is Dashan?" Online at http://www.dashan.com/en/index.htm [consulted January 14, 2011].

Statistics Canada. (2006a). "2006 Census Data Products." Ottawa: Statistics Canada. Online at http://www12.statcan.ca/census-recensement/2006/dp-pd/index-eng.cfm [consulted January 14, 2011].

Statistics Canada. (2008, December 9). "Special Interest Profiles, 2006 Census." Ottawa: Statistics Canada. Online at http://www.statcan.gc.ca/bsolc/olc-cel/olc-cel?lang=eng&catno=97-564-X2006007 [consulted January 14, 2011].

Wang, Shuguang, and Lucia Lo. (2005). "Chinese Immigrants in Canada: Their Changing Composition and Economic Performance." International Migration 43:3, 35–71.

Woo, Yuen Pau, and Huiyao Wang. (2009, June 23). "The Fortune in Our Future." *Globe and Mail.*

Zhang, Kenny, and Yuen Pau Woo. (2006, March 23). "Recognizing the Canadian Diaspora." *Canada Asia Commentary* no. 41. Vancouver: Asia Pacific Foundation of Canada. Online as http://www.asiapacific.ca/sites/default/files/archived_pdf/oped/diaspora_oped2006.pdf [consulted January 14, 2011].

Zhang, Kenny. (2009, September). "Portrait of Canadians Abroad: Hong Kong SAR." Canadians Abroad Project Portrait Report. Vancouver: Asia Pacific Foundation of Canada. Online as http://www.asiapacific.ca/sites/default/files/filefield/Portrait_Report_HK.pdf [consulted January 14, 2011].

Zhang, Kenny. (2010a, January). "Why Gaining the ADS is Just the Beginning." *China Business Magazine* Vol. 13, 20–22.

Zhang, Kenny. (2010b, May). "Flows of People and the Canada–China Relationship." *China Papers* no. 10. Toronto: Canadian International Council.

Chapter 14

Transnational Intergenerational Support: Implications of Aging in Mainland China for the Chinese in Canada

Ghazy Mujahid, Ann H. Kim
and Guida C. Man

This chapter explores the potential impacts of population aging in mainland China on patterns and experiences of caring among Chinese immigrants in Canada, particularly women. (Throughout the rest of this chapter, references to "China" are to mainland China, excluding Hong Kong, Macau or Taiwan, except where otherwise stated.) We situate the study in the literature on transnational, globalized and flexible families, concepts that refer to the separation of family members who preserve a sense of familyhood across national borders, and to the internationalization of the household (see Bryceson and Vuorela 2002 and Douglass 2006). Definitions of the transnational family and of global householding are suitably broad, and encompass multiple family forms, including families with adult children in Canada, and their own children and aging parents in China.

Over the past twenty years we have observed the burgeoning of the literature on Chinese "astronaut" families and "parachute" children, demonstrating how this transnational family form affects family relationships and individual members in both positive and negative ways (see Alaggia, Chau, and Tsang 2001, Aye and Guerin 2001, Gardner 2006, Ho 1999, Irving, Benjamin, and Tsang 2000, Lam 1994, Landolt and Da 2005, Man 1995a and 2007, McKeown 2000, Ong 1992 and 1998, Preston, Kobayashi, and Man 2006, Preston, Kobayashi, and Siemiatycki 2006, Pribilsky 2004, Salaff, Shik, and Greve 2008, Siemiatycki and Preston 2007, Skeldon 1994,

Tsang et al. 2003, Waters 2002, 2003, and 2005, Wong and Ho 2006, and Zhou 1998). However, more recently, the Chinese transnational family has shifted to a pattern in which working-age immigrants leave aging parents in China and also leave, or send back, their young children (see Da 2003, Liu 2008, and Man 2002, 2004, and 2008). It is their experiences that form the focus of this chapter. In particular, we examine intergenerational relations among Chinese immigrants, focusing on the evolving gamut of mutual care and support mechanisms that take place across borders.

Population Aging in China

The proportion of seniors in the population of China has been increasing rapidly since the beginning of the 21st century (see Table 14.1). While this demographic change is happening in almost every country, in China it has been more marked due to the decline in fertility as a result of the one-child policy, combined with the impact of rapid improvements in health care facilities on increased longevity. Between 1970 and 2010 China's population has increased from 816 million to 1.35 billion, that is, by around a little over 530 million. While the child population (between zero and fourteen years) declined from forty to twenty percent, the working-age population (between fifteen and sixty-four years) increased from fifty-six to seventy-two percent. The population of seniors also increased from 4.3 to 8.2 percent. The decline in the child population is explained by the decline in the number of births, from an estimated annual average of 25 million in the early 1970s to the current annual average of 18 million. The increasing proportion of seniors is explained by the increase in life expectancy at birth from sixty years in 1970 to seventy-three years in 2010 (see United Nations 2008).

The demographic trends during the next forty years are projected to be quite different. Population is projected to increase at a much slower rate, and to start declining after 2030. The total population is projected at 1.42 billion in 2050, that is, at only around 70 million more than the total as of 2010. By 2050, the number of births is projected to decline to an annual average of 14 to 15 million. The long-drawn decline in the birth rate is finally projected to start affecting the size of the working-age population, the proportion of which is projected to decline from seventy-two percent in 2010 to sixty-one percent by 2050. Seniors are the only section of China's population whose proportion within the total population is projected to increase over the next forty years, from eight percent in 2010 to more than twenty-three percent by

Table 14.1 Trends in Age Groups within the Population of Mainland China, 1970–2000, with Projections for 2010–2025

	Population	Proportion in age groups (%)		
	(thousands)	0 to 14	15 to 64	65 and over
Official Figures for Past Years				
1970	815,951	39.7	56.0	4.3
1980	980,928	35.5	59.8	4.7
1990	1,142,089	28.4	66.1	5.5
2000	1,266,954	25.7	67.5	6.8
Projections for Future Years				
2010	1,354,148	19.9	71.9	8.2
2020	1,431,156	18.7	69.6	11.7
2030	1,462,468	16.9	67.2	15.9
2040	1,455,057	15.3	63.0	21.8
2050	1,417,044	15.3	61.4	23.3

Source: United Nations 2009.

2050. The number of seniors in China increased from 35 million in 1970 to 111 million in 2010, and is projected to increase to 330 million by 2050: the increment during the next forty years is thus projected to be almost three times the increment during the past forty years.

The increasing proportion of seniors in the total population and their increasing numbers can be explained by further increments in life expectancy, which is projected to increase to almost eighty years by 2050 as a result of continuing improvements in lifestyle and health services. Both the proportion of the total population expected to survive to age sixty-five years and the number of years a senior is expected to live on average are projected to increase over the next forty years (see Table 14.2). Within the cohort of seniors the percentage of those reaching eighty years and the average number of years they can be expected to live after reaching age eighty years are also projected to go up (see United Nations 2008).

These projected demographic trends, if the projections are realized, would result in a larger number of seniors leading longer and healthier

Table 14.2 Indicators of Longevity in Mainland China in 2007, with Projections for 2025 and 2050

	2007	2025	2050
Life expectancy at birth (years)	72.6	75.3	78.7
Proportion expected to reach age 65 (%)	79.3	82.2	87.3
Life expectancy at age 65 (years)	15.2	16.9	18.3
Proportion expected to reach age 80 (%)	39.9	47.8	56.1
Life expectancy at age 80 (years)	6.8	7.7	8.6

Source: United Nations 2008.

lives. One remarkable reflection of this projected trend is the projected increase in the population of centenarians, from an estimated 33,000 in 2010 to 450,000 in 2050 (see United Nations 2009).

The significance of these projected changes in the age structure of China's population for the family structure is reflected in changes in the parent–support ratio, which is the ratio of the number of seniors aged eighty-five years or more per 100 persons aged between fifty and sixty-four years (see Figure 14.1). Those aged eighty-five years and more are assumed to be the hypothetical parents of the population aged fifty to sixty-four years, that is, those who were born to them when they were in their twenties and thirties.

Figure 14.1 Parent–Support Ratios in Mainland China, 1970–2000, with Projections for 2010–2050 (%)

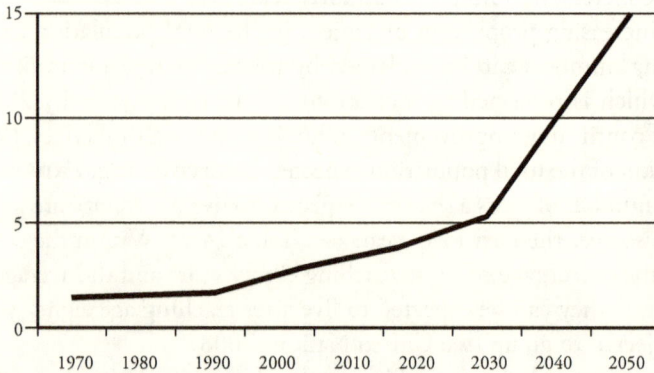

Source: United Nations 2009.

The parent–support ratio indicates the approximate trend in the percentage of the population aged fifty to sixty-four years whose parents are living.

The increase in the parent–support ratio over the forty years from 2010 to 2050 is projected to be much larger than the increase over the preceding forty years from 1970 to 2010 was. While the proportion of those aged fifty to sixty-four years having elderly parents increased from 1.4 percent in 1970 to 3.4 percent in 2010, it is projected to increase to 14.9 percent by 2050. Demographic evidence thus strongly indicates that increasing proportions of the Chinese already in Canada and of future immigrants will have elderly parents.

Another characteristic of the population of elderly parents is the higher proportion of women than of men, because women have longer life expectancy. In 2010, among China's population of those aged eighty-five years and older, there were 170 women for every 100 men, and this ratio is projected to remain almost unchanged until 2050. Further, a majority of these elderly people, and a larger majority of the women, are widowed. The Census of China conducted in 2000 showed that fifty percent of the men and eighty percent of the women aged eighty years and over were widowed (see China Center for Research on Aging 2007). A much higher proportion of senior women than of senior men is therefore projected to become dependent on offspring and other relatives.

Chinese Immigration to Canada after 1947

Chinese immigration into Canada was banned by the Canadian government under the Chinese Immigration Act of 1923, which remained in force until 1947. Following its repeal, while Chinese immigrants came to Canada from Taiwan, Hong Kong and other countries, emigration from China itself remained restricted as a result of the "closed door" policy of the newly established Communist regime. Two significant events during the 1970s paved the way for a resumption of migration from China to Canada: the establishment of diplomatic relations between Canada and China in 1970, and the end of the Cultural Revolution in 1976, following the death of Mao Zedong. Although emigration from China to Canada started following the establishment of diplomatic relations, it was not until after the rise of Deng Xiaoping to power in 1978 that China moved towards an "open door" policy, which eased the mobility of its citizens.

During the first ten years following the establishment of diplomatic relations between Canada and China, only 600 citizens from China emigrated to Canada (see Rafael 2007). Immigration then gathered pace during the 1980s and continued to increase after that (see Figure 14.2). Since 1998 China has been the single largest source country of migrants to Canada. The second highest number of immigrants to Canada has been from India, and the gap between the two has been narrowing, but the number of migrants from China exceeded those from India by more than 34,000 during the period from 2005 to 2008 (CIC 2009).

The growing inflows of migrants have contributed to a rapid increase in the population of Chinese in Canada. From a total of 119,000 in 1971, the number of Chinese in Canada increased to 289,000 in 1981 and to 634,000 in 1991 (see Li 2007). The Censuses of 1996 and 2001 showed that the Chinese population in Canada had increased to 860,000 by the former year and to 1.03 million by the latter year, while the Census of 2006 gave a total of 1.22 million Chinese in Canada based on visible minority counts. Given that 557,000 immigrants from China entered Canada between 1970 and 2006, migrants from China constituted roughly forty-five percent of the total Chinese population in Canada in 2006, and their proportion has presumably increased since then, as more than eighty percent of Chinese immigrants who entered Canada in 2007 and 2008 came from the mainland (CIC 2009).

Figure 14.2 Chinese Immigrants to Canada by Place of Origin, 1980–2006

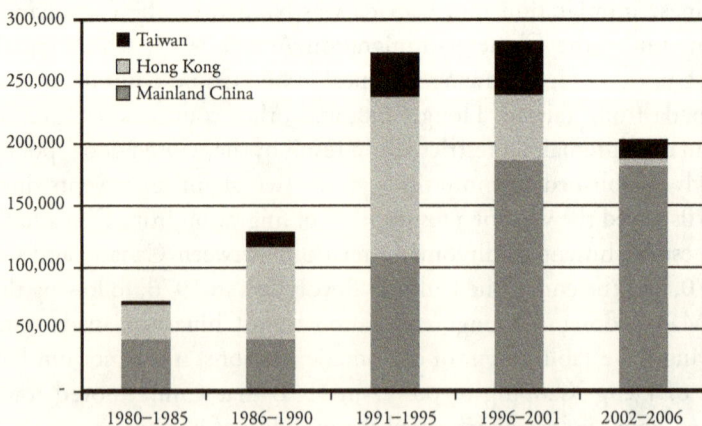

Source: CIC 2009.

According to the Census of 2006, the population of immigrants from China in Canada stands at more than 450,000 (see Table 14.3). Around seventeen percent are under the age of twenty-five years and a slightly higher proportion, nineteen percent, are aged sixty-five years or older, giving the Chinese immigrant population in Canada a much older age structure than that of China itself. These immigrants are geographically concentrated in Toronto (forty-one percent), with Vancouver being a close second destination. While Montreal is the third largest city of immigrants from China in Canada, it has attracted a much smaller number, with just over 16,000 immigrants.

A large proportion of this immigrant population as of 2006 were recent arrivals, with well over half having arrived since 1996. Most had arrived as working-age adults (forty-nine percent were aged twenty-five to forty-four years), but the relatively large presence of immigrants forty-five years or older (twenty-one percent) suggests that many immigrants from China were sponsored family members, given that very few points are awarded to applicants over the age of fifty years in Canada's immigration point system.

While this profile informs us of the general characteristics of the Chinese immigrant population, it does not provide detailed information on migration trends by age groups. For data on this matter we may turn to the Public Use Microdata File of Individuals, a 2.7 percent sample of the Canadian Census of 2006. Cross-tabulating age at arrival with period of arrival (see Table 14.4) shows how the ages of immigrants from China have changed over time.

It seems clear that since 1970 Canada has attracted older immigrants, who are likely to have fewer children of their own; that since 1981 there has been a steady increase in the arrival of working-age adults (twenty-five to forty-nine years); and that since 1990 fewer seniors as a proportion have been migrating. These trends suggest that more and more immigrants may belong to the "sandwich" generation, that is, they are adults supporting both children and elderly parents, and face various challenges while caring for aging parents (and sometimes children) in China.

Given the strong family structure, intergenerational relations and filial piety in Chinese culture, one can expect that an increasing number of immigrants coming to Canada will have to maintain strong links with elderly parents in China. Further, as the offspring of the one-child policy come of age, an increasing proportion of China's adult population migrating to Canada will fit into the "four–two–one" family pattern of one adult supporting two parents and four grandparents. Being the only child increases the responsibilities of filial piety.

Table 14.3 Selected Characteristics of Immigrants from Mainland China to Canada, 2006

		%
Total number	466,945	
Gender		
Male	213,950	45.8
Female	252,995	54.2
Age group		
Under 25 years	78,695	16.9
25 to 44 years	178,330	38.2
45 to 54 years	66,945	14.3
55 to 64 years	52,750	11.3
65 years and over	90,225	19.3
Period of immigration		
Before 1991	133,910	28.7
1991–1995	69,635	14.9
1996–2000	108,290	23.2
2001–2006	155,105	33.2
Age at immigration		
Under 25 years	140,935	30.2
25 to 44 years	229,800	49.2
45 years and over	96,215	20.6
Citizenship		
Only Canadian	303,045	64.9
Dual	13,895	3.0
Only non-Canadian	150,005	32.1
Destination		
Toronto	191,120	40.9
Vancouver	137,245	29.4
Montreal	16,180	3.5
Other	122,400	26.2

Source: Statistics Canada, 2006a.

**Table 14.4 Age at Arrival of Samples of Immigrants from Mainland China
to Canada, by Period of Arrival, as Reported in 2006**

	Before 1970	1970–1980	1981–1990	1991–2000	2001–2006
Under 25 years	64.6	34.5	24.3	27.4	33.2
25 to 49 years	35.0	52.6	47.8	51.8	57.0
50 years and over	0.5	13.0	27.9	20.8	9.8
Total sample	661	1,100	1,564	4,459	3,840

Source: Statistics Canada, 2006b, Public Use Microdata File on Individuals, Persons Born
in the People's Republic of China, 25 Years and Over.

Continuing Intergenerational Relations

The interaction between the Chinese diaspora in Canada and their elderly
parents in China can be expected to manifest itself in various ways. First,
an increasing number of Chinese residents in Canada will likely be called
on to provide support to elderly parents in China. This could include
remittances as well as more frequent visits to China than would otherwise be the case. Second, cases of newly arriving immigrants from China
sending infant offspring back to China to be taken care of by grandparents, so that both the husband and wife can work towards settling down,
can be expected to increase. An increasing number of immigrants will
have aging parents who are sufficiently active and healthy to look after
the infants, who would more likely than not be their only grandchildren.
Third, given that their parents are active and in good health, Chinese in
Canada may well be encouraged to bring them to Canada as visitors, as
well as under family sponsorship arrangements.

The extent to which immigrants from China in Canada have ties to
China can be gleaned from public use data from the Ethnic Diversity Survey conducted by Statistics Canada, in partnership with the Department of
Canadian Heritage, in 2002. These data reveal that seventy-eight percent
of immigrants from China aged twenty-five years and older had relatives
in China, and that sixty-four percent had visited China since immigrating
to Canada. While the survey uses a broad definition of "family," it suggests
that the majority of immigrants continue to have family ties in China. The

existence of family ties in China, and potential intergenerational relationships by extension, also differ by gender and marital status, as the survey
data show that more married females and single males than single females
and married males had families in China (see Figure 14.3).

When we examine trips to China for those who had family in China by
gender and period of arrival (see Table 14.5), it is clear that women who
had family in China were more likely to have visited at least once compared
to men, regardless of when they arrived in Canada, and women were far
more likely to visit China than males who arrived during the same period.
These data suggest that women, particularly married ones, bear the challenges associated with maintaining transnational family relationships, since
not only are women more likely to have family in China, but those women
with family in China are also more likely to travel there.

Caring for Elderly Parents in China

Some of the challenges in Chinese immigrant women's lives are examined
in this section, which in part is based on research data from a study on
Chinese immigrant women and precarious work conducted in 2004–2005

**Figure 14.3 Chinese in Canada with Family in Mainland China by Gender
and Marital Status, 2002**

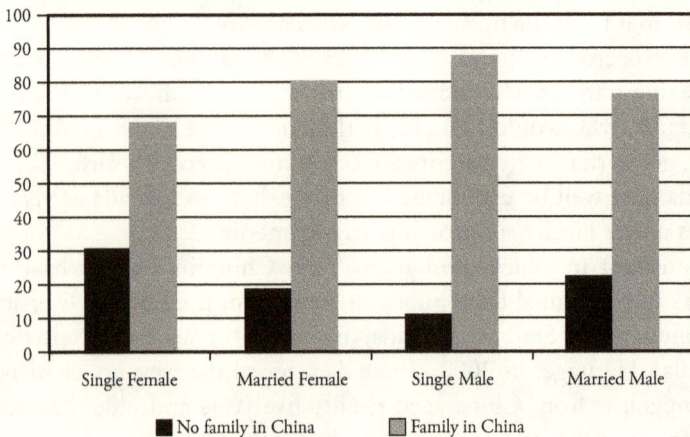

Source: Statistics Canada, 2003.

Table 14.5 Number of Trips to China by Chinese in Canada since Arrival (% of Samples)

	Before 1991		1991–2001	
	Female	Male	Female	Male
Never	19.7	26.5	40.1	52.4
Once	24.7	19.3	31.4	25.8
Two to four times	30.0	40.3	19.2	13.9
Five to nine times	17.6	8.5	8.7	5.1
Ten or more times	8.0	5.4	0.7	2.7
Total sample	91	83	123	100

Source: Statistics Canada, 2003.

(Man 2005). The research included two focus groups, one with immigrant women from (mainland) China, and the other with immigrant women from Hong Kong, and individual in-depth interviews were carried out with seven women from China and four from Hong Kong. The women had arrived in Canada between 1998 and 2004. They were all married and had at least one child, either in Canada or in their home country. They were also highly educated. All the women from China had bachelor's or master's degrees, and more than half of the women from Hong Kong had university or other post-secondary education. The women from China ranged in age from twenty-five to thirty-six years, and had young children who were pre-schoolers and required child care. The women from Hong Kong were older, ranging from twenty-nine to fifty-three years. While the focus of the analysis is on women from China, the experiences of some of those from Hong Kong are also described for comparative purposes.

New immigrants from China have typically immigrated to Canada in nuclear family units. Members of their extended families, such as parents or in-laws who are often elderly, have been either unable or unwilling to emigrate with their adult children and grandchildren (see Da 2003 and Man 2009). Immigration policy makes it difficult for such members of extended families to come, and some elderly parents are reluctant to move to a foreign country where they face social, cultural and linguistic challenges.

In China, the Confucian belief in filial piety obliges children to care for elderly parents, and in return grandparents, especially grandmothers, often help to care for grandchildren (see Man 1995b, Liu 2008 and Spitzer et al. 2003). While some men do participate in care-giving, in both Western and Asian cultures, the bulk of caring work is still done by women (see Corman and Luxton 2001, Devault 1991, Luxton 1990 and Waring 1999). Despite their household and employment difficulties, cultural ideology also informs immigrants from China to care for their parents or in-laws in China (see Man 1997 and Spitzer et al. 2003).

Since it is expensive and time-consuming for new immigrants to visit their elderly parents in China, many cannot engage in the day-to-day physical work of caring, but the work of emotional and economic caring continues. The Chinese immigrant women in this study phoned their parents long distance on a regular basis. Other studies have also found that immigrants from Hong Kong used the telephone and internet to communicate with their relatives transnationally (see Kobayashi et al. 2005 and Liu 2008).

Some immigrants send remittances to their family members in the home country, a practice that is also common among other immigrant groups (see Wong 2003). Periodically, when their budget permits, they pay visits to their elderly parents in China, or send money for their parents to visit them in Canada. The task of caring for family members in the home country always falls on the women. When the elderly parent is ill, the daughter or the daughter-in-law is the one who arranges for their care and calls them long distance from Canada (see Liu 2008 and Man 2008). When the family can afford it, the daughter or daughter-in-law typically travels to China to visit and care for elderly parents or in-laws. Gender ideology and cultural imperative prevail even when a professional Chinese woman in her forties has followed her husband to Toronto and may compromise her own career by travelling back and forth between Canada and China (see Man 2008). Her class status affords her the financial freedom to do so since transcontinental airfares are costly.

For Chinese immigrants who have aging parents and elderly in-laws residing in different geographical spaces, it is a constant struggle to accomplish the work of caring. As a woman from Hong Kong confided: "[M]y mother-in-law and my father-in-law are very old. We live with them [in Toronto]. We don't feel comfortable leaving them behind if we go back to Hong Kong. ... Well, if I do decide to go back to Hong Kong, it would be because I want to take care of my parents." Their struggle is not unlike that of those members of the "baby boomer" generation in Canada whose parents do not live in the same city or province as they do, and have to fly back and forth between cities in Canada.

Transnational Care of Grandchildren in China

In China it is customary for retired grandparents, particularly grandmothers, to take care of their grandchildren, alleviating the child care burden
on their adult children, male and female, to enable them to pursue their
career aspirations and economic advancement through participation in the
labour force. A Chinese woman reflected on the support she was able to
procure from her parents, and the ingenuity of extended family members in
cooperating in the accomplishment of social reproduction in China: "My
daughter lived with her grandma. My husband and I had our own place,
but we would go over to my mother's place for dinner and to see our daughter every evening. After dinner we would go back to our own place."

Although the prevalence of grandchildren living with and being cared
for by grandparents is not known, the general acceptance of this arrangement provides a space for the development of transnational parenting/
grandparenting practice. It reveals the cultural and organizational processes
in China that allow for this pragmatic approach.

Previous studies have asserted the interpenetration of household work and
paid work, and women's primary responsibility for this work (see Armstrong
and Armstrong 2002, Man 2002, Luxton 2006, Neysmith and Chen 2002
and Duffy, Mandell and Pupo 1989). For new immigrants in Canada, particularly women, the task of juggling paid work, housework and child care
is intensified (see Man 2002, Preston and Man 1999, Salaff and Greve 2006
and Wan 2003). Some Chinese immigrant couples who are unable to obtain
subsidized child care, and who have had difficulties juggling child care and
paid work, have resolved to send their children back to China to be taken care
of by their grandmothers or other family members.

It has been well-documented that Chinese immigrants encounter difficulties in employment (see Basran and Zong 1998, Li 2000, Wang and Lo
2003, Man 2004, Preston and Man 1999 and Reitz, 2003). Employers'
lack of recognition of the previous experience and credentials of immigrants makes it very difficult for them to find employment commensurate with their qualifications and experience. Immigrants, particularly the
Chinese immigrant women who were interviewed, have a propensity to
be channelled into menial and precarious positions. Compounded with
the lack of affordable child care, this has prompted some women to send
their children back to China to be cared for by grandparents so that they
can focus on job search and pursue better job opportunities. As this
woman explained:

My son was sent back to China already. I feel it's very stressful doing the
job search and taking care of the kid at the same time, both mentally and
physically. Sometimes this affected my attitude towards my son, and he
would feel confused when I easily lose my patience. After sending my son
back to China, I have more time studying and working, so I think it's a
right decision to make.

For many immigrants from China, the deterioration of their material conditions in the new country necessitated transnational practices to
continue their productive and reproductive processes, that is, maintaining
employment and the raising of children in separate geographical spaces
through transnational familial networks and linkages.

Care and Support between Chinese Immigrants and
Their Elderly Parents in Canada

Many immigrants found it difficult to care for elderly parents in China.
While the telephone was used frequently, and was a relatively convenient
and inexpensive way to connect with family members, it is inadequate
compared to face-to-face interaction. Visits to China prove to be costly,
exhausting and time-consuming. Chinese immigrant women therefore
expressed their desire for their parents to join them in Canada. A woman
from China whose mother was laid off from her job in a factory wanted
to apply for her to come to Canada so that she could provide for her. At
the same time she also hoped to benefit from her mother's help with child
care: "My mother works in a factory that was not run very well. Many
workers were dismissed.... I want my mother to come. She can help me
with child care."

Chinese immigrants who came to Canada without extended family
members lose the household and childcare support they obtained from
their parents when they were in China. The absence of this support has led
to the transformation of gender relations and household division of labour
between spouses in the new country. Another Chinese woman reminisced
about the support she was able to procure from her parents when they were
in China:

In China I didn't have to worry about the housework. We went to our
parents' to have dinner every working day, and did some cleaning at our

own home during the weekends. My parents helped take care of my children too. Now we have changed a lot. We need to cooperate very well to finish all the housework and take care of our daughter.

In a study that focuses on immigrants from China coming to Toronto, the majority of female seniors interviewed admitted that they were motivated to come to Canada in order to reunite with family members (see George et al. 2000). The vast majority of the senior participants who made the decision to emigrate had children living in Canada. Some elderly Chinese came to Canada to provide household help and child care for their grandchildren while their adult children went out to work. Chinese immigrant families who are financially qualified to sponsor their elderly parents to come to Canada are able to recreate in Canada the extended family support network they enjoyed in China.

In another study, a Hong Kong woman whose parents had also immigrated to Canada and lived close by was able to obtain child care assistance from her mother. Her daughter went to the grandparents' place after school, and stayed there until she and her husband got off work. The whole family then ate dinner at the grandparents' place every evening, and on the weekends they all went out for dinner. It was in this way that this family was able to replicate the mutual care and support they had provided for each other when they were in their home country (see Man 2009).

At the same time, some seniors reported experiencing difficulties with the English language and the isolation that ensued (see George et al. 2000). They commented on the ramifications of the lack of interpretation services in hospitals for their health care, since they were unable to describe their health problems fully to doctors, nor could they understand the doctors' advice (see George et al. 2000). Often, children were unable to accompany elderly parents to their medical examinations because they were engaged in two or more part-time jobs to make ends meet.

While intergenerational mutual support is common for many seniors and their children, intergenerational conflict within the family also occurs. The stress of unemployment of adult children is often seen as a major cause of a family's problems. Some elderly parents moved out of their children's home because of family conflicts and/or financial problems. Elder abuse, although very much underreported due to the shame perceived within the Chinese community, is also a reality for some (see George et al. 2000). The same study found that those elderly Chinese who are able to participate in seniors programmes at community centres found a reduction in their sense of isolation.

Conclusion and Recommendations

The analysis of data and research presented in this chapter suggests that transnational intergenerational support among the Chinese diaspora in Canada may become considerably more widespread. Given that the proportion of the elderly in the population of China is rapidly increasing, the mechanisms of support between the Chinese diaspora in Canada and their elderly parents in both Canada and China are expected to become more entrenched and prolonged. It is not certain what potential long-term effects the different sectors of the Chinese population (adults, children and the elderly) will encounter as a result of demands for intergenerational support. Given the increasing size of the Chinese population in Canada, it would be prudent for the governments of both Canada and China to take account of the situation by cooperating in a concerted effort to formulate measures to alleviate the hardship of families engaged in transnational intergenerational support.

In light of the above analysis, a multi-pronged approach is recommended. On the Canadian end, government policies that enable new immigrants to achieve social and economic integration and independence in the new country, while at the same time recognizing and supporting family and extended family commitments both at home and overseas, would be welcome. On the one hand, this would entail introducing measures that would enhance the labour market integration of Chinese immigrants, such as working with employers and regulatory bodies to recognize international credentials and experience, and making profession-specific language courses available to all immigrants. On the other hand, it would also mean providing affordable and culturally sensitive child care programmes to accommodate new immigrant families' needs, facilitating the sponsorship of extended family members and introducing incentives to employers to allow flexible family leaves, including leaves for caring for family members overseas.

More specific measures geared toward Chinese seniors in Canada are also warranted. Chinese seniors would benefit directly from initiatives such as facilitating and expediting sponsorship arrangements, providing language courses for seniors visiting family, making health services more culturally sensitive, and regularizing the most frequently used traditional Chinese medicines. Further, in view of the aging population in Canada, there is a need to put more emphasis on health care reform already in process, with a focus on encouraging Chinese immigrants to access health services so as to avoid more serious health problems, disability and the need for long-term care in the future.

At the same time, the government of China could, on its part, facilitate the emigration of Chinese seniors sponsored by their adult offspring in Canada, and offer support to seniors in China whose adult children have emigrated, particularly if the seniors are caring for their grandchildren. It is recommended that the government recognize grandchildren left in China in the care of seniors as dependents eligible for state benefits. The liberalization and facilitation of pension benefit payments to seniors emigrating to Canada would also greatly benefit those who made contributions during their years of employment in China. Together with the Canadian government, the government of China might be encouraged to negotiate a social security agreement, which would mean that eligible seniors would receive social security benefits from China or Canada. To date, Canada has signed social security agreements with fifty-four countries, including three in East Asia: Japan, South Korea and the Philippines. Again, in terms of priorities the government of China should extend support to seniors looking after grandchildren whose parents are abroad and initiate negotiations for a social security agreement with Canada.

According to Canada's Department of Foreign Affairs and International Trade, one of Canada's four main policy goals in China is "to work with China to advance shared interests such as health, the environment, and regional peace and security" (see Holden 2008). Given that the Chinese populations in both China and Canada are aging, population aging could be identified as a "shared interest," and the two governments should jointly tackle issues relating to seniors and transnational intergenerational support. There is a need to promote dialogue and information exchange on aging-related issues between the two countries, as well as collaborative research and exchanges between Canadian and Chinese geriatric specialists, to enable them to obtain firsthand experience of how best to cater to the needs of Chinese seniors.

Acknowledgements

This chapter draws in part on data from two research projects: "Transnational Citizenship and Social Cohesion: Recent Immigrants from Hong Kong to Canada," conducted by Audrey Kobayashi, David Ley, Guida Man, Valerie Preston and Myer Siemiatycki, which was funded by a grant from the Social Sciences and Humanities Research Council (2000–2004); and "Chinese Immigrant Women in Toronto: Precarious Work, Precarious Lives," conducted by Guida Man, which was funded by a small grant from the Social Sciences and Humanities Research Council and an Atkinson Minor Research Grant from York University (2004–2005).

References

Alaggia, Ramona, Shirley B. Y. Chau, and A. Ka Tat Tsang. (2001). "Astronaut Asian Families: Impact of Migration on Family Structure from the Perspective of the Youth." *Journal of Social Work Research* 2, 295–306.

Armstrong, Pat, and Hugh Armstrong. (2002). "Thinking it Through: Women, Work and Caring in the New Millennium." *Canadian Woman Studies* 21/22:4, 44–50.

Aye, Alice M.M.M.T., and Bernard Guerin. (2001, June). "Astronaut Families: A Review of their Characteristics, Impact on Families and Implications for Practice in New Zealand." *New Zealand Journal of Psychology* 30:1, 9–15.

Basran, Gurchan S., and Li Zong. (1998). "Devaluation of Foreign Credentials as Perceived by Visible Minority Professional Immigrants." *Canadian Ethnic Studies* 30:3, 6–23.

Bryceson, Deborah Fahy, and Ulla Vuorela. (2002). "Transnational Families in the Twenty-first Century," in *The Transnational Family: New European Frontiers and Global Networks*, ed. Bryceson and Vuorela. Oxford: Berg, 3–30.

Corman, June and Meg Luxton. (2001). "Families at Work: The Dynamics of Paid Employment and Unpaid Domestic Labour," Chapter 2 in their *Getting by in Hard Times: Gendered Labour at Home and on the Job*. Toronto, Buffalo, NY, and London: University of Toronto Press, 36–63.

China Center for Research on Aging. (2007). *Demographic Change in China: Ageing of the World's Largest Population*. Bangkok: United Nations Population Fund.

CIC. (2009). Facts and Figures 2008: Immigration Overview – Permanent and Temporary Resident. Ottawa: Communications Branch of Citizenship and Immigration Canada.

Da, Wei Wei. (2003). "Transnational Grandparenting: Child Care Arrangements among Migrants from the People's Republic of China to Australia." *Journal of International Migration and Integration* 4:1, 79–103.

Devault, M. L. (1991). *Feeding the Family: The Social Organization of Caring as Gendered Work*. Chicago: University of Chicago Press.

Douglass, Mike. (2006). "Global Householding in Pacific Asia." *International Development Planning Review* 28, 421–45.

Duffy, Ann, Nancy Mandell, and Norene Pupo. (1989). *Few Choices: Women, Work, and Family*. Toronto: Garamond Press.

Gardner, Katy. (2006). "The Transnational Work of Kinship and Caring: Bengali–British Marriages in Historical Perspective." *Global Networks* 6, 373–87.

George, Usha, Ka Tat Tsang, Guida Man, and Wei Wei Da. (2000). *Needs Assessment of Mandarin-Speaking Newcomers*. Unpublished report. Toronto: South East Asian Services Centre.

Ho, Christine G. T. (1999). "Caribbean Transnationalism as a Gendered Process." *Latin American Perspectives* 26, 34–54.

Holden, Michael. (2008). "Canada's Trade Policy and Economic Relationship with China." Ottawa: Parliamentary Information and Research Service of the Library Parliament. Online as http://www2.parl.gc.ca/content/lop/researchpublications/prb0432-e.pdf [consulted January 14, 2011].

Irving, Howard H., Michael Benjamin, and A. Ka Tat Tsang. (2000). "Asian Satellite Children: An Exploration of their Experience," in *Social Work Around the World*, ed. Ngoh-Tiong Tan and Elis Envall. Singapore: International Federation of Social Workers, 165–90.

Kobayashi et.al. (2005). Transnational Citizenship and Social Cohesion: Recent Immigrants from Hong Kong to Canada (2000-04). Analysis of data of strategic research funded by SSHRC.

Lam, Lawrence. (1994). "Searching for a Safe Haven: The Migration and Settlement of Hong Kong Chinese Immigrants in Toronto," in *Reluctant Exiles?: Migration from Hong Kong and the New Overseas Chinese*, ed. Ronald Skeldon. Armonk, NY: M. E. Sharpe, 163–79.

Landolt, Patricia, and Wei Wei Da. (2005). "The Spatially Ruptured Practices of Migrant Families: A Comparison of Immigrants from El Salvador and the People's Republic of China." *Current Sociology* 53, 625–53.

Li, Peter S. (2000). "Earning Disparities between Immigrants and Native-born Canadians." *Canadian Review of Sociology and Anthropology* 37:3, 289–312.

Li, Peter S. (2007). "Business Engagement of Chinese Immigrants in Canada," in *Handbook of Research on Ethnic Minority Entrepreneurship: A Co-evolutionary View on Resource Management*, ed. Léo-Paul Dana. Cheltenham and Northampton, MA: Edward Elgar.

Liu, W. (2008). "Carework in a Transnational Context among New Chinese Immigrants in Canada." Paper presented at the Canadian Sociology Association Annual Meeting, University of British Columbia, Vancouver, June 2–5.

Luxton, Meg. (1990). "Two Hands for the Clock: Changing Patterns in the Gendered Division of Labour in the Home," in *Through the Kitchen Window: The Politics of Home and Family*, ed. Meg Luxton, Harriet Rosenberg, and Sedef Arat-Koç. 2nd ed. Toronto: Garamond Press, 39–55.

Luxton, Meg. (2006). *Social Reproduction: Feminist Political Economy Challenges Neoliberalism.* McGill–Queen's University Press.

Man, Guida. (1995a). "The Astronaut Phenomenon: Examining Consequences of the Diaspora of the Hong Kong Chinese," in *Managing Change in Southeast Asia: Local Identities, Global Connections*, ed. Jean DeBernardi, Gregory L. Forth, and Sandra Niessen. Montreal: Canadian Council for Southeast Asian Studies.

Man, Guida. (1995b). "The Experience of Women in Recent Middle-Class Chinese Immigrant Families from Hong Kong: An Inquiry into Institutional and Organizational Processes." *Asian and Pacific Migration Journal* 4:2–3, 303–25.

Man, Guida. (2002). "Globalization and the Erosion of the Welfare State: Effects on Chinese Immigrant Women." *Canadian Woman Studies* 21:4/22:1, 26–32.

Man, Guida. (2004). "Gender, Work, and Migration: Deskilling Chinese Immigrant Women in Canada." *Women's Studies International Forum* 27:2, 135–48.

Man. (2005). Chinese Immigrant Women in Toronto: Precarious Work, Precarious Lives. Report of project funded by a SSHRC Small Grant (2004-05) and an Atkinson Minor Research grant (2004-05) at YorkUniversity.

Man, Guida. (2007). "Racialization of Gender, Work, and Transnational Migration: The Experience of Chinese Immigrant Women in Canada," in *Race and Racism in 21st-century Canada: Continuity, Complexity, and Change*, ed. Sean P. Hier and B. Singh Bolaria. Peterborough, ON: Broadview Press, 235–52.

Man, Guida. (2008) "Globalization, Transnational Migration, and Women's Work: Exploring Chinese and Indian Immigrant Women Professionals' Experiences in Canada." Paper presented at Women's World Conference, Universidad Complutense de Madrid, July 3–9.

Man, Guida. (2009). "From Hong Kong to Canada: Immigration and The Changing Family Lives of Middle-Class Women from Hong Kong," in *Family Patterns, Gender Relations*, ed. B. J. Fox. 3rd ed. Toronto: Oxford University Press.

McKeown, Adam. (2000). "From Opium Farmer to Astronaut: A Global History of Diasporic Chinese Business." *Diaspora* 9, 317–60.

Neysmith, S. M, and X. Chen. (2002). "Understanding How Globalization and Restructuring Affect Women's Lives: Implications for Comparative Policy Analysis." *International Journal of Social Welfare* 11:3, 243–53.

Ong, Aihwa. (1992). "Limits to Cultural Accumulation: Chinese Capitalists on the American Pacific Rim," in *Towards a Transnational Perspective on Migration: Race, Class, Ethnicity, and Nationalism Reconsidered*, ed. Nina Glick Schiller, Linda Basch, and Cristina Blanc-Szanton. New York: New York Academy of Sciences, 125–43.

Ong, Aihwa. (1998). *Flexible Citizenship: The Cultural Logics of Transnationality.* Durham, NC: Duke University Press.

Preston, Valerie, and Guida Man. (1999). "Employment Experiences of Chinese Immigrant Women: An Exploration of Diversity." *Canadian Woman Studies* 19:3, 115–22.

Preston, Valerie, Audrey Kobayashi, and Guida Man. (2006). "Transnationalism, Gender, and Civic Participation: Canadian Case Studies of Hong Kong Immigrants." *Environment and Planning* 38, 1,633–51.

Preston, Valerie, Audrey Kobayashi, and Myer Siemiatycki. (2006). "Transnational Urbanism: Toronto at a Crossroads," in *Transnational Identities and Practices in Canada*, ed. Vic Satzewich and Lloyd Wong. Vancouver: University of British Columbia Press, 91–110.

Pribilsky, Jason. (2004). "'*Aprendemos a convivir*': Conjugal Relations, Co-Parenting, and Family Life among Ecuadorian Transnational Migrants in New York City and the Ecuadorian Andes." *Global Networks* 4, 313–34.

Rafael, Alacorn. (2007). "The Free Migration of Skilled Workers in North America," in *Migration without Borders: Essays on the Free Movement of People*, ed. Antoine Pecoud and Paul du Guchteneire. Paris: UNESCO Publishing, and New York and Oxford: Berghahn Books.

Reitz, Jeffrey G. (2003). "Immigration and Canadian Nation-Building in the Transition to a Knowledge Economy," in *Controlling Immigration: A Global Perspective*, ed. Wayne A. Cornelius, Philip L. Martin, and James F. Hollifield. 2nd ed. Palo Alto, CA: Stanford University Press.

Salaff, Janet, and Arent Greve. (2006). "Why Do Skilled Women and Men Emigrating from China to Canada Get Bad Jobs?" in *Women, Migration, and Citizenship*, ed. Evangelia Tastsoglou and Alexandra Dobrowolsky. Ashgate Press.

Salaff, Janet, Angela Shik, and Arent Greve. (2008). "Like Sons and Daughters of Hong Kong: The Return of the Young Generation." *China Review* 8, 31–57.

Siemiatycki, Myer, and Valerie Preston. (2007). "State and Media Construction of Transnational Communities: A Case Study of Recent Migration from Hong Kong to Canada," in *Organizing the Transnational: Labour, Politics, and Social Change*, ed. Luin Goldring and Sailaja Krishnamurti. Vancouver: University of British Columbia Press, 25–39.

Skeldon, Ronald. (1994). "Hong Kong in an International Migration System," in *Reluctant Exiles?: Migration from Hong Kong and the New Overseas Chinese*, ed. Ronald Skeldon. Armonk, NY: M. E. Sharpe, 21–51.

Spitzer, Denise, Anne Neufeld, Margaret Harrison, Karen Hughes, and Miriam Stewart. (2003). "Caregiving in Transnational Context: 'My Wings Have Been Cut; Where Can I Fly?'" *Gender and Society* 17:2, 267–86.

Statistics Canada. 2003. Ethnic Diversity Survey (EDS) 2002. Public Use Microdata File. Ottawa, ON.

Statistics Canada. 2006a. 2006 Census of Population, Census Tabulations. Ottawa, ON. http://www12.statcan.ca/census-recensement/2006/dp-pd/index-eng.cfm

Statistics Canada. 2006b. 2006 Census of Population: Public Use Microdata File. Ottawa, ON.

Tsang, A. Ka Tat, Howard Irving, Shirley B. Y. Chau, and Michael Benjamin. (2003). "Negotiating Ethnic Identity in Canada: The Case of the 'Satellite Children.'" *Youth and Society* 34:3, 359–84.

United Nations. (2008). *World Population Ageing 2007*.New York: United Nations Department of Economic and Social Affairs, Population Division.

United Nations. (2009). *World Population Prospects: The 2008 Revision*. New York: United Nations Department of Economic and Social Affairs, Population Division.

Wan, Fung-Ling Mary. (2003). "Language, Social Networks, and Parenting in the Lived Experiences of Five Working-Class Chinese Immigrant Women in Toronto: An Ethnographic Study." PhD dissertation, University of Toronto.

Wang, Shuguang, and Lucia Lo. (2003). "Chinese Immigrants in Canada: Their Changing Composition and Economic Performance." Research paper presented to the Conference on Sub-Ethnicity in the Chinese Diaspora, University of Toronto, September 12–13. Online as http://www.chass.utoronto.ca/~salaff/conference/papers/ChineseImmigrantsInCanada-Wang-and-Lo.pdf [consulted 14 January 2011].

Waring, Marilyn. (1999). *Counting for Nothing: What Men Value and What Women are Worth*. 2nd ed. Toronto, Buffalo, NY, and London: University of Toronto Press.

Waters, Johanna L. (2002). "Flexible Families?: 'Astronaut' Households and the Experiences of Lone Mothers in Vancouver, British Columbia." *Social and Cultural Geography* 3:2, 117–34.

Waters, Johanna L. (2003). "'Satellite Kids' in Vancouver: Transnational Migration, Education, and the Experience of Lone Children," in *Asian Migrants and Education: The Tensions of Education in Immigrant Societies and among Migrant Groups*, ed. Michael W. Charney, Brenda S. A. Yeoh, and Tong Chee Kiong. Dordrecht: Kluwer Academic Publishers, 165–84.

Waters, Johanna L. (2005). "Transnational Family Strategies and Education in the Contemporary Chinese Diaspora." *Global Networks* 5:4, 359–78.

Wong, Lloyd, and Connie Ho. (2006). "Chinese Transnationalism: Class and Capital Flows," in *Transnational Identities and Practices in Canada*, ed. Vic Satzewich and Lloyd Wong. Vancouver: University of British Columbia Press, 241–60.

Wong, Madeleine. (2003). "Borders that Separate, Blood that Binds: Transnational Activities of Ghanaian Women in Toronto." PhD dissertation, York University, Toronto.

Zhou, Min. (1998). "'Parachute Kids' in Southern California: The Educational Experience of Chinese Children in Transnational Families." *Educational Policy* 12:6, 682–704.

Chapter 15

The Bridge Too Far?:
Language Retention, Ethnic Persistence
and National Identification among the
Chinese Diaspora in Canada

Jack Jedwab

Successful cultural and commercial exchanges often depend on the ability
to function in a common language. Personal knowledge of two or more
languages represents a form of human capital that enhances opportunities
for interaction across cultural boundaries. Despite the expansion of English
as a second language, global communication barriers persist. Even where
translation resources abound, the presence of substantial majorities each
speaking only one language can be an important barrier to bilateral and
multilateral interaction. In Canada there has been much attention directed
at the level of knowledge and acquisition of English and/or French on the
part of the population whose mother tongue, the first language learned and
still understood, is neither of the country's two official languages. Those
individuals in Canada whose first language is Chinese and who acquire
English and/or French, those whose first language is English and/or French
and who have learned Chinese languages, and residents of China who have
learned either of these languages collectively strengthen the capacity for
cultural bridging between people in the two countries.

Some observers contend that the persistence of minority languages and
ethnic cultures detracts from identification with Canada. An inability to
speak an official language can be an important barrier to accessing certain
public services and for this reason most Canadians regard the acquisition
of English and/or French as essential towards integration. To the extent
that such persistence facilitates ethnic bonding it presumably undercuts the
"good" social capital arising from interaction that transcends ethnic ties.

Measuring the loss of non-official languages across generations is seen as an indicator for adaptation to the host or majority culture. Nevertheless, little attention has been paid to the use of non-official languages by immigrants and or their retention by their descendants. This chapter looks at the extent to which Chinese languages are being preserved in Canada, and the potential impact of their retention on ethnic Chinese and Canadian identities. Does the retention of the non-official language diminish identification with Canada?

Canada's Changing Non-Official Language Landscape

In 1969, the Canadian Parliament legislated to make English and French the nation's two official languages. However, it refused to legislate official cultures and instead, in 1971, introduced a policy of multiculturalism. At that time a strong message was conveyed to the effect that there was no contradiction between maintaining one's ethnic identity and being Canadian. Then Prime Minister Pierre Trudeau observed during debate in the House of Commons (on October 8, 1971) that the "question of cultural and ethnic pluralism in this country, and the status of our various cultures and languages, [is] an area of study given all too little attention in the past by scholars." He contended that: "adherence to one's ethnic group is influenced not so much by one's origin or mother tongue as by one's sense of belonging to the group, and by the group's collective will to exist."

During the early 1970s the foreign-born population of Canada was predominantly white and European in origin. Since that period, however, the composition of the population has been considerably modified, and some three quarters of new Canadians are of non-European origin. As a consequence, the pattern of non-official languages has shifted significantly with the increase in the numbers of persons whose first language is neither English nor French (see Table 15.1). In 2008 the number of immigrants whose mother tongue was English hit a ten-year high, at just over 26,600, and eclipsed Mandarin as the leading mother tongue of immigrants to Canada. Arabic, Tagalog and Spanish held the next three spots. Immigrants whose mother tongue was Cantonese formed the eighteenth largest language group as their numbers fell from 5,322 in 2000 to 3,434 in 2008. In eleventh spot was a group referred to as "Other Chinese," at 5,693 in 2008, a decline from 8,761 in 2000. These changes in numbers reflected the shift in the regional origins of Chinese immigrants to Canada.

Table 15.1   New Permanent Residents in Canada by Top Five Mother Tongues, 2000–2008

	Total number	English	Mandarin	Arabic	Spanish	Tagalog
2000	227,458	19,560	31,389	15,492	8,719	9,612
2001	250,638	22,135	36 ,78	20,216	10,143	12,557
2002	229,049	18,868	28,127	18,049	10,462	10,610
2003	221,349	18,694	31,715	17,218	12,489	11,442
2004	235,823	22,031	31,456	18,985	14,319	12,443
2005	262,240	22,906	37,321	19,515	17,016	16,332
2006	251,643	24,884	28,049	20,009	17,059	16,099
2007	236,758	26,616	23,208	18,998	16,913	16,537
2008	247,243	28,751	26,086	21,925	16,292	20,835

Source: Citizenship and Immigration Canada 2008.

Among the non-official languages of Canada, Cantonese is the fifth most widely used mother tongue and Mandarin the ninth most widely used (see Figures 15.1 and 15.2). The combination of all Chinese languages into one category in the Census of 1996 made "Chinese" appear to be the most widely spoken non-official language in the country, but the Census of 2001 split the category up, so that Mandarin and Cantonese appeared in fourth and ninth place, respectively, that year. In 2006 Cantonese dropped to fifth place, while Mandarin moved up to seventh place. The most widely spoken non-official language in Canada remains Spanish, though it is spoken more often as a second language rather than as a mother tongue.

Mandarin versus Cantonese

The Census of 2006 showed that Cantonese continued to be the first language of the majority of the Chinese Canadian population, as 361,450 Canadians reported Cantonese as their mother tongue that year, and around 73,000 others reported that they spoke Cantonese as a second language. However, between 1996 and 2006 the number of immigrants arriving in

Figure 15.1 Selected Non-Official Mother Tongues of Canadians, by Thousands of Users, 1996, 2001, and 2006

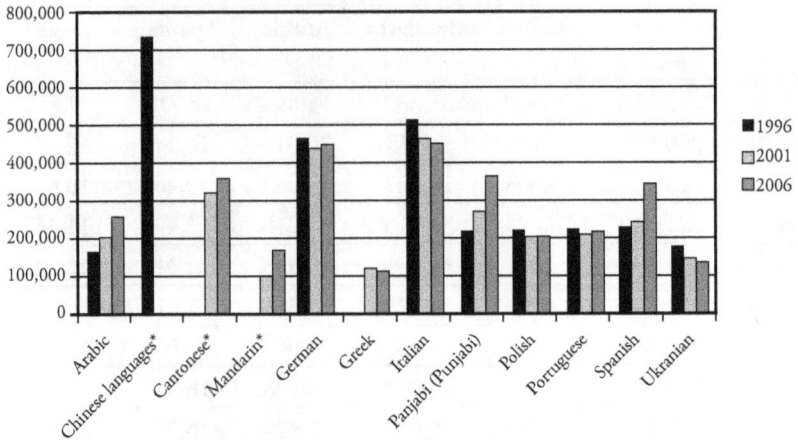

Figure 15.2 Selected Non-Official Languages Spoken in Canada, by Thousands of Speakers, 1996, 2001 and 2006

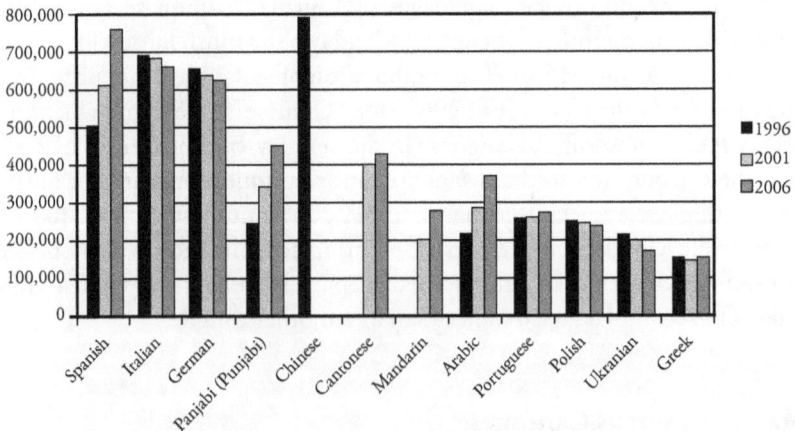

Source: Statistics Canada, Censuses of 1996, 2001 and 2006.

Canada from China whose mother tongue was Mandarin, the dominant language of mainland China, exceeded the number whose mother tongue was Cantonese (see Table 15.2).

Table 15.2 Canadians with Mandarin, Cantonese and Other Chinese Languages as Mother Tongues, 2006

Canada 2006	Cantonese	Mandarin	Chinese, n.o.s.	Total
Total	361 450	170 950	456 705	989 105
Non-immigrants	74 600	17 695	75 650	151 300
Immigrants	282 410	143 820	362 030	788 260
Before 1991	138 780	16 095	145 975	300 850
1991 to 2000	123 440	67 795	128 695	319 930
1991 to 1995	79 855	19 670	58 200	157 725
1996 to 2000	43 585	48 120	70 500	162 205
2001 to 2006	20 180	59 925	87 360	167 465
Non-permanent residents	4 435	9 435	19 025	32 895

Source: Statistics Canada, Census of 2006.

The majority of Cantonese speakers had come to Canada from Hong Kong between the late 60's to mid 70's and in significant numbers in the 80's to late 90's. Immigrants from Guangdong, Vietnam and Southeast Asia also form an integral part of the Canada's Cantonese speaker population. But since the 1990's, the vast majority of new Chinese immigrants have come from mainland China, especially Fujian Province, and tend to speak Mandarin along with their regional languages.

As China's global influence increases, it is likely that immigrants of Chinese origin will urge the younger generation to learn Mandarin. The decline of Cantonese purportedly represents a challenge for the older generation who speak only that language. Nonetheless, the Cantonese language still dominates Chinese Canadian television, and most events organized by the media are still conducted in Cantonese. If you want to get a job in the Chinese service sector in Canada, you still need to know Cantonese.

In 2006, immigrants represented nearly one in five Canadians. Of those with neither English nor French as their mother tongue, some seventy percent were immigrants. Nearly eighty-five percent with Mandarin as their mother tongue were immigrants and this was also the case for seventy-eight percent of those whose mother tongue was

Cantonese. There are nearly twice as many first-generation speakers of mother-tongue Cantonese as there are first-generation speakers of mother-tongue Mandarin, and more than ten times as many in the second generation, while in the third generation there are about sixty percent more speakers of mother-tongue Cantonese than there are speakers of mother-tongue Mandarin (see Table 15.3). For every non-immigrant under the age of fifteen whose mother tongue is Mandarin, there are nearly 2.5 whose mother tongue is Cantonese, but among immigrants under the age of fifteen more than twice as many have Mandarin as their mother tongue as have Cantonese as their mother tongue.

Table 15.3 Generational Status of Mandarin and Cantonese as Mother Tongues among Canadians, 2006

Canada mother tongue 2006	Mandarin	Cantonese
Total	173 730	369 645
1st Generation - subtotal above the age of 15 years	130 090	278 745
1st Generation	116 220	232 140
1.5 Generation*	13 875	46 605
2nd Generation - subtotal above the age of 15 years	3115	39 560
2nd Generation**	2865	38 110
2.5 Generation	250	1 445
3rd + Generation	1240	1 985
Immigrants under 15 years of age	14 940	7 345
Non-immigrants under 15 years of age	14 820	37 540

Notes: The term "1.5 generation" refers to persons who were born outside Canada to parents who were also born outside Canada, and who arrived in Canada, either as citizens or as immigrants, before the age of 12; or to persons who were born outside Canada with one Canadian parent and arrived in Canada as immigrants after the age of 12. The term "2.5 generation" refers to persons who were born in Canada with one parent who was also born in Canada.

Source: Statistics Canada, Census of 2006.

Knowledge of Official Languages among the Chinese Population

Almost all immigrants whose mother tongue is neither English nor French retain their languages of origin. Exceptions arise among immigrants who have arrived in Canada at a very young age, for whom knowledge of the non-official language tends to be eroded over time. However, those monitoring the process of immigrant integration have been particularly interested in the pace at which one or other of the official languages is acquired by persons with neither English nor French as their mother tongue.

In 2006 some 6.4 percent of all immigrants reported speaking neither English nor French (see Figures 15.3 and 15.4). Among those who had arrived before 1991, some 4.8 percent spoke neither official language, among those who had arrived between 1991 and 2001 the proportion was 7.8 percent, and among those who had arrived between 2001 and 2006 the proportion was 9.2 percent. Of the approximately 520,000 Canadians who in 2006 reported speaking neither English nor French, the majority were over the age of fifty-five. Some one fifth of those persons whose mother tongue was Cantonese reported knowledge of neither English nor French, while one sixth of those whose mother tongue was Mandarin did so. As among immigrants in general, most of those whose mother tongue was either Cantonese or Mandarin and who knew neither English nor French were over the age of fifty-five. Some thirty-eight percent of those immigrants who had Cantonese as their mother tongue and had arrived in Canada between 2001 and 2006 reported knowing neither English nor French, as compared to nearly nineteen percent of those whose mother tongue was Mandarin and twenty-one percent of those with other Chinese mother tongues.

The largest communities of Chinese-language-speakers are in Toronto and Vancouver, where their critical mass allows them to work in Chinese languages rather than, or as well as, in English. In 2006 some forty-six percent of Canada's mother-tongue Cantonese population resided in the Toronto region (170,495 people) and another thirty-five percent resided in Vancouver (128,550 people). Among the mother-tongue Mandarin population, some forty-one percent resided in Vancouver (70,410 people) compared to thirty-seven percent in Toronto (63,820 people).

In 2006, around 7.5 percent of Canadians whose mother tongue was neither English nor French used a non-official language at work. Among the mother-tongue Mandarin population, some 18.8 percent used Mandarin most often in the workplace, a proportion that was at twenty-seven

Figure 15.3 Knowledge of English and French among Canadians with Chinese Mother Tongues, 2006 (%)

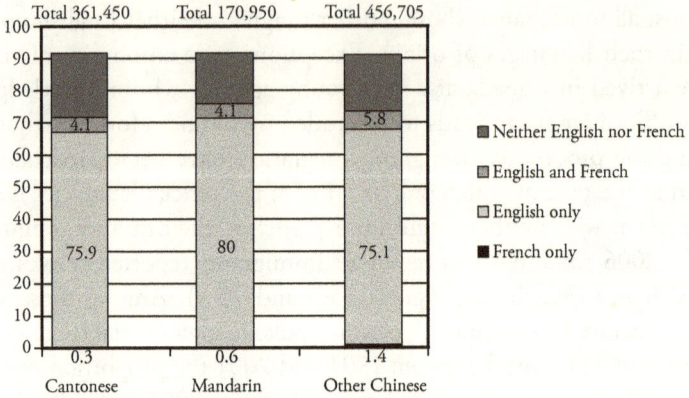

Source: Statistics Canada, Census of 2006.

Figure 15.4 Canadians with Chinese Mother Tongues Having Knowledge of Neither English nor French, 2006 (%)

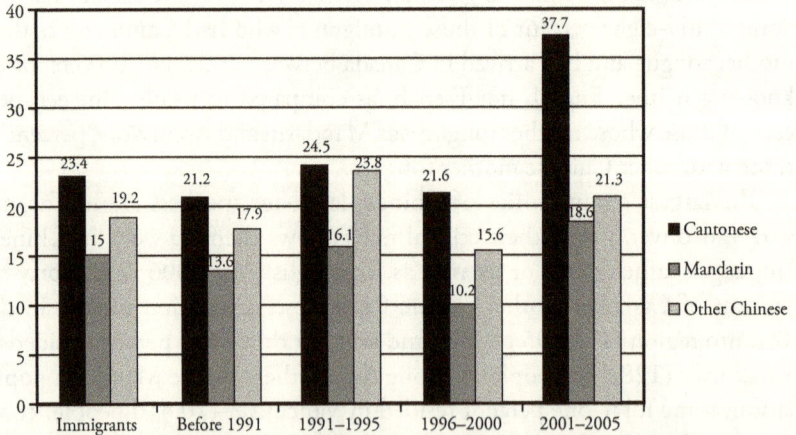

Source: Statistics Canada, Census of 2006.

percent in Vancouver and seventeen percent in Toronto. Among the mother-tongue Cantonese population, some 37.4 percent used Cantonese most often in the workplace, the same percentage did so in Toronto, and nearly twenty-five percent did so in Vancouver.

Language Retention, Ethnic Identification, and Belonging to Canada

Observers of language integration are generally concerned with the extent to which the children of immigrants retain their language of origin, particularly if they believe that retention of the non-official language impedes acquisition of one of the official languages. Canadian Census data support the idea that non-official languages become eroded in the second generation.

Among the second generation in groups of Canadians with non-official mother tongues, there is a broadly similar rate of language transfer, that is, of changing from the language first learned to the use of another language in the home (see Figure 15.5). In 2006, those reporting Punjabi as their mother tongue had the highest rate of home language retention, with some 37.4 percent continuing to speak it most often in their homes, while among those whose mother tongue was Greek only twenty percent continued to speak it in their homes, but overall about one in three persons in the second generation reported speaking their mother tongue most often at home.

The Ethnic Diversity Survey, conducted by Statistics Canada in partnership with the Department of Canadian Heritage in 2002, offers some insight into the use of non-official languages in various contexts, and permits an examination of how language may influence other expressions of identity. The survey reported that, among persons whose mother tongue was neither English nor French, some 68% used a non-official language, with siblings the figure drops to 51% and with friends some 30% use a non-official language while 54% use English only. The survey also provides data about the use of non-official and official languages, and about feelings of belonging, among the Chinese population in Canada (see Table 15.4). There was not much impact on the strength of feeling of belonging to Canada among those Chinese who used mainly English or a non-official language most often with siblings, parents or friends. However, those who used a non-official language most often reported somewhat higher rates of belonging to their ethnic or cultural group.

Figure 15.5 Use of Mother Tongues in the Home by Members of Second Generations in Selected Language Groups for Age Cohorts 15 to 24 and 25 to 34, 2006 (%)

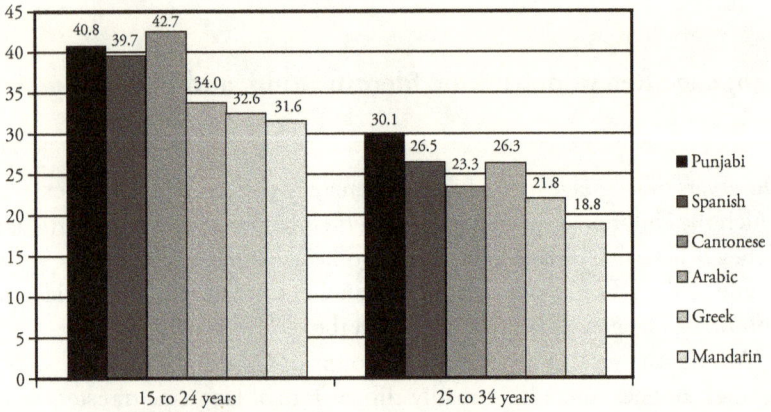

Source: Statistics Canada, Census of 2006.

Table 15.4 Visible Minority Chinese Reporting Belonging to Canada and Belonging to an Ethnic or Cultural Group, 2002 (%)

Percentage 4 and 5 on a five point scale where 5 is very strong	Belonging to Canada		Belonging to ethnic or cultural group	
Chinese Visible Minority	**English**	**Non-official language**	**English**	**Non-official language**
Language of Interview	74.4%	70.1%	51.6%	58.4%
Language Used Most Often with Siblings	76.2%	71.3%	47.1%	57.2%
Language Used Most Often with Parents	75.4%	72.1%	41.8%	58.0%
Language Used Most Often with Friends	76.0%	67.1%	48.6%	58.3%

Source: Ethnic Diversity Survey, Statistics Canada and the Department of Canadian Heritage, 2002.

Before the Census of 1991, a campaign was conducted to encourage the population to write in "Canadian" as their response to the question on ethnic origins. Until then, "Canadian" had not been among the suggested responses on the list provided on the Census form. In the view of the architects of the campaign, ethnicity was divisive and the very reporting of it encouraged interethnic conflict, so writing in "Canadian" was seen as a means of asserting a strengthened Canadian identity. Some 700,000 persons responded to the appeal and made "Canadian" the sixth most popular response to the Census question on ethnic origins. In 1996 the Census form itself listed "Canadian" sixth among the suggested responses to the question, and that year it emerged as the most popular response, with 5.3 million persons declaring "Canadian" their single ethnic origin and another 1.7 million including it as part of a multiple response.

The Census of 2001 saw a further increase in the number of "Canadian" responses, but analysis of these responses suggested that the vast majority of those giving them had previously reported French and British origins, and the vast majority of the members of minority ethnic groups had not shifted to the "Canadian" response, although many had included it in a multiple response. Among those respectively reporting Cantonese or Mandarin as their mother tongue, nearly every person identifying as first- or second-generation identified solely with a minority ethnic origin. Among those in the third or later generations, forty-nine percent of the mother-tongue Cantonese population identified solely with a minority ethnic origin, while thirty-seven percent of the Mandarin mother-tongue population did so. One in five of the persons in the third generation with Cantonese as their mother tongue made "Canadian" part of their response to the question on ethnic origin. Nearly one in three in the third generation with Mandarin as their mother tongue made "Canadian" part of their response.

On the basis of the Census data on the degree of self-identification as "Canadian," some might contend that Canadian identity gets stronger from one generation to the next. It should not be assumed, however, that nominal ethnic Canadianness implies a greater sense of belonging to Canada. Including "Canadian" as part of the response to the Census question on ethnic origin is most prevalent in the third generation. Some analysts are persuaded that self-identifying as ethnically "Canadian" implies a greater sense of belonging to Canada (see Hassman-Howard 1999), while Jeffrey G. Reitz and Rupa Banerjee (2007), working on the basis of the responses to the ethnic self-identification question in the Ethnic Diversity Survey, point to a presumed gap in self-identifying as Canadian between second-generation white Canadians and second-generation visible-minority Canadians. Yet the survey data reveal that, despite much less frequently self-identifying as "Canadian," immigrants had a stronger sense of belonging to Canada than their descendants did. The majority of the Chinese, South Asian and Black respondents to the survey reported a strong sense of belonging to their ethnic or cultural group, yet members of all these groups reported an even stronger sense of belonging to Canada (see Figure 15.6).

As for differences in the sense of belonging to Canada between first-generation and second-generation members of visible minorities, they were not very substantial (see Figure 15.7), although it is possible to make the gap appear wider by focusing only on those who reported "very strong" feelings of belonging (see Reitz and Banerjee 2007).

It is often assumed that where the sense of belonging to Canada is weak, it is due to the persistence of identification with an ancestral culture or ethnic origin. Following such logic, it might be assumed that Chinese Canadians possess a weaker sense of belonging to Canada than members of other groups do because of the persistence of their ties to Chinese culture. Such explanations are at the root of social integration theory, which assumes that

Figure 15.6 Proportions of Members of Selected Visible Minority Groups Reporting Belonging to Canada and Belonging to Ethnic or Cultural Groups, 2002 (%)

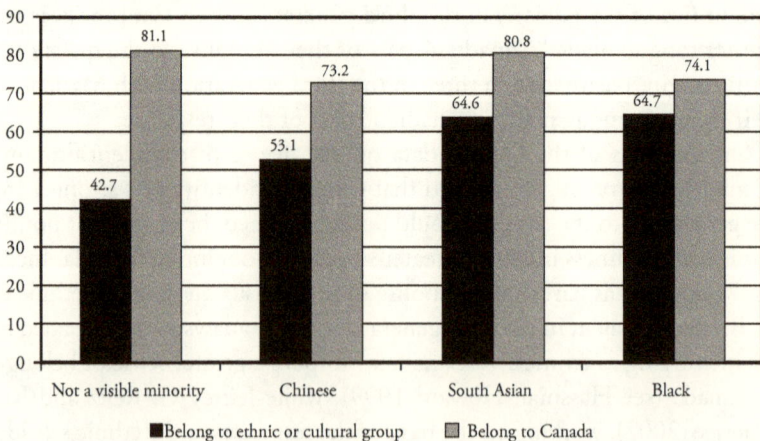

Source: Statistics Canada, Ethnic Diversity Survey, 2002.

Figure 15.7 Proportions of Members of Selected Visible Minority Groups Aged 30 to 44 Years, and in First and Second Generations, Reporting Belonging to Canada, 2002 (%)

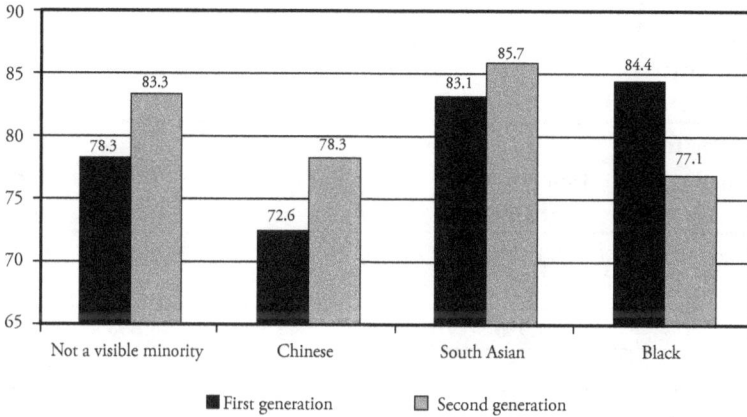

Source: Statistics Canada, Ethnic Diversity Survey, 2002.

ties to countries of origin are an important obstacle to cultural adjustment. Yet the data from the Ethnic Diversity Survey do not support this notion (see Table 15.5). Around eighty-five percent of those Chinese respondents who reported strong rates of ethnic belonging also reported a strong sense of belonging to Canada. By contrast, some sixty-three percent of those who reported a very weak sense of belonging to their ethnic group reported a strong sense of belonging to Canada.

Among those who identified as Chinese in the Ethnic Diversity Survey, 11 percent reported that all their friends were of the same first ancestry as themselves and 38 percent reported that most of them were. The combined total, 49 percent, compared with 37 percent of the South Asian population and twenty-two percent of the white population reporting that all or most of their friends had the same first ancestry. Social capital theorists contend that there is a distinction between "good" and "bad" social capital, the former referring to bonding between members of the same ethnic group and the latter to bridging across ethnic groups. Yet the data from the survey indicated that one's share of friends of the same ancestry had virtually no bearing on the strength of one's sense of belonging to an ethnic group or to Canada (see Figure 15.8).

Table 15.5 Sense of Belonging to an Ethnic or Cultural Group Correlated with Sense of Belonging to Canada among the Visible Minority Chinese Population, 2002 (%)

Visible Minority Chinese	Belonging to ethnic or cultural group				
Belong to Canada	1 (not strong at all)	2	3	4	5 (very strong)
Total 4 and 5 combined	63.5%	70.5%	65.8%	79.9%	85.5%
4	29.9%	31.2%	31.9%	44.6%	20.6%
5 - very strong	33.6%	39.3%	33.9%	35.3%	64.9%

Source: Statistics Canada, Ethnic Diversity Survey, 2002.

Figure 15.8 Correlation between Having Friends of the Same First Ancestry and Having a Strong Sense of Belonging to Canada for the Visible Minority Chinese Population, 2002 (%)

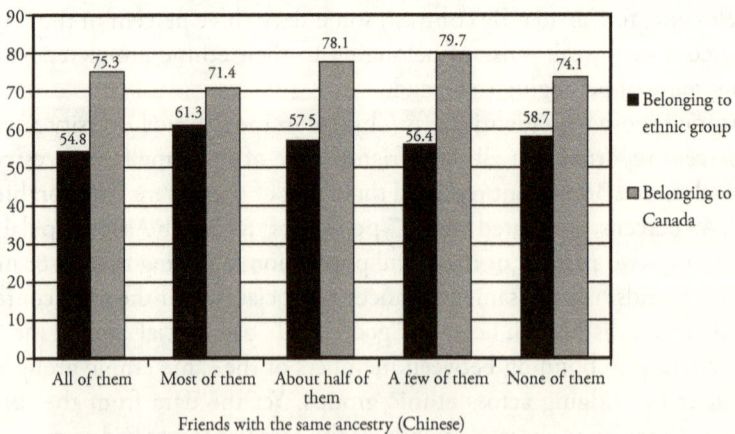

Source: Statistics Canada, Ethnic Diversity Survey, 2002.

Finally, the number of trips taken back to the country of origin by Chinese Canadians did not have much influence on their sense of belonging to Canada (see Figure 15.9).

Citizenship is one area where there appeared to be significant differences among Canadians of Chinese origin in the strength of their sense of belonging to Canada. Chinese respondents reporting Canadian citizenship indicated a stronger sense of belonging to Canada than those holding dual citizenship, that is, citizenship of Canada as well as citizenship in their country of birth. Some seventy-five percent of the former had a strong sense of belonging to Canada, compared with nearly sixty-six percent of the latter.

Models of Diversity and Cultural Bridging between Canada and China

Overseas migrants play an important role in the relationship between Canada and China. Although most migrants would not describe themselves as cultural brokers, very often persons of Chinese origin in Canada establish bridges between the cultures, and, while their numbers are relatively few,

Figure 15.9 Correlation between Number of Trips to Country of Birth and Sense of Belonging to Canada for the Visible Minority Chinese Population, 2002 (%)

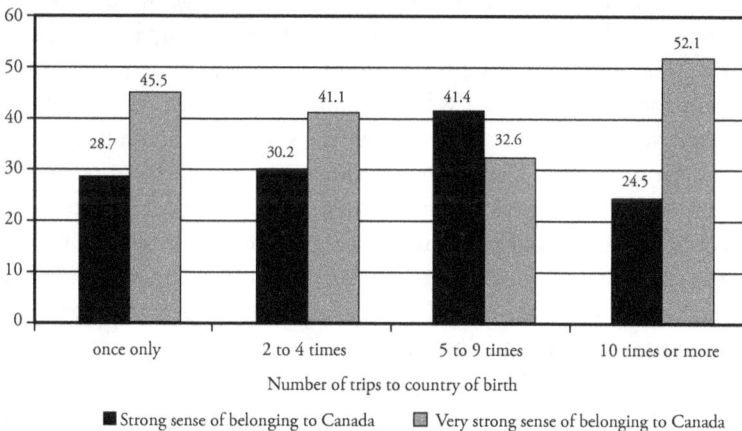

Source: Statistics Canada, Ethnic Diversity Survey, 2002.

persons of Canadian origin living and working in China also play a role in the bridging process. However, cultural brokerage requires that those making up the bridge possess dual or multiple attachments. The persistence of such attachments remains at the very centre of the debate in Canada over the nation's approach to managing diversity. While some feel that adjustment to life in Canada does not require that minority ethnic cultures and traditions be abandoned, others insist that if Canada is to build a cohesive society, immigrants and, more importantly, their descendants need to give up their ethnic and cultural ties to countries of origin. There is a need to understand better how the persistence of migrant ties influences cultural and commercial ties between countries, and specifically, in the case of Chinese migration, the ties between Canada and China.

Critics of the Canadian multicultural model believe that the persistence of ethnic cultures undercuts national identification, but very often their criticism has fallen short of providing evidence for the ways in which this undercutting happens. Too often, it is assumed that if the sense of belonging to Canada is insufficient, it must be because the sense of belonging to a minority ethnic culture is too strong. As demonstrated above, however, in the case of Canada's Chinese population their sense of ethnic belonging does not in fact diminish their sense of belonging to Canada, nor does the degree of contact with members of the same group (the "bad" social capital) have that effect. Only the holding of dual citizenship appears to make a noticeable impact on the strength of the sense of belonging to Canada, and even in these cases the difference is not so very great.

In the Canadian multicultural paradigm, knowledge of non-official languages has not been deemed essential to ethnic belonging: in effect, a strong sense of belonging to one's ethnic origins is not seen to require knowledge of the associated language. While members of ethnic communities may disagree with this view, it has not been the subject of much public debate. That is not to say that Canadian government policy does not recognize the importance of language as an expression of culture. It does so, after all, with respect to the country's French and Aboriginal communities. Yet there is no historic commitment to the preservation and enhancement of non-official languages, and there seems to be no strong reason for the government to extend support to such an objective.

As for the role of Chinese languages, whether as mother tongues or second languages, they do not appear to have a considerable effect on the strength of the Canadian Chinese population's sense of belonging to Canada. On the other hand, they do influence the strength of the sense of belonging to the ethnic or cultural group. In other words, for the Chinese population language retention is an important element of ethnic belonging. Again, however, that does not mean that Chinese Canadians cannot feel a strong sense of ethnic belonging without knowledge of any of the Chinese languages.

The Chinese population of Canada is often wrongly presumed to be linguistically monolithic. In fact, its linguistic diversity to some extent reflects the historic migration patterns of the Chinese in Canada. It is also in part a microcosm of the ethnic diversity in China, which is not well-known to many Canadians. Understanding the internal diversity of the Chinese Canadian population and the diversity of the population of China will be extremely useful to those engaged in building bridges between the two countries.

References

Citizenship and Immigration Canada. (2009). "Facts and Figures 2008—Immigration Overview: Permanent and Temporary Residents." Ottawa: Citizenship and Immigration Canada. Online at http://www.cic.gc.ca/english/resources/statistics/facts2008/index.asp [consulted January 14, 2011].

Howard-Hassman, Rhoda E. (1999). "Canadian as an Ethnic Category: Implications for Multiculturalism and National Unity." *Canadian Public Policy* 25:4, 523–37.

Reitz, Jeffrey G., and Rupa Banerjee. (2007). "Racial Inequality, Social Cohesion, and Policy Issues in Canada," in *Belonging?: Diversity, Recognition and Shared Citizenship in Canada*, ed. Keith Banting, Thomas J. Courchene, and F. Leslie Seidle. Montreal: Institute for Research on Public Policy, 489–545.

Statistics Canada. (1996, 2001, 2006). *Census of Canada*. Ottawa: Statistics Canada.

Statistics Canada. (2002). "Ethnic Diversity Survey (EDS)." Ottawa: Statistics Canada. Online at http://www.statcan.gc.ca/imdb-bmdi/4508-eng.htm [consulted January 14, 2011].

Chapter 16

Changing Territorial Strategies: Chinese Immigrants in Canada

Huhua Cao and Olivier Dehoorne

Canada is a country whose demographic evolution has depended upon immigration. In 2006 19.6 percent of its total population, or 6.2 million people, had been born outside Canada, and 3.8 million had settled in Canada after 1980. These new migration flows were part of a broader immigration boom in Canada, reflecting important changes in the country's immigration policies. First, in 1967 the policy of giving Europeans preferential access to Canada was abandoned. Second, the official objectives of immigration policy were broadened beyond responding to Canada's need for workers to include reuniting families and respecting the humanitarian tradition of admitting refugees. In addition, since the end of the 1970s the provincial governments have been responsible for policy-making and management with respect to the selection and integration of immigrants. Against this changing backdrop, the average number of immigrants increased annually throughout the 1980s and 1990s. While 102,000 people migrated to Canada between 1981 and 1985, 823,925 settled in the country between 1991 and 1995, and then 1,109,980 came between 2001 and 2006.

This movement of recent immigrants is also characterized by a profound change in the source countries of immigration: Europe is no longer the main source of immigrants, having been replaced by the Asia–Pacific region. In 2008, forty-six percent of immigrants in Canada came from this region, including those from mainland China, India, the Philippines, Pakistan, South Korea, Sri Lanka, Taiwan and Hong Kong. The highest proportion of Asian immigrants was from the world's two most populated countries, China and India. For instance, between 1999 and 2008 393,941 Chinese settled in Canada, 87.3 per cent of them being from mainland China and the rest from Hong Kong, Macau or Taiwan (see Citizenship and Immigration Canada 2009).

From a quantitative perspective the evolution of Chinese nationals' migration to Canada is particularly interesting. Mainland China (refers to the Chinese population living in People's Republic of China, excluding Hong Kong and Macao) has become the country with the largest proportion of citizens migrating to Canada since the mid-1990s (see Shi 2004). The specific motivations of Chinese migrants to Canada have also evolved considerably over time. While those who arrived around the beginning of the 20th century left their country of origin in the hope of escaping poverty and political instability, recent migration flows have been more selective, mostly consisting of students, entrepreneurs and investors (see Lai 2003).

Chinese Immigration to Canada: A Historical Overview

Chinese immigration to Canada started in the middle of the nineteenth century (see Lai 1988, Li 1998 and Wickberg 1984). These flows were essentially composed of single men, and were part of a broader wave of immigration to Canada that had started through the colonial empires in Southeast Asia. Migrants from mainland China sought to escape misery in a country where the population had nearly doubled from 200 to 250 million in 1750 to 410 million in 1850, while access to agricultural land remained limited (see Li 1998). Military defeat, political instability, famines and natural disasters, including floods, were also crucial motivations for migrating to North America.

Migratory procedures were of two kinds. The first was by means of a work contract, which was the procedure through which the labourers known as "coolies" migrated to Canada. Coolies, who were at the bottom of the socio-economic ladder, were hired on contract to work in the country of destination for a certain period of time, and had to reimburse the person involved in paying for and facilitating their migration to the relevant country. Once the contract was over, coolies could find themselves jobs on their own (see Wickberg 1984). The second procedure was migration in stages, meaning that migrants would, first, work in the country of destination until they had enough money to return to their country of origin; then they would usually get married there; and later they would return to their host countries, taking sons, nephews or other male relatives along with them. A migratory network slowly emerged out of such flows. Depending on their financial circumstances and the opportunities available in the host country, migrants also brought their spouse along and rebuilt their households in the host country.

The first Chinese immigrants were mostly coolies hired in groups to work on construction projects or in mining, but after 1900 migration in stages became the more common procedure (see Wickberg 1984). The first wave of Chinese immigrants came from British colonies, including those in what is now Eastern Canada, as well as from California, and settled in British Columbia, especially on Vancouver Island, in response to the Fraser River Gold Rush of 1858–1860 (see Lai 1988). The second wave of Chinese migration into the province started during the construction of the transcontinental railway at the end of the 1870s. Around 1,500 Chinese arrived in Canada from the United States to work on the construction of the line between 1880 and 1881, and they were joined by more than 16,000 other Chinese immigrants, including 10,000 who came directly from China (see Lai 1988 and Wickberg 1984).

By the beginning of the 20th century an average of 2,000 Chinese immigrants were settling in Canada each year. The vast majority of them were in British Columbia, although starting in 1880 a minority went all the way to Eastern Canada. As their professions diversified, Chinese enterprises moved beyond making, importing and/or selling goods exclusive to the needs of the Chinese immigrant community, as in the case of laundry businesses that dispatched Chinese pioneers across Canada. Some Chinese also opened western-style restaurants, especially in Manitoba and those parts of the Prairies that are now Alberta and Saskatchewan. Starting in the 1890s, however, the Chinese faced an increasingly limited job market, due to pressures from trade unions and politicians, British Columbia's Legislative Assembly even passed a law prohibiting the use of Asian labour, which its supporters justified as a response to an explosion at a coalmine in Nanaimo for which Chinese workers were apparently responsible, and which killed 200 people (see Wickberg 1984). Next, succumbing to pressures from groups in British Columbia and elsewhere, the federal Parliament also legislated to restrict Chinese immigration, in effect from January 1, 1902. (It is worth noting that during this period Asian immigrants were facing similar forms of exclusion elsewhere in North America: the U.S. Chinese Exclusion Act was passed in 1882 and became permanent in 1902.) Laws deterring Chinese immigration had already been in effect since the completion of the Canadian Pacific Railway in 1885, including a CA$ 50 head tax. The Canadian legislation of 1902 stated that a ship could transport only one Chinese migrant for every fifty tons of merchandise and increased the head tax, effectively an entry fee for Chinese migrants, to CA$ 100. In 1903, Parliament increased it to 500 dollars, but exempted those in six special categories from having to pay it: established tradesmen (a rather vague term that led to many abuses), diplomats, religious ministers, tourists, students and scholars (see Wickberg 1984). The head tax was the subject of a public apology by Prime Minister Stephen Harper in 2006 (see Office of the Prime Minister 2006).

The restrictions on Chinese immigration did not have significant effects, and the Chinese population of Canada, which had been 4,383 in 1881 and 9,129 in 1891, rose to 17,312 in 1901 and to 27,831 in 1911 (see Li 1998). The number of Chinese immigrants into British Columbia in particular also continued to increase, although many of them left the province by train to settle in the East. This diffusion, however, fuelled the rise of powerful anti-Chinese movements throughout the country and led the federal Parliament to legislate a total ban on Chinese immigration into Canada in 1923. During the period of exclusion, which lasted from 1924 to 1947, only a few Chinese were able to enter Canada (see Lai 1988), and the Chinese population of Canada declined by around twenty-five percent between 1931 and 1941.

From 1945 onward the Chinese communities in Canada pressured the Canadian government on two issues: the repeal of the ban on further immigration and the right of Chinese citizens in British Columbia to vote, which only the Cooperative Commonwealth Federation had supported until then (see Wickberg 1984). The repeal of the immigration ban in May 1947 constituted a significant moral victory for the Chinese Canadian population, and the introduction of Canadian citizenship the same year gave the right to vote to all citizens. Nevertheless, institutional restrictions on Chinese immigration continued until 1962, illustrating the racial prejudices that still underlaid Canadian immigration policy in relation to non-white populations. In particular, the only category of immigration available to Chinese was that of relatives sponsored by Chinese Canadians. During the 1950s, many Chinese immigrants were women and children who had been separated from their husbands or fathers during the long period of exclusion.

In 1962, the government of Canada changed immigration policy by creating four categories of admission (see Li 1998). The first two allowed independent migration by educated individuals entering the liberal professions, while the third was for immigrants who had privileged relationships with Canadian citizens or permanent residents, and in all three of these categories, immigrants' racial background or country of origin no longer constituted a criterion for admission into Canada. The fourth category, however, enabled Canadian citizens or permanent residents to sponsor only Europeans or US citizens seeking admission. The new policy of 1962 enabled the Chinese without family ties in Canada to enter the country as independent immigrants for the first time since 1923.

Changes in the composition and characteristics of the Chinese Canadian population were becoming obvious by the mid-1960s, but the last remnants of racial discrimination against the Chinese were not abandoned until 1967, the same year in which the Cultural Revolution directly affected Guangdong and made some impact on Hong Kong too (see Wickberg 1984). Direct migration from mainland China remained restricted because of the "closed door" imposed by Mao Zedong's regime since 1949, so most Chinese migrating to Canada came from Hong Kong, Taiwan and diaspora communities in Southeast Asia, Southern Africa, Latin America (especially Peru) and the West Indies. It was only starting in 1974, under the family reunification programme initiated during Prime Minister Pierre Trudeau's visit to China in 1973, that immigration from mainland China became a significant factor (see Liu 1997). Between 1974 and 1988 most of the mainland Chinese who migrated to Canada did so with the help of their already established families or through social networks. Additionally, as a result of Deng Xiaoping's economic reforms and "open door" policy, introduced from December 1978, around 50,000 mainland Chinese students studied in Western democratic countries between 1978 and 1987, 40,000 of whom were funded by the Chinese government, the other 10,000 being self-supporting (see Gittings 1989). Starting in the 1990s, the level of education of immigrants from mainland China to Canada was higher than that of other immigrants settling in the country (see Liu 1997). It is worth noting that, as a result of a change in Ottawa's immigration policy following the Tiananmen incident in 1989, many mainland Chinese immigrants during this period were admitted as independent immigrants.

The specific motivations of Chinese migrating to Canada have changed considerably over the past 150 years. While the need to escape poverty and misery constituted the primary motivation for the first wave of Chinese immigrants, by the 1960s, and especially in the 1980s and 1990s, migration became much more targeted, involving students, qualified professionals, and entrepreneurs and business owners looking for an economic environment favourable to investment and private sector employment (see Lai 2003). Nevertheless, the general theme of pursuing economic opportunity has remained dominant through the decades.

Chinese Immigrants on Canadian Territory

Chinese immigration to Canada took on a different dimension starting in the 1980s, following the historical developments outlined above, and the spatial diffusion that had occurred around the beginning of the 20th century became more obvious as the century ended. In particular, Vancouver used to be the main gateway through which Chinese immigrants entered Canada, but in recent years other migratory trends have developed. First, immigration from mainland China increased rapidly from the 1970s onward. Second, Chinese immigrants are now most likely to live in the largest and most dynamic urban areas of Canada, and around ninety-five per cent of them are located in just fourteen of Canada's thirty-three Census metropolitan areas, or CMAs (see Table 16.1).

Until the mid-1990s Chinese immigrants gave priority to just two urban centres in Canada: Toronto and Vancouver (see Table 16.2). Their geographical concentration became more and more obvious from one Census to another: less than sixty-one percent of Chinese Canadians lived in one or the other of these two cities in 1961, but by 2006 more than seventy percent of them did. From the beginning of 1970s, Vancouver gradually lost its status as first-choice Canadian host city for Chinese immigrants.

Table 16.1 **Numbers and Main Destinations of Immigrants from Mainland China to Canada, in Successive Periods from before 1961 to 2001–2006**

	Canada	14 CMAs	Proportion in the 14 CMAs (%)
Before 1961	13,865	12,325	88.9
1961–1970	17,745	16,435	92.6
1971–1980	39,355	37,405	95.0
1981–1990	62,940	60,395	96.0
1991–2000	177,925	169,645	95.3
1991–1995	69,640	66,800	95.9
1996–2000	108,290	102,845	95.0
2001–2006	155,105	146,690	94.6

Source: Statistics Canada, Census of 2006.

Table 16.2 Immigrants from Mainland China Going to Fourteen Canadian CMAs, in Successive Periods from Before 1961 to 2001–2006

	Total	Before 1961	1961–1970	1971–1980	1981–1990	1991–1995	1996–2000	2001–2006
Toronto	191,120	3,280	5,535	14,945	26,860	29,065	47,575	63,855
Vancouver	137,245	4,895	5,950	13,230	19,505	23,525	30,350	39,790
Montreal	34,475	950	1,005	1,825	3,465	4,085	6,970	16,180
Calgary	24,710	955	1,070	2,615	3,420	3,300	3,830	9,510
Edmonton	14,630	700	895	2,105	2,960	1,810	2,255	3,905
Ottawa–Gatineau	14,055	315	600	815	1,225	2,220	4,980	3,905
Hamilton	4,900	135	140	290	645	490	1,300	1,910
Victoria	4,355	470	420	480	720	600	835	835
Winnipeg	4,060	215	335	385	525	440	775	1,375
Kitchener	4,015	45	60	210	280	315	1,300	1,795
Windsor	3,780	115	130	185	285	455	1,255	1,350
London	2,525	60	110	85	210	180	715	1,165
Saskatoon	1,575	145	135	125	125	205	340	500
St. Catharines–Niagara	1,470	45	50	110	170	110	365	615

Source: Statistics Canada, Census of 2006.

In 1961, it was home to thirty-five percent of the Chinese immigrant population of Canada, but by 2006 it was home to only twenty-nine percent.
However, this proportionate decline does not imply a numerical decrease in
the Chinese population of the city: while there were 23,255 newly arrived
Chinese immigrants in Vancouver in the period 1991–1995, there were
39,790 of them in the period 2001–2006. Since the 1980s, the Greater
Toronto Area has been the most popular destination, accommodating
forty-one percent of newly arrived Chinese immigrants, or 63,855 people,
during the period 2001–2006.

Since the beginning of the 1990s, the other twelve CMAs, particularly
Montreal, Calgary, Edmonton and Ottawa–Gatineau, have had significantly increasing numbers of Chinese immigrants (see Figure 16.1). The
Census of 2006 showed that, for the first time, the total number of newly
arrived Chinese immigrants in these twelve CMAs exceeded the number
in Vancouver, and that the rate of increase in that total number between
2001 and 2006 was almost the same as in Toronto between 1996 and 2000.

**Figure 16.1 Increase in Numbers of Chinese Immigrants in Toronto,
Vancouver and Twelve Other CMAs, in Successive Periods from
before 1961 to 2001–2006**

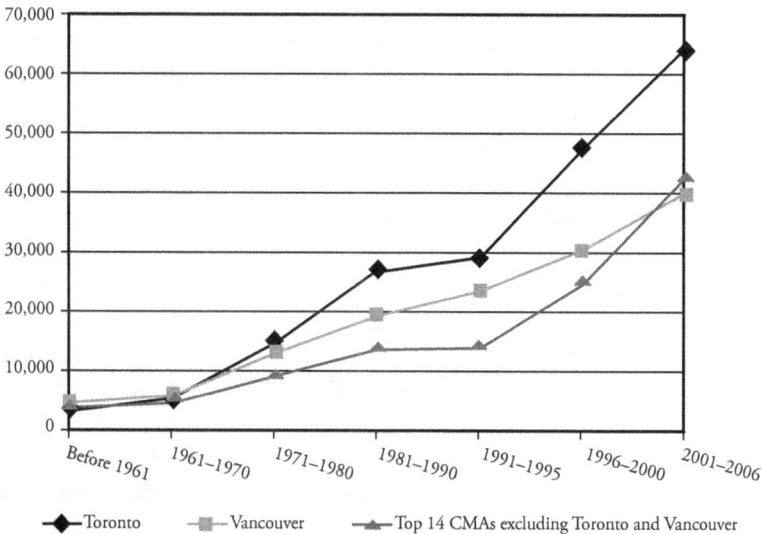

Source: Statistics Canada, Census of 2006.

It is clear, therefore, that recent Chinese immigrants have tended to spread further throughout Canada, particularly its urban centres.

Given the urban concentration of Chinese immigrants, the findings on their presence in these fourteen CMAs correlate with observable changes in their distribution across the provinces of Canada (see Figure 16.2 and Map 16.1). British Columbia was historically the main host area for the newly arrived Chinese population, but is now behind Ontario, where the numbers of new Chinese immigrants doubled between the period 1996–2001 and the period 2001–2006, accounting for more than fifty percent of all new Chinese immigrants in Canada in 2006. The flows of Chinese immigrants thus suggest an increasing tendency to favour Ontario, especially the Greater Toronto Area and neighbouring cities. For instance, Ottawa–Gatineau, Hamilton, Kitchener, Windsor and St. Catharines–Niagara all witnessed considerable rises in their Chinese populations from the 1990s onward. In Hamilton, the number of newly arrived Chinese immigrants went from 645 between 1981 and 1990 to 3,210 between 1996 and 2006, while the cities of Kitchener, Windsor and London received 3,095, 2,605 and 1,880 newly arrived Chinese immigrants, respectively, between 1996 and 2006, compared to fewer than 300 during the 1980s. The most significant increase was in the Ottawa–Gatineau area, with 8,885 new Chinese immigrants between 1996 and 2006, eight times as many as between 1981 and 1990. The Chinese population in Ontario has undeniably benefited these cities, particularly those located along the urban corridor stretching toward Montreal (see Map 16.1). The economic dynamism of the region, especially in the area of new technologies, was presumably a decisive factor in this choice of geographical location.

In contrast, Chinese immigration into the province of Quebec and the three Prairie provinces of Alberta, Saskatchewan and Manitoba illustrates a more nuanced pattern, with stable flows until the 1990s, and then a significant increase in both the numbers and proportions of Chinese immigrants since the year 2000. This new increase largely comprises concentrations of Chinese immigrants in Montreal for Quebec, and in Calgary, Edmonton, Winnipeg and Saskatoon for the Prairies. The number of newly arrived Chinese immigrants in Montreal went from 3,465 in the 1980s to 23,150 in the period 1996–2006, a near-sevenfold increase. Similar tendencies were observed in Calgary and Edmonton: these two cities were host to 13,340 and 6,160 new Chinese immigrants, respectively, in the period 1996–2006, compared to only 3,420 and 2,960, respectively, during the 1980s. Montreal attracted a lot of Chinese immigrants mainly because the

**Figure 16.2 Increase in Numbers of Chinese Immigrants in the Canadian
Provinces, in Successive Periods from before 1961 to 2001–2006**

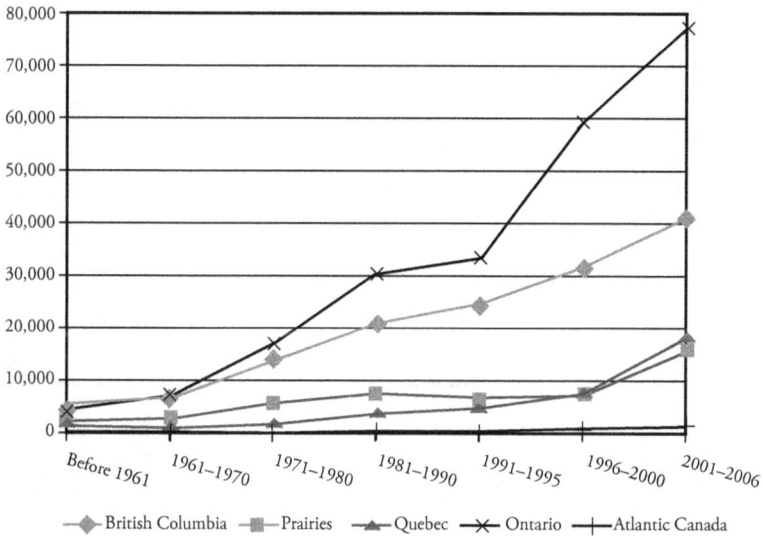

Source: Statistics Canada, Census of 2006.

city is part of the dynamic urban corridor stretching from London to Montreal, and is also bilingual. As for Calgary and Edmonton, the economic
boom and rapid growth experienced in Alberta was no doubt the main
factor attracting new Chinese immigrants.

Between Chinatown and the Suburbs: Plural Immigrant Communities

As part of the institutional expression of significant racial discrimination,
the concept of "Chinatown" was initially associated with the building of an
enclave that culturally and geographically isolated Chinese immigrants from
the rest of the Canadian population. It was also at the heart of the larger
process of assimilation of Canadian-born Chinese and their adaptation to the
host society. Then, as discussed above, new dimensions in Chinese immigration started to develop in the 1960s, and became more evident during the

**Map 16.1   Evolution of Spatial Distribution of Immigrants from Mainland
China in Selected Canadian CMAs, 1990 and 2006**

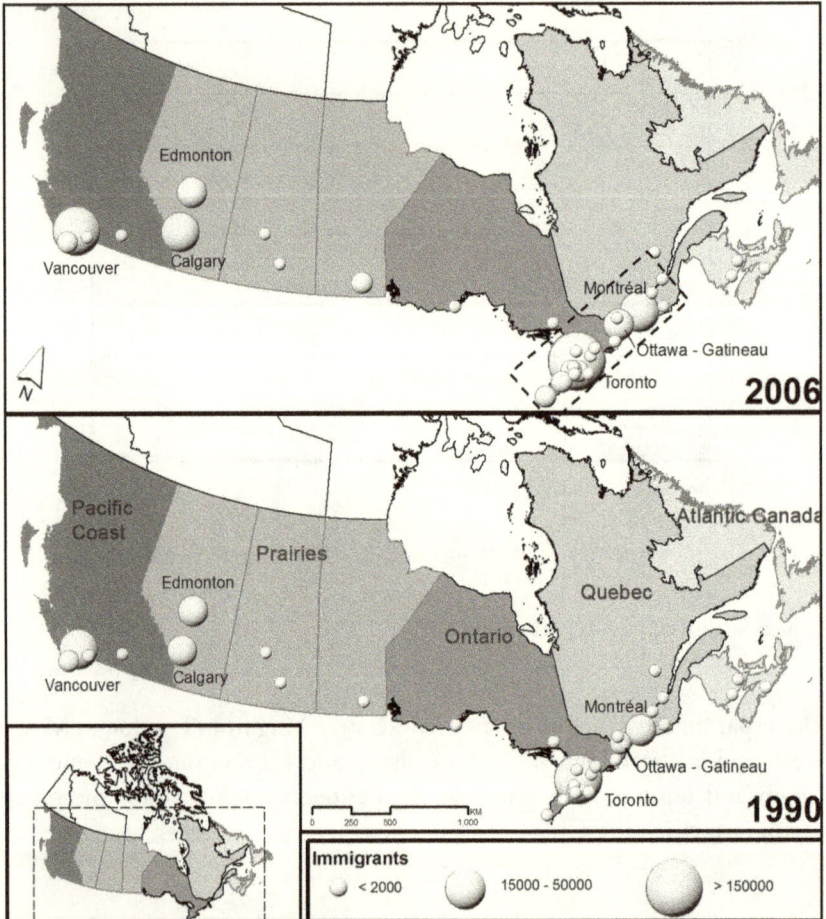

Source: Statistics Canada, Census of 2006.

1980s and 1990s. Accompanied by investment, they facilitated the revitaliza-
tion of old Chinatowns, and contributed to the development of new ones
(see Lai 2003), enabling the opening of Chinese or Asian shopping centres in
suburbs, especially in the Greater Toronto Area and in Vancouver. These new
development projects were made possible by transnational capital originating
from China. Chinatown became a symbolic cultural and commercial centre

for the Chinese communities in Canada, although it was not necessarily a residential area for new immigrants (see Li 2000).

Suburbanization began in major urban centres in North America in the 1960s and had a considerable impact on new Chinese immigrants' choice of residential area. In New York, Los Angeles and San Francisco the spatial mobility of Chinese immigrants stretches all the way to suburbs, which for a long time were considered ethnically and racially homogenous residential areas for the most socioeconomically privileged (see Fang and Brown 1999). Chinese Americans have increasingly left areas with high concentrations of ethnic groups, and chosen to settle in neighbourhoods where work opportunities are better. Chinese living in suburbs also seem to have a higher socioeconomic status than those who live in downtown Chinese neighbourhoods. Residents of Chinatowns are often older, have lower levels of education, and have lower incomes, and are distinct from the younger generation of Chinese who have benefited from greater geographical mobility, better education and better knowledge of English.

In Toronto, Vancouver and Montreal the number of "visible minority neighbourhoods"—defined as Census sectors where more than thirty percent of the population comprises members of visible minorities (Statistics Canada, 2004)—rose from six in 1981 to 254 in 2001, and slightly more than sixty percent of these neighbourhoods were Chinese (see Keung 2004). In Toronto, however, most Chinese have chosen to live in the suburbs and less than ten percent live downtown. Some Chinese have settled in certain suburbs of Toronto as a result of the development of high-technology industries and better job opportunities.

Comparisons between Chinese living in ethnic enclaves and those living outside them indicate that there are significant socioeconomic differences, which are particularly marked in Toronto (see Lo and Wang 1997). Suburban Chinese have benefited from higher levels of human capital, especially since the mid-1980s. At that time the majority of them came from Hong Kong and Taiwan, but since the 1990s more and more Chinese have migrated from mainland China as independent migrants, investors and/or business owners. In contrast, Chinese who live in downtown Toronto are predominantly from the southern parts of mainland China, Hong Kong or Vietnam and arrived before the 1960s. They are on average older, were either refugees or settled in Canada under the family reunification programme, and suffer from a higher unemployment rate.

A detailed look at the Chinese in one Canadian city will illustrate these broader developments. In Ottawa, one person out of five is now an immigrant and one person out of seven is a member of a visible minority, and it has been projected that these proportions will double over the next twenty years. The Chinese community in the city comprises more than 30,000 people and constitutes the largest visible minority (see O'Neill 2003). In the period 1991–2006 more than 11,105 new immigrants from mainland China settled in Ottawa, representing around thirty percent of the total Chinese population of the city. The first Chinese arrived in Ottawa near the end of the 19th century, following their involvement in railway construction (see Li 2000), but as recently as the early 1960s there were still only around 1,000 Chinese residents, of whom 315 were from mainland China. By 1981 an estimated 3,800 Chinese people lived in the city and by 1991 there were 7,600, settled in most of the neighbourhoods all over Ottawa, although there was already a clear tendency to concentrate in suburban neighbourhoods (see Map 16.2). Some Chinese still prefer to live around Chinatown, but suburbanization has become more and more prominent since the late 1990s.

Effectively, the Chinese immigration boom started in the mid-1990s in Ottawa. Opportunities in high-technology industries were among the main motives for immigration. Many Chinese engineers from mainland China settled in Kanata, where information technology corporations such as Nortel had their headquarters. Nortel alone hired more than 10,000 Chinese immigrants between the mid-1990s and the beginning of 2000. There was a very important presence of Chinese immigrants in Kanata, and the community also opened Chinese food stores and small enterprises specializing in subcontracting. Kanata became one of the residential areas most preferred by the Chinese population in Ottawa. However, this changed suddenly with the downfall of Nortel and other high-tech companies around the beginning of the 21st century. Many of the Chinese workers who had migrated to Canada from the mid-1990s were left unemployed, many of them left, and some of them returned to China, indicating that they lacked roots in the city (see Rao 2001). However, in 2010 the Chinese multinational corporation Huawei Technologies announced a partnership and investment of CA$ 50 million in the Ottawa Centre for Research and Innovation, bringing in 180 jobs in research and development alone (see CTV News 2010). The arrival of this Chinese firm may help to breathe new life into a struggling industry and give new opportunities to the pre-existing pool of skilled labour.

Compared to other Chinatowns in Canada, Ottawa's Chinatown has had a short history, which started when 4,000 immigrants from Indochina settled in the city during the 20th century, opening restaurants, grocery

Map 16.2   Spatial Distribution of Chinese toward Suburban Areas of Ottawa, 1960, 1990, and 2006

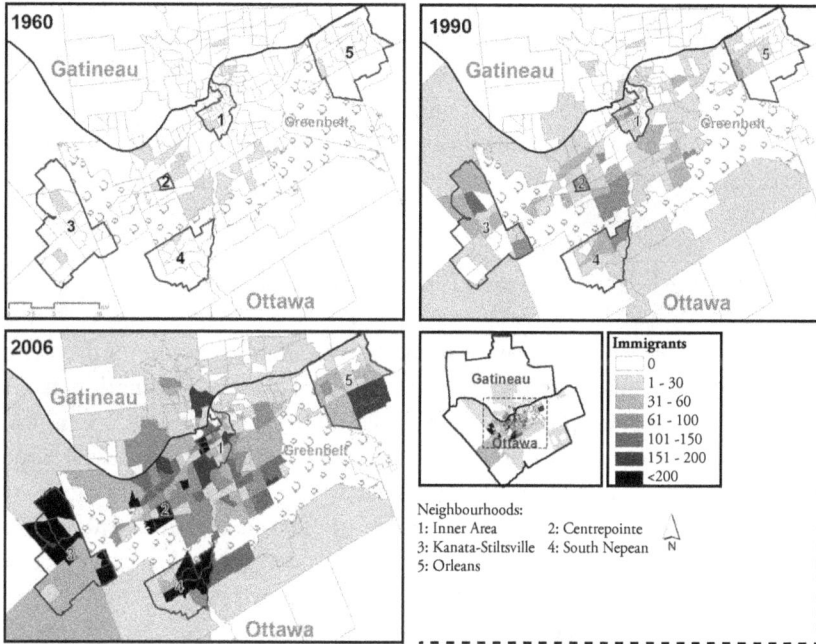

Source: Based on data from Statistics Canada, Census of 2006.

stores and laundromats downtown (see Li 2000). The first waves of Chinese immigrants in Ottawa came from areas of China other than the mainland, such as Hong Kong and Taiwan, which had been more influenced by the West. They were much more market-oriented, spoke Cantonese and English, and in many cases were Christians. Unlike these earlier cohorts, the recent waves of Chinese tend to be non-religious, are often highly qualified as doctors, engineers or professors, and come from mainland China. As most of them speak Mandarin, this has become the main language for communication among the Chinese in Ottawa.

As the example of Ottawa suggests, the immigrant communities in Canada that are aggregated under the term "Chinese" are in fact very diverse culturally and historically, in terms of their geographical origins, socioeconomic status, lifestyles and residential locations. In the context of such a diverse population, individual motivations have become more central to

Chinese decisions to migrate to Canada. Consequently, in urban centres such as Ottawa–Gatineau where the Chinese population is highly diverse, they are more geographically dispersed than in other parts of Canada. Most of them are no longer geographically segregated and live outside Chinatown, although there are some new concentrations of Chinese in suburbs near to their workplaces. Suburbanization, which accelerated in the early 1990s, has thus facilitated integration into Canadian society and impeded the expansion of Chinatown.

Concluding Discussion and Policy Implications

The history of immigration to Canada was marked at the end of the 20th century by an increase in the scale of migration originating from Asian countries, and particularly mainland China. Since 1996, Chinese languages as a group have replaced Italian as the most commonly spoken non-official mother tongue in Canada, being the mother tongues of 3.3 percent of Canada's population. In the Census of 2006, 1,034,085 people reported speaking these languages, including Cantonese and Mandarin. There has also been an increasing polarization of the Chinese population in Canada in favour of the most dynamic urban areas, primarily Toronto and Vancouver, but also increasingly other cities. However, Chinese immigrants' choices of geographical location suggest that the causes of immigration to Canada have not changed over the decades: most Chinese immigrants are still primarily motivated by the quest for better living conditions and higher incomes, regardless of their qualifications and level of education, although it is noteworthy that around thirty-four percent of recent Chinese immigrants aged between twenty-five and forty-four had completed their academic studies, compared to nineteen percent of Canadian citizens in the same age category.

The Chinese community in Canada today is highly diverse, socially, culturally and economically. The new generation has more post-secondary education and is better prepared for successful migration and economic integration in Canada. The Chinese community today is composed of individuals with very diverse geographical origins, and is also politically divided as a result of recent events in mainland China. There is a significant gap between the older generation of migrants, who tended to live in British Columbia and were originally from Hong Kong, and the newer generations of Chinese, who were educated in mainland China following the economic reforms launched in the late 1970s. In the context of such a diverse Chinese population, "Chinatown" has acquired various meanings. Recent migrants have chosen not to live in these neighbourhoods, giving priority instead to a suburban lifestyle and Chinese grocery stores on the urban periphery. Chinatown nonetheless remains symbolic for those Chinese, and Asian immigrants more generally, who are less socioeconomically privileged, as well as for Chinese youth born in Canada, who use it as a site for cultural events and gatherings. The socio-economic, cultural and historical heterogeneity of the Chinese Canadian population is particularly notable in Ottawa, where the Chinese community has slowly disaggregated into various sub-communities as the choice of residential location has become the product of individual preferences.

As discussed above, increasing numbers of Chinese immigrants have decided not to settle in Toronto or Vancouver, and have dispersed to other cities across Canada. As more Chinese immigrants take on these new territorial strategies, residing in cities with less established Chinese communities while in search of employment, there will be an increasing demand for policy targeted at retaining their talents for a longer term. Economic factors are the primary motivators for the mobility of Chinese immigrants. The wealth maximization thesis in migration studies states that "migrants move to countries where economic returns to their human capital are higher than in their home country" (see Wang and Lo 2005). While this theory refers to international migration, it also holds true for intranational migration and illuminates, for example, Ottawa's experiences following the decline of high-tech industries in the west end of the city. This raises the question of how cities with smaller and more recently expanded Chinese populations can retain the newer members of the community, given fluctuations in employment. Municipalities without large Chinese communities may find it beneficial to increase their efforts to include Chinese immigrants in community activities where possible, since creating connections with non-Chinese members of Canadian society is very important to a feeling of inclusion (see Wang and Lo 2005).

One obstacle to inclusion in the larger community is the language barrier, particularly for Chinese immigrants who have, on average, less ability in either of the two official languages of Canada than other immigrant groups (see Sakamoto, Ku and Wei 2009). Communication ability is directly correlated with increased income, and is therefore an issue for those Chinese immigrants in transition who have less language ability (see Wang and Lo 2005). This is particularly a problem in Ottawa: communication in the workplace may not be of primary importance for those working at home using information technology, but it becomes an issue when seeking new employment or pursuing further involvement in the community.

At the more general level, smaller Canadian cities that are receiving more Chinese immigrants need to focus on creating an environment that will enhance inclusiveness and increase communication between Chinese and non-Chinese, by finding entry points to non-Chinese communities and networks, and targeting improvements in the language abilities of recent Chinese immigrants. Both sides of this line of policy are mutually reinforcing, and can have benefits in adding a non-economic dimension to the reasons for living in a particular city. A particularly viable contribution to helping with this issue is to create partnerships between Mandarin-speaking immigrants and local institutions that offer Mandarin-language programmes. Initiating sustained language and cultural exchanges, as well as opportunities for skills improvement, can go a long way toward helping mutual understanding and learning, and developing local friendships and networks.

While such social and cultural policies may assist in the development of connections, they do not directly address the problem of employment. In the case of Ottawa, for example, in the early 2000s the lack of suitable employment for skilled workers specialized in high technologies led many Chinese immigrants to move away to Canadian cities with better prospects, or back to mainland China, with its increasingly prosperous information technology sector. Policy measures are required to attract new employers at the local level, using the available body of labour that exists in each city. These, of course, would have benefits not only for recent Chinese immigrants, but for the community as a whole, although recent immigrants may be more prone to relocate as a result of unemployment.

Since the beginning of the 21st century, Chinese firms have increasingly become global competitors and sources of local investment, which may be particularly attracted to areas with large pools of sector-specific labour. Chinese members of these labour pools may have linguistic, cultural and network advantages in attracting this sort of investment, and these skills should not go unnoticed. There may also be opportunities for Chinese immigrants in Canada, particularly more recent immigrants, to use networks in China to promote Canadian business in China. Further, when investment does occur, Chinese immigrants may have the same "bridge" advantages in helping Chinese companies to operate in the Canadian context, and vice versa. Nurturing the development of integrated communities in Canada with links to China will not only help to retain skilled Chinese immigrants, but may also help to draw in the investment needed to create the jobs sought by Chinese immigrants. It is now up to policy-makers, locally, provincially and nationally, to acknowledge the new territorial strategies of Chinese immigrants in Canada, recognize their new demands for inclusion, and focus on opportunities for transnational partnerships.

References

Citizenship and Immigration Canada. (2009). "Canada—Permanent Residents by Source Country." Ottawa: Citizenship and Immigration Canada. Online at http://www.cic.gc.ca/english/resources/statistics/facts2008/permanent/10.asp [consulted January 14, 2011].

CTV News. (2010, April 20). "Huawei Plans to Triple Number of Ottawa Employees." Ottawa: CTV Television Network. Online at http://ottawa.ctv.ca/servlet/an/local/CTVNews/20100420/OTT_Huawei_100420/20100420/?hub =OttawaHome [consulted January 14, 2011].

Fang, Di, and David Brown. (1999, Spring). "Geographic Mobility of the Foreign-Born Chinese in Large Metropolises, 1985–1990." *International Migration Review* 33:1, 137–55.

Gittings, John. (1989). *China Changes Face: The Road from Revolution, 1949–1989*. Oxford: Oxford University Press.

Keung, Nicholas. (2004, March 10). "Ethnic Mini-Cities on Rise: Statscan Study Finds Immigrants Settle in Enclaves: Concerns Raised about Isolation." *Toronto Star*.

Lai, David Chuenyan. (1988). *Chinatowns: Towns within Cities in Canada*. Vancouver: University of British Columbia Press.

Lai, David Chuenyan. (2003). "From Downtown Slums to Suburban Malls: Chinese Migration and Settlement in Canada," in *The Chinese Diaspora: Space, Place, Mobility, and Identity*, ed. Laurence J. C. Ma and Carolyn Cartier. Lanham, MD, and Oxford: Rowman & Littlefield, 311–36.

Li, Peter S. (1998). *The Chinese in Canada*. 2nd ed. Toronto: Oxford University Press.

Li, Qiang. (2000). "Ethnic Minority Churches: The Case of the Canadian Chinese Christian Churches in Ottawa." PhD thesis, University of Ottawa.

Liu, X.-F. (1997). "Refugee Flow or Brain?: The Humanitarian Policy and Post-Tiananmen Mainland Chinese Immigration to Canada." *International Journal of Population Geography*, vol. 3, 15–29.

Lo, Lucia, and Shuguang Wang. (1997). "Settlement Patterns of Toronto's Chinese Immigrants: Convergence or Divergence?" *Canadian Journal of Regional Science* vol. 20, 49–72.

Office of the Prime Minister. (2006). "Prime Minister Harper Offers Full Apology for the Chinese Head Tax." Online at http://pm.gc.ca/eng/media.asp?id=1219 [consulted January 14, 2011].

O'Neill, J. (2003, October 18). "Crossing Canada's 'Racial Divide': Series: Our Town: In Living Colour." *Ottawa Citizen*.

Rao, Badrinath. (2001). "Economic Migrants in a Global Labour Market: A Report on the Recruitment and Retention of Asian Computer Professionals by Canadian High-Tech Firms." Ottawa: Canadian Policy Research Networks.

Sakamoto, I., J. Ku, and Y. Wei. (2009). "The Deep Plunge: Luocha and the Experiences of Earlier Skilled Immigrants from Mainland China in Toronto." *Qualitative Social Work* 8, 427–47.

Shi, Yan. (2004). "The Impact of Canada's New Immigration Act on Chinese Independent Immigrants." *Canadian Journal of Urban Research*, 13:1, 140–54.

Statistics Canada. (2004). "Document de recherche: Immigration récente et formation de quartiers de minorités visibles dans les grandes villes canadiennes", *Division de l'analyse des entreprises et du marché du travail*, Ottawa: Statistics Canada.

Statistics Canada. (2006). "Census of 2006", Ottawa: Statistics Canada.

Wang, Shuguang, and Lucia Lo. (2005). "Chinese Immigrants in Canada: Their Changing Composition and Economic Performance." *International Migration* 43:3, 35–71.

Wickberg, P. (1984). *Histoire des peuples du Canada. "De la Chine au Canada" : Histoire des communautés chinoises au Canada*. Ottawa: Centre d'édition du gouvernement du Canada, Ministère des Approvisionnements et Services.

Chapter 17

Causes and Consequences: Overeducated Chinese Immigrants in the Canadian Labour Market

Tony Fang

More than thirty years have passed since Richard Freeman's influential book *The Overeducated American* (1976) described the growing tendency for workers to have more formal education than their jobs require, a tendency that Freeman suggested generated a pattern of declining returns to higher education within the United States. While a similar pattern was initially confirmed for Canada (see Dooley 1986), this trend seems to have been reversed more recently in both countries, and certainly so for younger workers (see Katz and Murphy 1992, Bar-Or et al. 1995 and Card and Lemieux 2001). Nevertheless, the extent of overeducation and its consequences remain of vital policy interest. It has been estimated at different periods that forty-one percent of workers in the United States are overeducated (see Sicherman 1991), that thirty-one percent of British workers are overeducated (see Sloane, Battu and Seaman 1999), and that twenty-seven percent of Canadian workers are overeducated (see Ying 2003), while comparative data on seventeen countries in Europe and North America put the Canadian rate of overeducation at second only to that of the United States (see Brisbois 2003). The overeducated are known to have lower earnings, lower job satisfaction and higher job turnover (see Allen and van der Velden 2001). Overeducation represents labour market mismatch, signals wasted public resources and gives rise to inefficient churning and job search (see Bender and Heywood 2006 and Wald 2005). Indeed, the variation in overeducation by degree programme has been used to suggest reallocations within Canadian higher education (see Frenette 2004).

While recent data confirm the impressions articulated above, the situation is even worse for disadvantaged workers in the labour market, such as immigrants, and especially recent immigrants to Canada. For example, in 2001 twenty-five percent of university-educated male immigrants and thirty-eight percent of university-educated female immigrants were working in jobs that required, at most, a high school education (see Galarneau and Morissette 2004). This compared with twelve percent of Canadian-born men and thirteen percent of Canadian-born women. Data from the Survey of Labour and Income Dynamics reveal that fifty-two percent of recent immigrants with university degrees worked in jobs requiring only high school education at some point during the period 1993–2001, nearly double the proportion among the Canadian-born (see Li, Gervais and Duval 2006). Data from the Longitudinal Survey of Immigrants to Canada also indicate substantial job mismatch for immigrants to Canada. For example, among working-age immigrants who arrived in Canada between April 2001 and May 2002, only forty-two percent found work in their intended occupations during their first two years in Canada (see Statistics Canada 2003).

While the study of racial and ethnic minorities deserves scrutiny, the imperative for Canada is to focus on the distribution of overeducation among immigrants. The education of immigrants has become a central labour market issue in Canada for a number of reasons. First, Canada selects economic immigrants on the basis of a system that heavily rewards educational attainment. In the most recent version of the "Point System," which came into effect in 2002, applicants in the "Skilled Worker" category can earn twenty-five of the sixty-seven points necessary for admission into Canada through their educational attainment. Given the policy emphasis on skill-based immigration, it becomes critical to measure the extent to which the education of immigrants is both used and rewarded.

Second, demographic projections show that the growth of the Canadian population will increasingly rely on immigration. According to one forecast, immigration is expected to account for all net labour force growth by 2011 (see Human Resources Development Canada 2002). Third, and more importantly, immigrants, particularly the recent cohort, suffer increasing difficulties in the Canadian labour market in the following three dimensions. The relative educational standing of immigrants has been falling compared to native-born Canadians; the return that immigrants earn on their education appears to be significantly lower (see Reitz 2001 and Aydemir and Skuterud 2005); and immigrants are less likely to be employed in the most highly skilled professions (see Reitz 2006). The second and third outcomes might well be expected if overeducation is more common among immigrants. Lack of information and failures in signalling make it likely that foreign credentials will be undervalued in the Canadian labour market. At the same time, lack of language fluency may make it genuinely difficult for immigrants to gain a return even on valuable education and credentials. While these points argue that immigrants are more likely to be overeducated (mismatched), they may also indicate that the economic consequences of overeducation may be smaller than anticipated if one controls for language ability. Further, since a very large share of Canada's visible minorities is comprised of immigrants, one might anticipate that discrimination by employers makes immigrants more willing to compromise in the job search process, resulting in mismatch. Similar concerns in Australia have resulted in at least one major study of the extent of overeducation among immigrants (see Green, Kler and Leeves 2004).

Although a variety of aspects of overeducation have been studied by labour market economists (see Belfield 2000 for a review of the literature), the distribution of overeducation and the differential consequences of overeducation have received much less study. Early work from the United States suggested that African Americans were more likely to be overeducated (see Duncan and Hoffman 1981). More recent work from the United Kingdom also indicates that members of ethnic minorities are more likely to be overeducated (see Alpin, Shackleton and Walsh 1998), although there is heterogeneity among those minorities (see Battu and Sloane 2002). There have been a number of studies examining returns to immigrants' education in the Canadian context (see Reitz 2001, Ferrer and Riddell 2008 and Sweetman 2004), but to my knowledge only two studies have directly considered the impact of overeducation (see Galarneau and Morissette 2004 and Wald and Fang 2008). This lack of attention is somewhat surprising, given the prevalence of immigrant overeducation as described above, as well as the well-developed body of literature that examines the earnings consequences of overeducation (see McGuinness 2006 for an up-to-date and thorough review). On the other hand, there were no published studies examining the relationship between educational mismatch and wages in Canada until quite recently (see Vahey 2000). Most Canadian studies of overeducation neglect the immigrant population, either because the focus of the particular research is on other issues, such as literacy or the Canadian post-secondary education system, or because there are unacceptably small numbers of immigrant observations, or even none at all, within the data sets employed (see Boothby 1999, Frenette 2001 and Green and Riddell 2001).

In this chapter I examine the impacts of overeducation on the earnings of immigrants, particularly Chinese immigrants, in the Canadian labour market from a slightly different perspective. Specifically, I use the framework most commonly appearing in the overeducation literature that enables one to examine returns to school contingent upon job requirements. In more precise terms, a decomposition of respondents' years of education permits the estimation of returns to schooling according to whether those years of education: are required for the job, exceed job requirements or are in deficit of job requirements. I also use a categorical version of mismatch measurement that contrasts overeducated and undereducated workers to those who are properly matched. Further, whereas Diane Galarneau and René Morissette (2004) examined one particular type of overeducation, albeit probably the most important type, the data set used here captures many different magnitudes of educational mismatch.

Explaining Overeducation

Why might recent immigrants face a heightened incidence of overeducation? A number of hypotheses have been developed. The first possible explanation, which renders the existence of overeducation consistent with the assumptions of human capital theory, is that, while immigrants may be categorized as overeducated, their "surplus" education compensates for education of inferior quality or other human capital "deficiencies." For example, a study for Statistics Canada examining the employment of immigrants four years after arrival concludes that there is a significantly positive relationship between the ability to speak English and the likelihood of having an "appropriate" job (see Statistics Canada 2007). Employed immigrants with the highest levels of spoken English (on a five-point self-reported scale) were more likely to have high-skill jobs, jobs in the intended field, jobs similar to the ones they had before migrating, jobs related to their training or education, and higher hourly wages.

The high incidences of overeducation among Asian immigrants can also be explained by the fact that Asians, especially Chinese, have historically placed a great emphasis on higher education as a stepping stone to social, political and economic advancement (see Stevenson and Stigler 1992). For example, according to one study comparing elementary school children and their families in mainland China, Taiwan and Japan with counterparts in Chicago, Illinois (see Stevenson 1992), the Chinese, Taiwanese and Japanese families were more likely to attribute success in school to the quality of teaching and the hard work of students, whereas the families in Chicago contended that innate talents and abilities beyond students' control had a greater influence. The families in Chicago tended to regard childhood as a time for a variety of activities, but in East Asia school work was seen as a child's primary task. When asked to fantasize about what they would like if they could have any wish, more than two thirds of the children in this study from mainland China, Taiwan and Japan wished for something related to education and educational success, while only one in ten of the students in Chicago did so, and the majority instead chose wealth, material objects or fun fantasies such as a trip to the Moon. The lives of the children in East Asia were clearly much more centred on school than those of the children in Chicago were, and the parents were much more involved in, and critical of, their local schools than the parents in Chicago were. These contrasts go a long way toward explaining why students in East Asia have more success in school than American children do. However, attitudes do not exist in a vacuum. There are structures in the societies and educational systems of East Asia that support and encourage them. For example, historically, individuals who excelled in the educational system in China were much more likely to be recruited and promoted into the higher ranks of government or industry even if they did not possess superior management or practical skills. (Nevertheless, the system of recruitment and promotion mainly based on educational attainment has been in transition since China adopted open-door and market reform policies, starting in 1978.) In theory, then, it is because immigrants from East Asia are more educated than Americans or Canadians that they are likely to experience a higher incidence of overeducation.

Third, if visible-minority immigrants are discriminated against by Canadian employers, they will find it harder to gain employment and will therefore become willing to make greater compromises in terms of job match (an argument advanced in relation to immigrants in Britain by Battu and Sloane 2002). Indeed, a case before the Canadian Human Rights Tribunal in 2006 focused squarely on this issue: the complainant, an immigrant from India with a PhD, argued that refusal to hire overqualified immigrants amounted to discrimination, since members of visible minorities face barriers at their appropriate levels of employment that force them to seek lower-skilled jobs instead (see Canadian Human Rights Tribunal 2006). Third, given their status as new labour market entrants, mismatches might be more prevalent as newcomers learn about the labour market, although overeducation among immigrants cannot be dismissed as a temporary phenomenon, but may persist even ten years after immigrants arrive in Canada (see Galarneau and Morissette 2004). Fourth, it might simply be that the quality of the job match is secondary to more pressing concerns. While it is not surprising that immigrants escaping political persecution would put a somewhat low priority on the quality of job match, survey responses reveal that even principal applicants in the "Economic Class" of immigrants cited reasons other than job prospects as the most important determinant behind their settlement location decision (Statistics Canada 2003, p. 15). Among principal applicant economic immigrants who settled in Vancouver, a number of reasons outranked "job prospects" as the most important, including family or friends, climate, lifestyle; and education prospects. In Toronto "family or friends" was cited by 49.7 percent of respondents, compared to 23.4 percent citing "job prospects." Finally, immigrant skills may not be fully used when Canadian licensing bodies or employers fail to recognize foreign credentials or work experience (see Reitz 2001).

Returns to Immigrant Education

As mentioned above, there have been a number of studies examining the returns to immigrants' education in the Canadian labour market. A finding common to most research is that immigrants receive a smaller earnings premium for formal education compared to the Canadian-born (see Reitz 2001 and Ferrer, Green and Riddell 2006). According to Jeffrey Reitz (2001), a generalization that can be drawn from this research is that the estimated return to an additional year of schooling for immigrants is about half what it is for the native-born. Why should immigrants' education be rewarded less than that of other Canadians? Again, one strand in the literature hypothesizes that the skills embodied in the education of immigrants are, in some respects, inferior to those of the native-born population and that the observed inferior returns are reflective of this. Research testing this hypothesis has examined heterogeneity in school quality and literacy skills (see Sweetman 2004 and Alboim, Finnie and Meng 2005).

Arthur Sweetman (2004), using data from multiple Censuses and school quality measures for eighty-seven countries, has explored the role of educational quality in immigrants' source countries in returns to schooling. He concludes that there is substantial correlation between average source country school quality and Canadian labour market earnings. For instance, parameter estimates implied that moving up from the twenty-fifth to the seventy-fifth percentile of the school quality index is associated with a ten percent increase in annual earnings.

Ana Ferrer, David Green, and Craig Riddell (2006), using the Ontario Immigrant Literacy Survey to examine the impact of literacy skills on immigrant earnings, find that differences in literacy account for a large amount of the higher earnings of Canadian-born workers. For example, among the university-educated literacy differences account for about two thirds of the earnings gap between immigrants and the Canadian-born. Naomi Alboim, Ross Finnie and Ronald Meng (2005) use the Survey of Literacy Skills Used in Daily Activities, conducted in 1989, and similarly find that an important factor related to the discounting of immigrants' foreign education is language ability.

Data and Methodological Approach

Data for this study are drawn from the Canadian Workplace and Employee Survey (WES), conducted by Statistics Canada in 2003. The WES is a linked file consisting of both employer and employee components, and covers a broad range of topics from both the demand and the supply sides of the labour market. Employers are sampled by physical location and employees are then sampled within each location from employer-provided lists. The survey excluded business locations in the Yukon, Nunavut and the Northwest Territories, along with agriculture, fishing, road, bridge and highway maintenance, government services and religious organizations. Responses were received from 6,565 business locations and 20,834 employees.

For the present study, the key WES data include information on earnings, workers' educational attainments, perceptions of job requirements, ethnic backgrounds and dates of immigration. Information pertaining to immigrants' countries of origin and measures of literacy—which, as discussed above are generally found to be important determinants of immigrant labour market earnings—is unfortunately absent from the WES data, but there is information on ethnicity and foreign language usage at home, which will serve as proxy measures.

The WES contains certain data that render it particularly well-suited for studying the impacts of overeducation on earnings. For instance, it contains a direct measure of individuals' total work experience in addition to a measure of job tenure with current firms. This is unavailable in most data sets, for which years of experience must be estimated (using the formula: experience = years of age – years of schooling – 5). The WES also contains detailed information on the incidence and amount of workplace training. These high-quality measures of work experience and training are particularly important in light of the hypothesis that overeducated workers possess lower levels of other forms of human capital, namely work experience and training.

The sample of interest consists of paid workers who were between the ages of eighteen and sixty-four in 2003. This results in a sample of 20,558 workers from 5,267 workplaces, among whom 17,270 were born in Canada and 3,288 were immigrants (including twelve percent Chinese). For this analysis I focus on the economic performance of those who immigrated after 1989. Of the 3,288 immigrants, 963 are what may be termed "recent" immigrants, having immigrated between 1990 and 2003. Chinese immigrants consist of 18.5 percent of these recent immigrant workers (see Table 17.1).

Key Variables and Measures

Four approaches are typically used in the overeducation literature to ascertain the match between a job's entry and/or performance requirements and an individual's educational attainment (see Wald 2005): (1) comparison of a worker's educational attainment with the education level that the worker believes is necessary for either job entry or performance; (2) the respondent's perception of being overeducated or overqualified; (3) comparison of a worker's educational attainment to the educational requirements for the position as specified by job analysts; and (4) deviation from the average level of educational attainment within a narrowly defined occupation. The third and fourth of these approaches cannot be used here, since WES data available to researchers via remote access are not coded with sufficiently detailed occupational information, but the first of these approaches can be used.

Specifically, an individual's educational attainment can be compared with responses to the following question: "What is the minimum level of education required for this job?" This question can be reasonably interpreted as asking either about the requirements for being hired or about those for job performance. However, Séamus McGuinness (2006) has pointed out that both interpretations have elicited similar responses. McGuinness cites results from a study using a data set of alumni of the University of Newcastle in the United Kingdom (Green, McIntosh and Vignoles 1999), which found that in the "vast majority of cases, the assessment of education levels needed to do the job tended to match those needed to get the job."

Based on the comparison between survey respondents' educational attainments and the perceived minimum levels of education required for their jobs, I derive a set of three dichotomous variables, characterizing the fit as either overeducated, matched or undereducated. The analysis focuses on the overeducated population, due to its policy relevance. I also derive a continuous version whereby years of schooling (Sa) are separated into three components: years of schooling required for the job (Sr); years of surplus education or overschooling (So); and years of deficit or underschooling (Su), so that Sa = Sr + So - Su.

For example, a PhD graduate assumed to have twenty years of schooling and driving a taxi would have twelve years of required schooling and eight years of surplus schooling if he/she responded that in order to drive a taxi; a high school education was required. On the other hand, a high school graduate working in a job perceived to require a college diploma would have fourteen years of required schooling and two years of deficit schooling.

While the self-assessed overeducation measure adopted here can reasonably be criticized for its subjectivity, I feel that it confers two major advantages over external measures. First, it is a job-specific measure rather than an occupation-specific measure, and thus avoids the risk of misclassification solely due to heterogeneity within an occupation. Second, external assessments often rely on occupational taxonomies that are infrequently updated by government analysts. According to analysis of Canadian policies aimed at developing skilled workers (see Baygan 2004), "occupational classifications are slow to incorporate newly emerging fields, particularly in science and technology, or changing skill requirements within occupations." Given the high number of recent immigrants in Canada employed in computer-related occupations, and the likely rapidity of change within these occupations, relying on respondents' assessments of the skill requirements of their jobs seems to be the preferable measurement approach.

Sample Characteristics

If one tabulates weighted sample means according to immigration status (see Table 17.1), one finds, consistent with other data sets, that the earnings of recent immigrants, at $17.81, were well below those of Canadian-born workers, at $20.73. However, recent Chinese immigrants made even less, at

Table 17.1 Weighted Means by Immigration Status

Variable	Canadian born	Non-recent immigrants	Recent immigrants	Recent Chinese	Total
Hourly wage ($)	20.73	22.46	17.81	16.49	20.77
Education–job match (continuous variables)					
Years of education	13.2	13.6	14.4	15.0	13.4
Years of required education	12.2	12.5	12.3	13.1	12.3
Years of overeducation	1.4	1.6	2.4	2.2	1.5
Years of undereducation	0.4	0.4	0.3	0.3	0.4
Education–job match (dichotomous variables)					
Education matched	0.505	0.454	0.350	0.313	0.489
Overeducated	0.331	0.368	0.509	0.559	0.347
Undereducated	0.164	0.178	0.141	0.128	0.164
Highest level of educational attainment					
Less than high school education	0.104	0.101	0.057	0.009	0.100
High school graduation	0.210	0.165	0.151	0.045	0.201
Some college	0.105	0.073	0.058	0.022	0.098
Some university	0.364	0.354	0.293	0.502	0.358
College diploma	0.051	0.052	0.030	0.007	0.050
Undergraduate degree	0.137	0.186	0.312	0.292	0.154

Professional degree	0.005	0.011	0.014	0.025	0.006
Graduate degree	0.025	0.058	0.085	0.099	0.032
Occupation					
Managers	0.125	0.173	0.098	0.048	0.129
Professionals	0.158	0.174	0.217	0.442	0.164
Technical/Trades	0.420	0.399	0.378	0.275	0.415
Marketing/Sales	0.084	0.051	0.096	0.064	0.080
Clerical/Administrative	0.152	0.126	0.138	0.162	0.148
Production workers	0.061	0.077	0.073	0.009	0.064
Observations	17,270	2,325	963	144	20,558

Note: The total sample size (23,296) does not equal the sum of categories (23,252) due to the exclusion of forty-four immigrants from the "most recent immigrant" category (those who entered Canada in 1998 or 1999).

Source: Statistics Canada, Workplace and Employee Survey, 2003.

$16.49, despite being the most educated in terms of years of education, at 15.0 years versus 13.4 years for the entire population. These inferior wages cannot be attributed to lower amounts of educational attainment, as recent immigrants were a very well-educated group. For example, 31.2 percent of recent immigrants were university graduates, compared to 13.7 percent of Canadian-born workers, and recent immigrants brought one more year of education to the labour market than the Canadian-born did (14.4 years versus 13.2 years). Strikingly, 50.9 percent of recent immigrants were labelled as overeducated according to the dichotomous measure of overeducation, compared to about one third of the Canadian-born. The proportion of the overeducated was even higher for the Chinese immigrant sample, at 55.9 percent. Recent immigrants had one additional year of overeducation compared to Canadian-born workers (2.4 years versus 1.4 years). In fact, despite their significantly higher levels of educational attainment, the jobs of recent immigrants were perceived to require levels of education almost identical to those of the Canadian-born (12.3 years compared to 12.2 years).

If one tabulates the sample according to education–job matches (see Table 17.2), the data once again indicate that recent immigrants were more likely to be overeducated than non-recent immigrants or the Canadian-born. Recent immigrants comprised 8.9 percent of the overeducated sample, in contrast to only 4.3 percent of workers who were matched. (Note that recent immigrants in this table include forty-four immigrants who entered Canada in 1998 and 1999, whereas these are excluded from the data sample for the purpose of regression analysis.) Individuals of Chinese descent (4.4 percent, compared to 2.8 percent of the overall sample) and individuals of other non-European descent (22.5 percent versus 20.0 percent) are overrepresented in the sample of overeducated workers.

Overeducated workers earned somewhat less than matched workers or undereducated workers. Compared to workers who were educationally matched, overeducated workers earned $2.27 less per hour on average, in spite of their higher levels of educational attainment, at 14.2 years compared to 12.9 years for matched workers. The positive relationship between the hourly wage rate and years of required education hints at the efficacy of decomposing years of education in this manner.

The argument that higher levels of education compensate for lower levels of experience and training seems plausible when examining these mean differences. For example, overeducated workers were younger than matched workers (38.6 years compared to 40.5 years), had fewer years of full-time work experience before the current job (9.0 years compared to 9.1 years),

Table 17.2 Weighted Means by Educational Match

Variable	Undereducated	Matched	Overeducated
Hourly wage ($)	24.57	20.97	18.70
Education–job match (continuous variables)			
Years of education	12.7	12.9	14.2
Years of required education	15.1	12.9	10.0
Years of overeducation	0.0	0.0	4.2
Years of undereducation	2.4	0.0	0.0
Highest level of educational attainment			
Less than high school education	0.234	0.127	0.000
High school graduation	0.128	0.244	0.174
Some college	0.150	0.104	0.065
Some university	0.263	0.344	0.423
College diploma	0.031	0.056	0.052
Undergraduate degree	0.194	0.098	0.212
Professional degree	0.000	0.009	0.005
Graduate degree	0.000	0.018	0.068
Immigration period			
Born in Canada	0.810	0.840	0.776
Immigrated before 1970	0.047	0.040	0.033
Immigrated between 1970 and 1979	0.049	0.039	0.044
Immigrated between 1980 and 1989	0.042	0.038	0.058
Immigrated between 1990 and 2003	0.052	0.043	0.089
[European Canadians]	0.794	0.795	0.731
Chinese	0.017	0.020	0.044
Other Non-Europeans	0.189	0.185	0.225
Occupation			
Managers	0.183	0.112	0.128

Professionals	0.260	0.167	0.114
Technical/Trades	0.365	0.450	0.389
Marketing/Sales	0.026	0.067	0.124
Clerical/Administrative	0.120	0.147	0.162
Production workers	0.046	0.057	0.083
Observations	3,532	10,271	6,755

Source: Statistics Canada, Workplace and Employee Survey, 2003.

and had lower levels of firm-specific job tenure (6.9 years compared to 9.0 years). Additionally, overeducated workers were employed in firms with lower training expenditures per capita ($281 compared to $318).

Overeducated workers do not appear to differ in a substantial manner from matched workers either along gender lines or according to the presence of children. Personal employment history does seem to affect the likelihood of over-education, as those with higher levels of unemployment and those who involuntarily left their previous jobs had heightened incidence of overeducation.

A number of other variables appear to have increased the likelihood of overeducation. For example, a higher proportion of workers in part-time positions were overeducated compared to those who were educationally matched (29.2 percent compared to 25.2 percent), as were workers in firms with a higher incidence of part-time work. Workers with postsecondary educational credentials comprised a relatively large share of the overeducated. For example, while 9.8 percent of the total sample of workers had undergraduate degrees (see Table 17.1), 21.2 percent of overeducated workers had them.

Findings

I use a multinomial logit model to investigate the probability of overeducation and undereducation. The multinomial logit estimation technique is appropriate where the discrete dependent variable covers two or more outcomes that do not have a natural ordering. I am particularly interested in whether the negative relationship between overeducation and time spent in Canada is statistically significant when the other potential determinants discussed above are considered.

I use survey estimation commands with the employee survey weights provided in the WES in all the estimations to account for the fact that, once an establishment has been selected in the survey, the assumption that a given worker is randomly sampled from the overall population of workers is no longer appropriate. In Stata Version 9, I use the "svyreg" and "svymlogit" commands, the counterparts to "reg" and "mlogit," which are inappropriate in the presence of complex survey data. That is, the errors generated are corrected for the common components associated with a cluster of workers from a given workplace. These estimation commands also return representative results and provide heteroskedasticity-robust standard errors.

If one tabulates coefficients and marginal effects (evaluated at the means) from the multinomial logit model (see Table 17.3), one finds, consistent with the bivariate relationships, that the likelihood of over-education was higher for recent immigrants, the marginal effect being 0.126. Being of Chinese descent increased the likelihood of overeducation by a slightly larger magnitude (0.147). Therefore it would be safe to conclude that recent immigrants from Chinese background were highly prone to overeducation.

Results from the multinomial logit are consistent with the hypothesis that overeducated workers may have been substituting formal education for work experience and workplace training. Higher level of job tenure significantly decreased the likelihood of overeducation. None of the demographic variables related to potential household constraints—such as marriage, the presence of children or gender interactions—were statistically significant. Despite the bivariate relationships between overeducation and a worker's previous job separation and unemployment history, the estimates from the multinomial logit failed to find a significant relationship. Working in establishments with higher part-time rates heightened the incidence of overeducation (marginal effect of 0.099).

To analyze the effect of educational mismatch on earnings, I rely on a standard Mincerian semi-logarithmic wage equation, with the modification that years of educational attainment are decomposed:

$$\ln W_{ij} = \alpha + \beta_1 S^r_{ij} + \beta_2 S^o_{ij} + \beta^3 S^u_{ij} + X_{ij}\gamma + Y_{ij}\,\delta + \varepsilon_{ij} \ (1)$$

where

$\ln W_{ij}$ = the natural logarithm of the observed hourly wage of the ith worker in the jth workplace,

S^r_{ij} = years of required schooling of the ith worker in the jth workplace,

Table 17.3 Determinants of Mismatch (Multinomial Logit)

Variable	Undereducation			Overeducation		
Mean dependent variable	Coef.	t-stat.	Marginal effect	Coef.	t-stat.	Marginal effect
Ethnicity						
[European Canadian]						
Chinese	-0.284	-0.79	-0.058	0.553	2.34**	0.147
Other Non-Europeans	-0.060	-0.54	-0.014	0.119	1.20	0.030
Immigration period						
[Born in Canada]						
Immigrated before 1970	0.047	0.24	0.000	0.108	0.62	0.022
Immigrated between 1970 and 1979	0.287	1.40	0.020	0.312	1.53	0.056
Immigrated between 1980 and 1989	0.297	0.98	0.015	0.409	2.02**	0.078
Immigrated between 1990 and 2003	0.472	1.91*	0.022	0.655	3.35***	0.126
Full-time work experience	0.019	3.79***	0.003	-0.003	-0.78	-0.002
Female	0.231	1.43	0.025	0.085	0.80	0.007
Married	0.296	2.12**	0.036	0.030	0.29	-0.008
Female x married	-0.427	-2.44***	-0.043	-0.172	-1.24	-0.018
Children aged 2 and under	-0.177	-0.81	-0.024	0.046	0.28	0.019
Female x children aged 2 and under	-0.263	-0.77	-0.015	-0.386	-1.50	-0.070
Children aged 3 to 5	-0.001	-0.01	-0.006	0.111	0.76	0.025

Female x children aged 2 and under	0.266	0.83	0.042	-0.079	-0.35	-0.032
Foreign language most often spoken at home	-0.122	-0.49	-0.015	-0.007	-0.04	0.004
Part-time job	-0.301	-1.95 *	-0.041	0.123	0.87	0.043
Union/collective bargaining agreement	-0.126	-1.19	-0.020	0.077	0.96	0.024
Reason left last job						
[Other reason]						
Laid off from last job or contract ended	-1.28	0.20	-0.023	-0.118	-0.90	-0.015
Left last job for current better job	-0.16	0.87	0.000	-0.068	-0.60	-0.014
Unemployment in previous five years	0.010	0.91	0.001	0.001	0.11	0.000
Job tenure	0.019	3.30 ***	0.004	-0.027	-4.48 ***	-0.007
Workplace size	0.021	0.88	0.004	-0.017	-0.49	-0.005
Per-capita training expenditures	0.000	0.53	0.000	0.000	-0.41	0.000
Workplace part-time rate	-0.089	-0.4	-0.033	0.420	2.22 **	0.099
Member of a team	0.192	1.94 *	0.023	0.033	0.32	-0.002
Job rotation	-0.033	-0.31	0.000	-0.074	-0.87	-0.015
Constant	-1.483	-5.40 ***	0.153	0.49		

Notes: N = 20,558, F-Statistic: 5.49***

Also included are dummy variables for six regions

*significant at 10%; **significant at 5%; *** significant at 1%

Source: Statistics Canada, Workplace and Employee Survey, 2003

S^{o}_{ij} = years of surplus schooling of the ith worker in the jth workplace (overeducation),

S^{u}_{ij} = years of deficit schooling of the ith worker in the jth workplace (undereducation),

X_{ij} = a vector of (other) personal characteristics for the ith worker in the jth workplace,

γ = a vector of estimated slope coefficients for worker characteristics,

Y_{ji} = a set of characteristics of the jth workplace for worker i,

δ = a vector of estimated slope coefficients for workplace characteristics, and

ε_{ij} = an error term.

If the results from the earnings regressions are tabulated with separate estimations for the Canadian-born, recent immigrants and recent immigrants of Chinese ethnicity (see Table 17.4), one finds that returns to years of overeducation were positive in all three samples, but were smaller than those to years of required education. Both returns to required education and returns to overeducation were smaller for Chinese recent immigrants and for all recent immigrants than for the Canadian-born (4.6 percent, 7.5 percent, 8.9 percent, 3.9 percent, 5.7 percent, 6.6 percent).

The estimates for the relative returns to overeducation, as compared with returns to required education, are at the high end of the range of typical results, whereas the estimates for recent immigrants are at the low end of the range. An analysis of forty-five studies from numerous countries covering various time periods found that returns to overeducation averaged about half to two thirds of the returns to required education (see Hartog 2000). In all estimates based on equation 1, the implicit assumption within human capital theory that returns to education are not contingent on job requirements (i.e. $\beta 1 = \beta 2 = \beta 3$) is rejected. For the three equations the relevant F statistics corresponding to the Wald tests are $F(2,5024) = 157.97$, Prob>F = 0.0000, $F(2,706) = 16.36$, Prob>F = 0.0000, and $F(2,117) = 7.99$ and Prob>F = 0.0006.

There were significant earnings differences among recent immigrants according to ethnic background. Relative to those of European descent, Chinese immigrants earned significantly less (12.7 percent, 15.3 percent for the dummy variable approach), followed by other non-Europeans (5.7 percent, 7.8 percent for the dummy variable approach). The impact of having a foreign language as the main language spoken within the household was significantly negative for other non-Europeans (15.5 percent), and was also negative for Chinese immigrants (7.2 percent), but was not significant. The returns to prior work experience differed across the three subsets: the Canadian-born reaped significant returns for their years of work experience, whereas recent immigrants, and especially recent Chinese immigrants, did not (returns per year were 0.8 percent, 0.5 percent and 0.3 percent for Canadian-born, recent immigrants and recent Chinese immigrants respectively). In other words, the prior work experience of recent immigrants, which is typically comprised largely of foreign work experience, was seriously discounted by employers. Unfortunately, due to the nature of the data, it was not possible to partition prior work experience into that specifically obtained in Canada and that obtained abroad. Specifically, while there are data of immigration and years of total work experience, there are no complete work histories of time spent in Canada. Accordingly, it is not known, for example, what part of the years since immigration was spent not in the labour force or in unemployment. However, I define prior work experience to exclude experience obtained in the current job (job tenure), which is by definition Canadian experience, thus partially rectifying this problem.

Conclusion

Analysis with the WES data supports findings from other data sets, as well as substantial anecdotal evidence, that recent Chinese immigrants have faced heightened levels of overduction in the Canadian labour market. Of all recent immigrants arriving between 1990 and 2003, fifty-one percent were overeducated in 2003, according to data from the WES, which was higher than the figure for 1999 (forty-eight percent). Among recent immigrants, the Chinese experienced a heightened level of overeducation, at fifty-six percent. Multivariate analysis confirmed the significance of this relationship when many other potential determinants of overeducation were considered.

This study has shown that, in addition to the high incidence of overeducation, recent immigrants suffered a larger earnings disadvantage from overeducation than the Canadian-born did, and that this was particularly the case for recent Chinese immigrants. This supports findings based on Canadian Census data (see Galarneau and Morissette 2004). The wage impact of overeducation was assessed in two ways. First, recent immigrants were found to receive lower economic returns both to years of required education (8.9 percent for the Canadian-born, 7.5 percent for recent immigrants and 4.6 percent for recent Chinese immigrants) and to years of surplus schooling (6.6 percent, 5.7 percent and 3.9 percent, respectively), compared to the Canadian-born.

Table 17.4 Wage Impacts of Educational Mismatch (Continuous Variable Approach)

Variable	Canadian-born		RCT Immigrants		RCT Chinese	
	Coef.	t-stat.	Coef.	t-stat.	Coef.	t-stat.
Ethnicity						
[European Canadian]						
Chinese	-0.049	-0.79	-0.127	-1.86 *		
Other Non-Europeans	0.016	1.16	-0.057	-1.09		
Education–job match						
Years of required education	0.089	25.35 ***	0.075	8.41 ***	0.046	2.74 ***
Years of overeducation	0.066	18.22 ***	0.057	6.67 ***	0.039	2.55 **
Years of undereducation	-0.035	-7.55 ***	-0.071	-3.59 ***	-0.056	-1.41
Full-time work experience	0.008	10.47 ***	0.005	1.91 *	0.003	1.08
Female	-0.158	-9.42 ***	-0.138	-1.99 **	0.465	3.50 ***
Married	0.097	5.61 ***	0.073	1.20	0.342	3.26 ***
Female x married	-0.014	-0.62	0.035	0.43	-0.494	-3.72 ***
Children aged 2 and under	0.066	2.39 **	-0.009	-0.18	-0.063	-0.44
Female x children aged 2 and under	0.007	0.15	-0.036	-0.34	0.107	0.52
Children aged 3 to 5	0.063	2.69 ***	-0.038	-0.70	-0.065	-0.68
Female x children aged 2 and under	0.038	1.13	0.115	1.28	0.209	1.83 *

Foreign language spoken most often at home	0.057	1.13	-0.155	-3.66 ***	-0.072	-0.70
Part-time job	-0.054	-2.76 ***	0.001	0.02	0.151	1.51
Union/collective bargaining agreement	-0.028	-1.69 *	0.062	1.56	-0.054	-0.62
Job tenure	0.015	18.15 ***	0.025	4.83 ***	0.027	2.47 ***
Workplace size	0.037	8.16 ***	0.012	0.99	0.058	2.60 ***
Non-profit firm	-0.002	-0.06	0.064	-1.34	0.262	2.39 **
Foreign-owned firm	0.015	0.75	-0.070	0.98	0.000	0.00
Member of a team	0.088	7.07 ***	0.087	-1.34	0.025	0.42
Job rotation	-0.062	-5.33 ***	-0.079	1.95 *	0.012	0.19
Incentive pay received	0.095	6.83 ***	0.048	-1.98 **	0.032	0.50
Per-capita training expenditures	0.000	5.44 ***	0.000	1.25 ***	0.000	2.62 ***
Workplace part-time rate	-0.249	-7.42 ***	-0.369	4.05 ***	-0.472	-3.50 ***
Constant	1.290	24.16 ***	1.680	-4.62 ***	1.159	2.60 ***
Observations	17,270		963		144	
R_2	0.574		0.515		0.825	

Notes: Also included are dummy variables for six regions and fourteen industry sectors.

*significant at 10%; **significant at 5%; *** significant at 1%

Source: Statistics Canada, Workplace and Employee Survey, 2003

Second, it was found that immigrants had a larger earnings penalty associated with overeducation in an estimation approach that measured the incidence, rather than the magnitude, of overeducation (-0.144 for the Canadian-born, -0.184 for recent immigrants and -0.280 for recent Chinese immigrants). Thus, with respect to earnings a proper job match was relatively more important for recent Chinese immigrants than for other recent immigrants and the Canadian-born. This is consistent with the evidence that, compared with recent immigrants from European background, Chinese immigrants earned 15.3 percent less, after controlling for other wage determinants.

The most plausible explanations for the earnings consequences of overeducation for recent Chinese immigrants are either non-recognition of foreign credentials, employment discrimination or, most likely, both. Although they are somewhat correlated, in this study I cannot disentangle these two types of effects. There might well be a disconnection between foreign education or training and the Canadian labour market, and/or genuine concerns about the quality of foreign education or training, which supports initiatives such as bridge programmes, especially in the medical and engineering fields, or language and skill training specific to the Canadian labour market, including job search skills. However, it is also possible that some employers simply used this possibility as an excuse to discriminate against recent immigrants in employment and/or earnings. Certainly, we cannot rule out this possibility of employer discrimination, including discrimination against foreign education and credentials. Fresh and convincing evidence supports this argument through a carefully designed field experiment (see Oreopoulos 2009): all qualifications being equal, job applicants with Chinese, Indian or Pakistani names were found to be forty percent less likely to be called for a job interview than otherwise equivalent applicants with English-sounding names (eleven percent versus sixteen percent).

Depending on the interpretations of the empirical findings—non-recognition of credentials or quality of education, which is again hard to measure and validate, or employment discrimination—there can be various different policy responses. If we are concerned about the quality of education, then the government may wish to develop a more vigorous selection system to validate the value of credentials, and add language proficiency test requirements in the selection process, rather than providing various bridge programmes or language training programmes after the immigrants have arrived. On the other hand, if the job–education mismatch is attributable to non-recognition of foreign education and experience, then it appears to be appropriate to provide skilled immigrants with bridge programmes, especially for those in the medical and engineering fields, and language and skill training specific to the Canadian labour market, including job search skills. In the case of employment discrimination, the government may want to tighten human rights legislation, employment equity legislation and other anti-discrimination laws, and make the enforcement more proactive, rather than mainly complaint-driven. There also appears to be a need to educate employers, especially small and medium-sized employers, about the benefits of hiring and rewarding skilled immigrants, such as population and labour force growth, creativity and innovation through workforce diversity, knowledge of emerging markets and links to international trade.

There is even a possibility that highly educated, highly skilled immigrants may be oversupplied in the Canadian labour market. If this is proved to be true through a thorough labour market analysis, then a shift from highly educated to relatively less educated immigrants or temporary foreign workers can be a reasonable policy option. In fact, such a policy change is occurring. The number of immigrant intakes from the Temporary Foreign Workers programme has increased dramatically in recent years, while the number of landed immigrants remains stable (see Citizenship and Immigration Canada 2009a and 2009b). However, the effect of such programmes on overeducation and job–education match remains to be seen.

Future studies should do a better job of teasing out the two potential causes of earnings penalty associated with overeducation of Chinese immigrants, that is, employment discrimination and non-recognition of foreign credentials, possibly by using Census data. For example, employment discrimination could be investigated by comparing Chinese and Caucasians with the same Canadian education and other qualifications in job–education match. Alternatively, non-recognition of foreign credentials could be examined by studying differences in job–education match between Canadian-born Chinese with Canadian education and immigrant Chinese with Chinese education. Although somewhat outside the scope of this chapter, these are certainly areas of research that are worth further exploration.

Given the greater rewards for proficiency in one or other of the official languages, and for work experience in Canada, potential immigration applicants should expose themselves to Canadian or equivalent experience as much as possible. They should also acquire skills and training that are unique to the Canadian market, including language and job search training, as well as targeting specific organizations for pre-arranged employment. In doing so, future immigrants from China may be able to expedite their assimilation into the Canadian labour market and maximize their career success in Canada.

References

Alboim, Naomi, Ross Finnie, and Ronald Meng. (2005). "The Discounting of Immigrants' Skills in Canada: Evidence and Policy Recommendations." *IRPP Choices* 11:2, 1–28.

Allen, Jim, and Rolf van der Velden. (2001). "Educational Mismatches versus Skill Mismatches: Effects on Wages, Job Satisfaction, and On-the-Job Search." *Oxford Economic Papers* 53:3, 434–52.

Alpin, C., J. R. Shackleton, and S. Walsh. (1998). "Over- and Undereducation in the UK Graduate Labour Market." *Studies in Higher Education* 23:1, 17–34.

Aydemir, Abdurrahman, and Mikal Skuterud. (2005, May). "Explaining the Deteriorating Entry Earnings of Canada's Immigrant Cohorts: 1966–2000." *Canadian Journal of Economics* 38:2, 641–71.

Bar-Or, Yuval, John Burbidge, Lonnie Magee, and A. Leslie Robb. (1995, October). "The Wage Premium to a University Education in Canada, 1971–1991." *Journal of Labor Economics* 13:4, 762–94.

Battu, Harminder, and P. J. Sloane. (2002). "To What Extent Are Ethnic Minorities in Britain Overeducated?" *International Journal of Manpower* 23:3, 192–208.

Baygan, Günseli. (2004). "Developing Highly Skilled Workers: Review of Canada." Report of the OECD Committee on Industry and Business Environment. Paris: OECD Publications.

Belfield, Clive R. (2000). *Economic Principles for Education: Theory and Evidence.* Cheltenham and Northampton, MA: Edward Elgar.

Bender, Keith A., and John S. Heywood. (2006). "Educational Mismatch among PhDs: Determinants and Consequences." Working Paper no. 12693. Cambridge, MA: National Bureau of Economic Research.

Boothby, Daniel. (1999). "Literacy Skills, the Knowledge Content of Occupations, and Occupational Mismatch." Hull, QC: Publications Office, Applied Research Branch, Strategic Policy, Human Resources Development Canada.

Brisbois, Richard. (2003, December). *How Canada Stacks Up: The Quality of Work—An International Perspective.* Research Paper W23, Work Network. Ottawa: Canadian Policy Research Networks.

Canadian Human Rights Tribunal. (2006). "Gian S. Sangha, Complainant, and Canadian Human Rights Commission and Mackenzie Valley Land and Water Board, Respondent: Reasons for Decision." Online at http://www.chrt-tcdp. gc.ca/search/files/sangha%20final%20decision.pdf

Card, David, and Thomas Lemieux. (2001, May). "Can Falling Supply Explain the Rising Return to College for Younger Men?: A Cohort-Based Analysis." *Quarterly Journal of Economics* 116:2, 705–46.

Citizenship and Immigration Canada. (2009a). *Facts and Figures 2009—Immigration Overview: Permanent and Temporary Residents, Permanent Residents.* Ottawa: Citizenship and Immigration Canada. Online at http://www.cic.gc.ca/english/resources/statistics/facts2009/permanent/01.asp [consulted January 14, 2011].

Citizenship and Immigration Canada. (2009b). *Facts and Figures 2009—Immigration Overview: Permanent and Temporary Residents, Temporary Residents.* Ottawa: Citizenship and Immigration Canada. Online at http://www.cic.gc.ca/english/resources/statistics/facts2009/temporary/02.asp [consulted January 14, 2011].

Dooley, Martin. (1986, February). "The Overeducated Canadian?: Changes in the Relationship among Earnings, Education, and Age of Canadian Men, 1971–1981." *Canadian Journal of Economics* 19:1, 142–59.

Duncan, Greg J., and Saul Hoffman. (1981). "The Incidence and Wage Effects of Overeducation." *Economics of Education Review* 1:1, 75–86.

Ferrer, Ana, David A. Green, and W. Craig Riddell. (2006, Spring). "The Effect of Literacy on Immigrant Earnings." *Journal of Human Resources* 41:2, 380–410.

Ferrer, Ana, and W. Craig Riddell. (2008, February). "Education, Credentials, and Immigrant Earnings." *Canadian Journal of Economics* 41:1, 186–216.

Freeman, Richard. (1976). *The Overeducated American.* New York: Academic Press.

Frenette, Marc. (2001, Spring). "Overqualified?: Recent Graduates, Employer Needs." *Perspectives on Labour and Income* 13:1, 45–53.

Frenette, Marc. (2004, February). "The Overqualified Canadian Graduate: The Role of the Academic Program in the Incidence, Persistence, and Economic Returns to Overqualification." *Economics of Education Review* 23:1, 29–45.

Galarneau, Diane, and René Morissette. (2004, June). "Immigrants: Settling for Less?" *Perspectives on Labour and Income* 5:6, 5–16.

Green, C., P. Kler, and G. Leeves. (2004). "Overeducation and the Assimilation of Recently Arrived immigrants: Evidence from Australia." Working Paper no. 4. Brisbane: Centre for Economic Policy Modelling, University of Queensland.

Green, David A., and W. Craig Riddell. (2001). "Literacy, Numeracy, and Labour Market Outcomes in Canada." [Canadian Component of the International Adult Literacy Survey]. Ottawa: Statistics Canada, Human Resources Development Canada, and National Literacy Secretariat.

Green, Francis, Steven McIntosh, and Anna Vignoles. (1999). "Overeducation and Skills—Clarifying the Concepts." Discussion Paper 435. London: Centre for Economic Performance, London School of Economics and Political Science.

Hartog, Joop. (2000). "Overeducation and Earnings: Where Are We, Where Should We Go?" *Economics of Education Review* 19:2, 131–47.

Human Resources Development Canada. (2002). "Knowledge Matters: Skills and Learning for Canadians: Canada's Innovation Strategy." Hull, QC: Human Resources Development Canada.

Katz, Lawrence F., and Kevin M. Murphy. (1992, February). "Changes in Relative Wages, 1963–1987: Supply and Demand Factors." *Quarterly Journal of Economics* 107:1, 35–78.

Li, Chris, Ginette Gervais, and Aurélie Duval. (2006). "The Dynamics of Overqualification: Canada's Underemployed University Graduates." Ottawa: Income Statistics Division, Statistics Canada.

McGuinness, Séamus. (2006). "Overeducation in the Labour Market." *Journal of Economic Surveys* 20:3, 387–418.

Oreopoulos, Philip. (2009, May). "Why Do Skilled Immigrants Struggle in the Labour Market?: A Field Experiment with Sixty Thousand Résumés." Working Paper no. 09–03. Vancouver: Metropolis British Columbia.

Reitz, Jeffrey. (2001). "Immigrant Skill Utilization in the Canadian Labour Market: Implications of Human Capital Research." *Journal of International Migration and Integration* 2:3, 347–78.

Reitz, Jeffrey. (2006, July). "Recent Trends in the Integration of Immigrants in the Canadian Labour Market: A Multidisciplinary Synthesis of Research." Unpublished paper. Online as http://www.utoronto.ca/ethnicstudies/trends.pdf [consulted January 14, 2011].

Sicherman, Nachum. (1991, April). "'Overeducation' in the Labor Market." *Journal of Labor Economics* 9:2, 101–22.

Sloane, P. J., Harminder Battu, and P. T. Seaman. (1999). "Overeducation, Undereducation and the British Labour Market." *Applied Economics* 31:11, 1,437–53.

Statistics Canada. (2003). "Longitudinal Survey of Immigrants to Canada: Process, Progress, and Process." Ottawa: Special Surveys Division, Statistics Canada.

Statistics Canada. (2007). "Knowledge of Official Languages among New Immigrants: How Important Is It in the Labour Market?" Ottawa: Special Surveys Division, Statistics Canada.

Stevenson, Harold W. (1992, December). "Learning from Asian Schools." *Scientific American*, 70–76.

Stevenson, Harold W., and James W. Stigler. (1992). *Learning Gap: Why Our Schools are Failing, and What We Can Learn from Japanese and Chinese Education*. New York: Simon & Schuster.

Sweetman, Arthur. (2004). "Immigrant Source Country Educational Quality and Labour Market Outcomes." Research Paper no. 234. Ottawa: Analytical Studies Branch, Statistics Canada.

Vahey, S. P. (2000). "The Great Canadian Training Robbery: Evidence on the Returns to Education Mismatch." *Economics of Education Review* 19, 219–27.

Wald, Steven. (2005). "The Impact of Overqualification on Job Search." *International Journal of Manpower* 26:2, 140–56.

Wald, Steven., and Tony Fang. (2008). "The Overeducation of Immigrants in the Canadian Labour Market: Evidence from the Workplace and Employee Survey." *Canadian Pubic Policy* 34:4, 457–80.

Ying, S. N. (2003). "Earnings and 'Skill' Allocation in the Canadian Labor Market." *International Journal of Manpower* 24:8, 964–80.

Chapter 18

Conclusion:
Reimagining Canada's Present and Future
in the Shadow of the Rise of China

Jeremy Paltiel

Senator Poy and Dr. Cao have assembled contributions from policy practitioners and academic commentators that critically examine the Canada–China relationship over the past forty years. In this brief concluding chapter I look at what we must do in light of these contributions to build a robust partnership that will benefit both our countries, and the world, over the next forty years.

Challenging Our Complacency

As B. Michael Frolic points out in his chapter, Canada's relations with China over most of the past forty years have been premised on a single idea: in partnering with China, a major power outside the mainstream of international society, Canada can play a valuable, even principal role in improving China's integration into international society and global governance, and might thereby advance Canada's own international stature. Having, in our own minds, rummaged in the wilderness to find the magic lamp that will yield the genie who will accede to our wishes, we have found along the way that the genie is no slave to our commands, and is not exactly grateful for being liberated.

There is a story told in the Mencius of two soldiers on a battlefield. When the attack drums sound, both take off to the rear. One soldier stops after fifty paces and, seeing that his companion has already retreated a hundred paces, laughs out loud. Mencius asks whether there is any difference in the coward-ice of either soldier. So too, China's leaders see no need to single Canada out among Western nations. China engages the world on its own terms.

Faced with this, Canadian leaders have played both ardent suitor and hard to get, in the mirror image policies of the Chrétien and Harper regimes. Arguably, neither path has yielded satisfactory results. Each has been premised on what China represents to us, rather than on where we are of interest to China, or on mobilizing latent resources that can be synergized through a more active partnership with China. Our policy has yet to move from a perception that we are closer to the fulcrum of global politics than the Chinese are, to a recognition that it is up to us to move ourselves closer to the fulcrum of global politics if we are to leverage our relatively modest power.

The past forty years have seen several important milestones. Even before diplomatic recognition, wheat sales were initiated through the Canadian Wheat Board under Prime Minister Diefenbaker. Canada's recognition ini-tiative was a milestone event in China's relations with the West, underlining Canada's understanding that China had the potential to be a significant global power, but that it had little experience in engaging the multilateral institutions created in the wake of the Second World War. The third mile-stone was our aid programme in China, put in place through a memoran-dum of understanding in 1983. The importance of this programme was the focus that it gave to human resources, and to enhancing the capacity of civil society in meeting the challenges of a China that was becoming more open and more globalized. This was an important leg of our China strategy in the 1980s, as so masterfully set out in Professor Frolic's chapter. Coming soon after Deng Xiaoping had launched the reform and opening process at the Third Plenum of the Eleventh Central Committee in December 1978, all along our programme was aimed at enhancing and reinforcing that process. We can fairly claim some credit for training at least some of China's agents of internationalization and, in the process, normalizing China's engage-ment with the world, through tools ranging from technical, managerial and language to legal reform and environmental capacity enhancement.

While our modest aid programme and our extensive welcoming of Chi-nese immigrants and students engaged a broad range of Chinese institutions and institutional actors, as well as fostering university linkages, these were not translated into lasting institutional bonds that could have transcended project funding or the human contacts among diverse individual actors. Canada remains well-regarded in China, but our role in China's opening is poorly appreciated and seldom commented on. Of the thousands of Canadians engaged by this process, only a minority remain engaged in China relations as a regular aspect of their careers, and there has been little or no effort to mobilize this latent source of *guanxi* in any systematic way.

A number of Canadian firms have been active in the Chinese market since the earliest days of its opening to the world, but few have established a significant footprint in any individual sector, with Bombardier Transportation and Manulife Financial being significant among those few. Nortel's adventures in China followed the bittersweet trajectory of that firm. Complementing this has been the rather timid and slow penetration of Chinese investment in our resources sector, which is only now assuming significant momentum and scale. All in all, despite quite significant and energetic efforts at various junctures by governments at the national and provincial levels, and with significant input at the municipal level, we remain fond acquaintances rather than fast friends or even active partners.

While there can be no gainsaying the cultural and linguistic barriers to closer ties, some fault for this modest achievement lies with our own parochial and smug self-satisfaction, rooted, perhaps, in a benign missionary condescension. Our reflexive insistence on seeing the Chinese as latecomer pupils in need of benign tutelage, or else as virgin market terrain whose superficial penetration should exact exorbitant rents, has belied the actual picture of our engagement. Few have followed in the footsteps of Mark Rowswell, the Canadian media celebrity known in China as Dashan, and bothered to invest the time and energy to establish a lasting presence in the intricate web of Chinese social, political and economic organization sufficient to yield the status of knowledgeable insiders with the capacity to recognize, and capitalize on, reciprocal interests and opportunities. Those who have , are reluctant to generalize their experience to others and in many cases are unable to because their success is intensely localized and particularistic, in keeping with the intricacy of the Chinese environment. As a result we are unaware of our resources and ignorant of our opportunities, except when they are spelled out directly by Chinese officials eager to transact specific deals in specific circumstances.

Charles Burton has highlighted some of these aspects of our underperformance in China, while Sonny Lo and Ming Chan both highlight the bridging role that Hong Kong has played in Canada's relations with China. However, they also critique our underexploitation of this potential aspect of our "soft power" in China, despite the fact that, as far back as the mid-1980s, it was an important element in the "China Strategy" that Professor

Frolic describes. Perrin Beatty again emphasizes the positive role played by Hong Kong in our relationship with China.

In general, this volume testifies to the potential of our soft power, but laments the lack of recognition by our policy-makers of our potential and capacity to mobilize this latent resource. Qiang Zha shows how education, traditionally one of the areas where Canadians prided themselves on being tutors of China's modernization, is increasingly a two-way street, in which our own high-tech firms are increasingly reliant on imported human resources. Indeed, one of the most important findings of this entire volume is that Canadians must be made more aware of, better appreciate and make better use of the two-way character of Sino-Canadian exchanges.

China is a terrain where local knowledge is crucial and can be scaled up only with care and experimentation. Here there is an obvious asymmetry between our vast and relatively sparse network, and China's simultaneous vastness and density. Our efforts to engage bump up awkwardly against a further instance of cultural inconsistency. Ours is a rule-bound society integrated through the rule of law, where teams of lawyers hash out agreements according to standard formulas recognizable in the common law and sanctified through precedent. China is a newly (re)born market society where rules are relative, policies are correlative and trust is intimate and personalized. Under the mantle of the general authority of the Communist Party of China, officials maximize their personal authority by using all the discretion granted them by law and policy to realize their personal interest. Nothing is possible unless those interests are met or that discretion is neutralized by the favour of a more powerful official. Contracts are only as valid as the interest and capacity of the party involved in the agreement. Court justices are officials with interests also. Legal boilerplate cannot make up for relations of trust at any level of the Chinese hierarchy. Trust grows from mutual commitment and is cemented through easy familiarity. It is not transferable and has a "best before" date. Given that neither our politicians nor our active entrepreneurs can spend more than a minor portion of their careers on the opposite side of the Pacific Ocean, our initiatives and interactions are destined to be sporadic at best. This necessary drawback must be compensated by intensity and consistency. Given our vast landscape and sparse population, we rarely achieve that kind of intimacy even in our domestic politics, let alone with our favoured allies. How much less is it possible for us to imprint ourselves on the consciousness of statesmen of a different language, culture and ideology?

And yet, over the decades since Canadian immigration laws removed the last vestiges of formal discrimination by race and country of origin, almost all our urban spaces have been transformed by infusions of Chinese culture. Kenny Zhang's chapter provides concrete data showing the visibility of Chinese communities in various major metropolitan centres, as well as their strong representation in a large number of professional and managerial categories. Chinese cuisine and public figures of Chinese ethnic origin have become commonplaces of our own landscape, from our municipal councils through to Parliament and even the office of Governor General. Where Chinese Canadians may once have represented the face of Canadian multiculturalism, they now represent unhyphenated Canada, full stop.

Transforming Our Imaginary

Unfortunately the same cannot be said of our Pacific imaginary. Twenty-five years after the establishment of the Asia Pacific Foundation of Canada, funded by all ten provinces and the federal government, we do not have a Pacific Council to focus the attention of civic leaders and policy-makers on the strategic challenges of forging trans-Pacific linkages. Our strategic culture still looks across the Northwest Atlantic and to our close neighbours to the South. Thus, for example, the website of the Canadian Defence and Foreign Affairs Institute shows only one article on East Asia (specifically, on China) for the past two years, and that by a non-expert (see Burney 2009), while a more recent study of the rise of the Chinese military was conducted by a colleague who has no expertise on China and largely recaps verbatim assessments coming from the United States (see Sloan 2010). The most recent statement of Canada's Defence Strategy, *Canada First*, contains a single sentence in the page about the Strategic Environment: "The ongoing build-up of conventional forces in Asia–Pacific countries is another trend that may have a significant impact on international stability in coming years" (see Ministry of National Defence 2010). We remain hostage to mainstream historiography on both sides of the Pacific, to a vision of Canada forged in the trenches of Flanders, and a vision of China that "stood up" by facing down the missionaries, adventurers and imperialist exploiters. Yet Norman Bethune was a relative latecomer in a long series of Canadians who made their efforts to contribute to China's re-emergence as a modern and dignified society in the community of nations.

Charles Burton's contribution to this volume applies a kind of revisionist twist to the self-congratulatory historiography of Sino-Canadian relations that was prevalent from the 1970s through the 1980s and, even after the trauma of the Tiananmen tragedy, extended beyond the 1990s. He reminds us that we have never shared a common ideological outlook with the Communist rulers of the People's Republic and that this difference forms a fact of life in our relationship. This sober outlook provides helpful background to changing perspective on Sino-Canadian relations under the current Harper government. Yet, despite the fact of different values, China's place in the world has radically changed and our policy must take account of this in the interest of all Canadians.

Canada's "Grand Strategy," as identified by David Haglund (2000) and re-emphasized by David Pratt (2008), has been securely nestled within a North Atlantic Triangle. Both these authors emphasize Canada's overlapping interests in maintaining close coordination with the United Kingdom and the United States, and maintaining a foreign policy based on multilateralism and internationalism, and anchored in liberal economic and political values, including the rule of law and individual rights. Over the more than sixty years that have passed since this foreign policy direction became institutionalized in Canada's commitments to NATO, NORAD and the UN, the economic and political centre of gravity has shifted towards the Asia–Pacific region. However, despite the formation of APEC, the institutions that frame the Asia–Pacific region lack the same nexus of values and institutions that cemented the North Atlantic Triangle in the past. In the early pages of his study, Haglund reviews Prime Minister Chrétien's conviction that the 21st century would be the Pacific Century and then, in a few words, simply dismisses it as an exaggerated fantasy about a remote future (Haglund 2000, pp. 2 and 67–72). While the contribution to this volume by that experienced practitioner of Canadian diplomacy, former Ambassador Fred Bild, may question the relevance and usefulness of grand ideas in the practical course of events, as the Sino-Canadian relationship has unfolded, those who shape and advise our country's foreign policy can only work on the assumption that the ship of state will go in the direction in which it is steered. Without a firm grasp of its destination, our country is quite literally lost.

Recent non-government reports, especially the Canadian International Council's *Open Canada: A Global Positioning Strategy for a Networked Age* (the Greenspon GPS project, 2010), along with the contributions to this volume, have highlighted the need to engage China more strategically.

Open Canada specifically recommends making Vancouver our Asia–Pacific Gateway, reaching an agreement on dual Canadian–Chinese citizenship and doing more to encourage Chinese investment and higher education in Canada. These are worthy goals, but unless our policy is anchored in a vision that places our identity within the Asia–Pacific region and ties our destiny to our trans-Pacific relationships, such efforts are likely to be crowded out by other priorities on either side of the Pacific Ocean. Fully supporting a Gateway oil pipeline to the Pacific coast would be a significant commitment that would demonstrate in material form our faith in strategic energy ties across the Pacific. This should be coupled with joint research and development efforts in green energy, and better environmental stewardship of oil sands energy resources. Collectively these efforts would have an impact in mutually indigenizing our trans-Pacific business cultures and broadening the social and economic stakes in maintaining a healthy relationship. We could jointly apply the profits of current energy technology to the search for a more sustainable future for the planet that would simultaneously sustain Sino-Canadian relations.

The main reason why our North Atlantic imaginary endures is because it is both anchored in history and reinforced by the enduring values underlying our federation and political life. Even the way in which we have integrated immigrants coming from diverse cultural origins is closely tied in with the evolving character of the liberal institutions that underpin our bilingual federation. While we have relationships that span the Pacific Ocean, the integration of our own society appears to owe more to the values transmitted across the Atlantic. Further, we staked our claim to nationhood largely on the battlefields of Europe during the two world wars. As the diplomat John Holmes pointed out in his survey of our foreign policy more than thirty years ago, even in the Second World War we left the fighting in the Pacific to our American allies.

Mobilizing Our Latent and Potential Resources

Few Canadians had ties to the Communist guerrilla elites that ruled China after 1949, and those who did fell under the shadow of the Cold War. Among the immigrants who have enriched Canada since the late 1960s, few have been able to retain influential ties back home while struggling to establish themselves in Canada. The hard work of the first generation, and the anxiety of the second generation to blend into their parents' new homeland, has not been conducive to forming ties that bind. At the same time, Canada has been considerably enriched by the contributions of Chinese immigrants from Hong Kong and other former British colonies, who have in turn served as a bridgehead for immigrants from mainland China. Senator Poy rightly emphasizes the catalytic role that Canada's relationship with Hong Kong has played in stimulating and developing our relationship with China as a whole. It may take another generation for a cohort to arise that can ride the jet stream and stride the dateline with equanimity and confidence, but, just as many Canadians travel the arc between homes in Vancouver and Hong Kong on a regular basis and divide family relations between the two port cities, the same kind of nexus of business, family and culture is gradually being woven between Vancouver and Shanghai, and various other gateways of Canada and China. *Open Canada* seeks to speed that process by proposing that Canada reach a formal agreement with China on dual citizenship. That may be a laudable objective, but it is unnecessary under Canadian law and too sensitive for Chinese legislation. We should instead work for some kind of framework bilateral agreement for visas for business executives and skilled workers, while working harder here at home to facilitate the integration of highly educated Chinese into the professional labour force. This laudable goal, articulated by Senator Poy and documented most notably by Tony Fang, along with others in this volume, must be backed up by practical measures that bring immigrant professionals into the workplace before their job experience in their home-land becomes stale. This will require cooperation, not only between federal immigration authorities and provincial credential-granting authorities, but also between the private sector and the voluntary associations assisting immi-grant settlement. As Ghazy Mujahid, Ann Kim and Guida Man point out in Chapter 14, socioeconomic pressures of aging in the transnational family create incentives for officials from both countries to ease the burden of the 'sandwich generation' caught between the caring for young children as well as elderly parents. The dividends, however, will flow to the country as a whole, not just because we benefit from the full applications of the human resources of immigrants, but because professional immigrants who are fully integrated into our private and public sectors form a human bridge back to China, as both Kenny Zhang, Huhua Cao and Olivier Dehoorne point out, and keep open the channels of technical cooperation and technology transfer, invest-ment and multinational management.

We must also do more to ensure that the welcome we have extended to Chinese students in our schools and universities, so that they can acquire sophisticated knowledge in our two official languages, as well as the thousands of language teachers we have dispatched to China over the past forty years, are matched by equal commitments by our provincial education authorities, not only to provide heritage language programmes, but to expand the learning of Mandarin Chinese as a second language, and a more robust commitment to acquainting our young people with the historic achievements of Chinese civilization. As Jack Jedwab has pointed out in his contribution to this volume, language retention enhances social capital, and thus increases the social capital available in this country to maintain and advance our relations with China and the world.

Professor Errol Mendez recommends our federal constitutional model for China as a method of resolving problems of minority rights. We are justly proud of our record of progress in multiculturalism, and our survival as a multiethnic and multilingual state largely free from violent confrontation. It might be better to use a different metaphor, for each country to use the other, not as a model, but as a mirror in which to examine its own practices to see whether they can improve. Without preaching, we can hold out our human rights culture and institutions as a mirror in which the Chinese may look at their own practice. We can admire and learn from Chinese practices in development and the eradication of poverty, while sharing experience in bringing prosperity to minorities and the historically disadvantaged. The challenge before us is to go beyond the instrumental ties of commerce to forge deep and abiding relationships, while holding fast to the cherished values that cemented our historic genesis in the North Atlantic Triangle. As China rises, we need to convince ourselves that our participation was integral to China's successful re-emergence on the global stage. Secure in this knowledge, we may then integrate our identity as a multicultural Asia–Pacific nation with China's rise. The challenge is to look at China not as a reflection of our values or as a favoured pupil, but as a complex reality in which our values are embedded in a configuration that is distinctive, but not identical. As the Chinese sage Confucius recommends, "the authoritative person seeks harmony without sameness, whereas the inferior one only attaches himself to the same."

Reorienting Our Partnership to a Post-Western World

Canada does have much to offer in the area of governance and the rule of law, and we have actively shared our experience through the programmes administered by CIDA in China. However, our experience both in the integration of skilled immigrants, and in the economic and social development of remote Aboriginal communities, leaves much to be desired. We can and should acknowledge China's success in economic development, while sharing experience in the management of minority issues. As our relationship matures after forty years, we should move away from the frame of teacher and pupil, and the frame of first encounters, into a new cooperative framework, where participants from both sides work together to tackle common problems in economic development, environmental sustainability and multiethnic governance in a globalized world. This cooperative framework is hinted at in the contribution by Thomas d'Aquino. We should encourage our government and business leaders to elaborate on this through the strategic working groups already established between our national governments, supplemented by other initiatives from the provinces and the private sector. We can not only encourage the "whole of government" approach to China recommended by former Minister Emerson, but add federal–provincial cooperation and the participation of the private and voluntary sectors. In looking to the next forty years of our bilateral relations, we must focus more strategically to reorient our vision across the Pacific Ocean, adapting without losing the values that have shaped our success so far, and looking to shape our mutual relationship in a way that enhances the building of a "harmonious world."

Prime Minister Harper has grown much keener on the relationship with China, as seen not just in the Joint Statement issued during his visit to China in December 2009, but in his reaffirmation of our strategic partnership during the state visit of President Hu Jintao in June 2010. The Prime Minister views China partly through the lens of his own self-proclaimed vision of Canada as an "energy superpower" and his recognition of Canada as a Pacific nation with important investment in an Asia–Pacific Gateway (see Harper 2009 and 2010). However, without a specific commitment to creating the infrastructure that will enable China to have strategic access to our petroleum resources, Canada cannot figure in China's calculations of energy security. In his speech to the Canada–China Business Council on June 24, 2010, President Hu expressed the need to deepen energy and resource cooperation and expand two-way investment, and also expressed China's willingness to participate in the Asia–Pacific gateway projects.

With China's rise and growing dependence on our resources, we have a unique opportunity to take advantage of China's "going out" strategy to forge new and more durable links that will bind us more intimately.

We have the mineral resources and China has vast financial resources, in addition to a growing market, but commodity exchange will not suffice to cement enduring relations. We also have the cultural and human resources that can be put together in common enterprises, projects, and institutions that will further build intimacy and trust. To achieve these goals, we must commit to better and fuller integration of Chinese immigrants into the mainstream of professional and managerial careers, and turn our strategic vision across the Pacific to achieve a complementary partnership of distinct actors with differing perspectives but common goals.

Rather than view our interests in strictly regional or hemispheric terms, we should promote Canada as a platform for all-round cooperation in China's global "going out" strategy. We should fully realize and utilize our unique advantages as a multicultural country of immigration, our open markets and our sophisticated and stable financial system, as Yuen Pau Woo points out in this volume. These advantages, like our social and political system, are grounded on a robust foundation of the rule of law that is open to innovation and the participation of new actors. Further, our advanced education and technology should be put to greater and better use, ensuring that our common ventures will be more energy-efficient, cleaner and more environmentally sustainable, as urged by Thomas d'Aquino. We can and should create new synergies in our areas of technological strength in energy, transportation systems, aerospace and telecommunications. However, the ultimate test of our relationship will be measured, not in profits or even common prosperity, but by the way that we will have transformed a cultural divide into a meeting point of mutual appreciation and a network of indissoluble bonds. Only then will we achieve the "harmony without sameness" that both sides sincerely yearn for.

References

Burney, Derek. (2009). "China Ascending: A Policy Update Paper." Calgary: Canadian Defence and Foreign Affairs Institute. Online as http://www.cdfai.org/PDF/China%20Ascending.pdf [consulted January 14, 2011].

Canadian International Council. (2010). *Open Canada: A Global Positioning Strategy for a Networked Age.* Toronto: Canadian International Council. Online at http://www.onlinecic.org/opencanada [consulted January 14, 2011].

Haglund, David G. (2000). *The North Atlantic Triangle Revisited: Canadian Grand Strategy at Century's End.* Toronto: Irwin.

Harper, Stephen. (2009, December 7). "Canada and Korea in the Asia–Pacific Era: Building a Stronger, Closer Partnership." Speech to the National Assembly of the Republic of Korea. Ottawa: Office of the Prime Minister. Online at http://pm.gc.ca/eng/media.asp?id=3025 [consulted January 14, 2011].

Harper, Stephen. (2010, June 24). "PM Welcomes Chinese President Hu." Speech to the Canada–China Business Council. Ottawa: Office of the Prime Minister. Online at http://pm.gc.ca/eng/media.asp?category=2&id=3504 [consulted January 14, 2011].

Hu Jintao. (2010, June 24). "Promote the All-Round Development of the China–Canada Strategic Partnership." Speech to the Canada–China Business Council, Ottawa. Online at http://www.chinese-embassy.org.uk/eng/zgyw/t712797.htm [consulted January 14, 2011].

Ministry of National Defence. (2010, March 12). "Strategic Environment." Canada First Defence Strategy. Online at http://www.forces.gc.ca/site/pri/first-premier/defstra/enviro-eng.asp [consulted January 14, 2011].

Office of the Prime Minister. (2009, December 3). "Canada–China Joint Statement." Ottawa: Office of the Prime Minister. Online at http://www.pm.gc.ca/eng/media.asp?id=3005 [consulted January 14, 2011].

Pratt, David. (2008, Winter). "Is There a Grand Strategy in Canadian Foreign Policy?" *Journal of Military and Strategic Studies* 10:2.

Sloan, Elinor. (2010, June). "China's Strategic Behaviour." Calgary: Canadian Defence and Foreign Affairs Institute. Online as http://www.cdfai.org/PDF/China%20Strategic%20Behaviour.pdf [consulted January 14, 2011].

The Greenspon GPS project (2010). Online at http://www.onlinecic.org/open-canada (consulted January 14, 2011)

Notes on Contributors

Author of the preface:

The Honourable Allan Rock. Born and raised in Ottawa, Allan Rock is a three-time graduate of the University of Ottawa. He attended the University of Ottawa high school before completing a Baccalaureate in Arts in 1968 and a law degree in 1971. For 20 years, Allan Rock conducted a varied practice in civil, commercial and administrative litigation. In 1993, he was elected as the Member of Parliament for Etobicoke-Centre and named Minister of Justice and Attorney General of Canada. He introduced significant improvements to the Criminal Code, the Canadian Human Rights Act and other federal legislation. In 1997 he became Minister of Health where he spearheaded the creation of the Canadian Institutes of Health Research (CIHR) and more than doubled annual health research funding on a national scale.

Subsequently, as Minister of Industry and Minister of Infrastructure, he introduced Canada's innovation strategy, was responsible for Canada's three granting councils and introduced legislation to create the Pierre Elliott Trudeau Foundation to promote applied research in the social sciences and the humanities.

Allan Rock was appointed Ambassador of Canada to the United Nations in December 2003. As the voice of Canadians at the United Nations, Allan Rock was an outspoken advocate of human rights, human security and reforming the UN. At the 2005 World Summit at the UN, he led the successful Canadian effort to secure the adoption by world leaders of the doctrine Responsibility to protect populations from genocide, ethnic cleansing, war crimes and crimes against humanity.

Editors:

Huhua Cao, is Professor of Geography at the University of Ottawa. He received his bachelor degree from Shanghai Tong-Ji University and his master and PhD from Laval University. Dr. Cao has been involved in extensive research and international cooperation projects in Canada and China. His research has focused on three axes: 1) Urbanization and Mobility; 2) Regional ethnic minority; 3) Spatial inequality and accessibility of social services. Dr. Cao's research has been funded several times by the Social Sciences and Humanities Research Council of Canada (SSHRC), Canadian Institutes of Health Research (CIHR), Canadian International Development Agency (CIDA), Human Resources and Skills Development Canada (HRSD) and also by Chinese Government ministries including the Ministry of Science and Technology and the Ministry of Education.

Along with his research experience, Dr. Cao has written numerous articles related to urban and regional development while collaborating with academics throughout the world. He is guest editor of the International Convention of Asia Scholars (ICAS) publication series: Ethnic Minorities and Regional Development in Asia: Reality and Challenges (Amsterdam University Press, 2009) and is also the co-editor of the books Inclusion and Harmony: Improving Mutual Understanding of Development in Minority Regions (The Ethnic Publishing House-民族出版社, 2008) and Regional Minorities and Development in Asia (Routledge, 2010). In 2010, Dr. Cao authored the book, Regional Disparity and Minority Inclusion: The Challenges of China after the Beijing 2008 Olympic Games (Disparités régionales et inclusion des minorités : *Les défis de la Chine de l'après Jeux Olympiques de Beijing)*, by Presses de l'Université du Québec.

Senator Vivienne Poy, Chancellor Emerita of the University of Toronto.

The Honourable Vivienne Poy is a historian, author, fashion designer, entrepreneur, corporate director and volunteer with a number of cultural, educational and social organizations. Born in Hong Kong, she was educated in Hong Kong, England, and Canada. She completed an Honours B.A. in history at McGill University, followed by an MA and PhD in history from the University of Toronto. She also completed a Diploma in Fashion Arts at Seneca College. Her academic interests, and her 4 books, focus on the history of the Chinese in Canada, the history of Hong Kong and of modern China.

In 1998, Senator Vivienne Poy was the first Canadian of Asian descent to be appointed to the Senate of Canada. Over the years, Vivienne Poy has been involved with many cultural, educational and philanthropic causes across Canada. As a Senator, and an active member of the Asian Canadian communities, she was instrumental in having May recognized by the federal government as Asian Heritage Month in Canada. She is also committed to building bridges of understanding between Canada, and the Asia Pacific region. As a result of her leadership in politics, the community and education, she has received many awards and honours including being voted by Canadians as one of 2010's Top 25 Canadian Immigrants in *Canadian Immigrant Magazine*, as well as receiving the inaugural Golden Mountain Achievement Award at the 150 Years in Golden Mountain Celebration in 2008 in Victoria.

In recognition of her national and international achievements, she has been awarded several honorary degrees from universities in Canada and around the world.

Authors:

Thomas Paul d'Aquino, B.A., LL.B., LL.M., LL.D.

Thomas d'Aquino is an entrepreneur, lawyer, author, educator and corporate director. He is Chairman and Chief Executive of Intercounsel Ltd, a private company engaged in providing strategic solutions and in advancing transformational change. He is also Senior Counsel at Gowlings, one of Canada's largest law firms, chairs the firm's Business Strategy and Public Policy Group and is a member of the Gowlings International Strategic Advisory Group.

Mr. d'Aquino serves on the Board of Directors of Manulife Financial Corporation, CGI Group Inc., and Coril Holdings Ltd. and is Chairman of the National Gallery of Canada Foundation.

He is associated with two of Canada's leading academic institutions: as Distinguished Visiting Professor, Global Business and Public Policy Strategies at Carleton University's Norman Paterson School of International Affairs; and as Honorary Professor at The University of Western Ontario's Richard Ivey School of Business. Earlier in his career, he served as Special Assistant to the Prime Minister of Canada and as Adjunct Professor of Law at the University of Ottawa lecturing on the law of international trade and global business transactions.

From 1981 to 2009, Mr. d'Aquino was Chief Executive and President of the Canadian Council of Chief Executives (CCCE), an organization composed of the chief executives of 150 of the country's leading enterprises and pre-eminent entrepreneurs. Mr. d'Aquino assumed leadership of the Council in its formative stages. Upon his retirement from the CCCE as of December 31, 2009, member companies accounted for $850 billion in annual revenues and $4.5 trillion in assets. With a combined Canadian stock market value of $675 billion, the companies are responsible for the majority of Canada's private sector exports, investment and training. In recognition of his exemplary leadership, he was named by the Canadian Council of Chief Executives Board of Directors, a Distinguished Life Time Member.

A native of Nelson, British Columbia, Mr. d'Aquino was educated at the Universities of British Columbia, Queen's and London (University College and the London School of Economics). He holds B.A., LL.B., and LL.M. degrees, and an Honorary Degree of Doctor of Laws from Queen's University and from Wilfrid Laurier University.

Mr. d'Aquino has been referred to as Canada's most influential policy strategist and the country's leading global business ambassador. He is the author of numerous publications including the influential book *Northern Edge: How Canadian Can Triumph in the Global Economy*. He is a regular commentator on radio and television, and a frequent speaker on platforms in Canada, the United States, Europe, Asia and Latin America. Mr. d'Aquino has addressed audiences in forty countries and in over one hundred cities worldwide.

The Honourable Perrin Beatty, P.C. has been the President and Chief Executive Officer of the Canadian Chamber of Commerce, since August 2007. Prior to joining the chamber Mr. Beatty was the President and Chief Executive Officer of Canadian Manufacturers & Exporters. He was elected to the House of Commons as a Progressive Conservative in 1972 and in 1979 he was appointed Minister of State (Treasury Board) in the government of Joe Clark, at the time the youngest person ever to serve in a federal Cabinet. He held six additional portfolios in subsequent Progressive Conservative governments, including Secretary of State for External Affairs in 1993. Following the 1993 federal election, he was an Honourary Visiting Professor with the Department of Political Science, University of Western Ontario, where he taught a course in Communications Technologies and Public Policy. Mr. Beatty was appointed President and CEO of the Canadian Broadcasting Corporation (CBC) in 1995. Mr. Beatty has served on a number of Canadian government advisory committees covering issues that include national security, border management, privacy and international trade. He is also a member of the Advisory Council of the Canadian Defence and Foreign Affairs Institute and served for five years as Business Co-Chair of the Canadian Labour and Business Centre.

Fred Bild is Adjunct Professor at the University of Montreal's Centre of East Asian Studies. A graduate of Concordia University (philosophy & sociology), University College London (diploma in international law), and École d' Administration, Paris. He joined DEA in 1961. Professor Bild has served in various posts at Headquarters, including Director of personnel and Administration, international political and security affairs. He has served abroad with the Canadian delegation to the International Control Commissions in Laos and at Embassies in Tokyo, Paris (3 times), Bangkok and Beijing. The latter two as Ambassador.

Charles Burton is Associate Professor at Brock University specializing in Comparative Politics, Government and Politics of China, Canada-China Relations and Human Rights. He served as Counsellor at the Canadian Embassy to China between 1991-1993 and 1998-2000. Prior to coming to Brock, he worked at the Communications Security Establishment Canada of the Department of National Defence.

Dr. Burton received his PhD in 1987 from the University of Toronto after studies at Cambridge University (Oriental Studies) and Fudan University (History of Ancient Chinese Thought Program, Department of Philosophy, class of '77). He held the Izaak Walton Killam Memorial Post-Doctoral Scholar in Political Science at University of Alberta from 1986 to 1988.

His recently published works include: "Response to Jeremy Paltiel's Article, 'Canada and China: An Agenda for the Twenty-First Century: A Rejoinder to Charles Burton'" *Canadian Foreign Policy*, 15 (2), 2009, *A Reassessment of Canada's Interests in China and Options for Renewal of Canada's China Policy* refereed report released by the Canadian International Council (A Changing World: Canadian Foreign Policy Priorities, No. 4), 2009, "Neoauthoritarianism, urban bourgeoisie, and China's democratization" in Wu Guoguang, and Helen Lansdowne (eds), *Zhao Ziyang and China's Democratic Future*, (Routledge, 2008), "The 'Beijing Consensus' and China's quest for legitimacy on the international stage" in André Laliberté and Marc Lanteigne (eds), *The Chinese Party-State in the 21st Century*, (Routledge, 2008).

Ming K. Chan was born in Hong Kong where he completed high school. He obtained three US degrees, including a Ph D in history from Stanford in 1975 at the age of 25.

He is a visiting fellow, Center for East Asian Studies, Stanford University, where he was Visiting Professor of Chinese History, 1992-93. As a Research Fellow at Stanford's Hoover Institution 1999-2008, he ran the Hong Kong Documentary Archives project. During 1980-97, he taught in the History Department, University of Hong Kong, where he was twice elected "Best Teacher" by the Students' Union. He served as the John Heath Professor at Grinnell College, 2006-07, and the Julian & Virginia Cornell Professor at Swarthmore College, 1993-94. He was also visiting professor at Duke University, Mount Holyoke College, UCLA and El Colegio de Mexico.

Ming Chan has published 12 academic volumes and over 60 articles/ book chapters on Chinese history, China- global links, and Hong Kong/ Macao studies. He is General Editor of the *Hong Kong Becoming China* multi-volume series published by M E Sharpe, New York, with 12 titles issued since 1991. His recent books are: *Crisis and Transformation in China's Hong Kong* (M.E. Sharpe, 2002); *Historical Dictionary of the Hong Kong SAR & the Macao SAR.* (Scarecrow Press, 2006); *China's Hong Kong Transformed: Retrospect & Prospects Beyond The First Decade* (City University of Hong Kong Press, 2008); and *Perspectives on Lingnan Modern History: Guangdong and its Hong Kong Links, 1900-38* (Commercial Press, 2010).

Presented 80 plus papers in international conferences, Ming Chan has lectured at over 90 universities in North America, Europe, Asia and Australia. As an Asian affairs commentator, he is frequently interviewed by television, radio and the printed media, including Canadian newspapers and TV/radio networks. He is a trustee & principal of the Hong Kong Oral History Foundation.

Olivier Dehoorne was born in Manciet, Gers, France. He received his PhD in 1996, with his research focusing on the development of mountainous areas and tourism development strategies. After a first post at l'Université de Poitiers, he came to settle in Martinique in 2002 at the University of the French West Indies and Guiana, where he teaches geography, geopolitics, development and tourism.

His research is devoted to development issues in less developed countries, on the themes of migration, tourism, and resource management and planning. His specialty is in Latin America, but he also has an interest in

Asian studies. He has co-authored several books, also co-editing a book (on the island) and authoring articles in several journals (REMI, Téoros, Etudes Caribéennes).

Dr. Dehoorne has had teaching and research positions in Eastern Europe since 2000, notably in relation with Romania and the University of Oradea. He is currently engaged in several research projects on tourism and heritage in partnership with Romanian colleagues. He also regularly collaborates with Canadian universities (co-organizing a summer school in 1998 with the University of Montreal), including the University of Moncton (conference in 1999, visiting scholar from 2000 to 2002) and Ottawa (Visiting Professor in 2004, co-organizer of a symposium on regional development in 2004).

Tony Fang is an Associate Professor of Human Resources Management and Industrial Relations at York University and a research associate with the Centre for Industrial Relations and Human Resources Management at University of Toronto. Currently he also serves as the Domain Leader in Economic and Labour market Integration at CERIS – Ontario Metropolis Centre and a past Board Member of the Chinese Economists Society. He is also a visiting professor at Fudan University, Southwest University of Finance and Economics, and China University of Geosciences, all in China. In 2010, he received the tile of "Chutian Scholar" of Hubei Province.

Professor Fang has a PhD in Industrial Relations and Human Resource Management from the University of Toronto, a MA in Economics from Memorial University of Newfoundland, and B.A. in economics from Shandong University. His areas of research interest encompass issues of compensation and benefits, high performance workplace practices, pension, retirement policy and the ageing workforce, education, immigration, and minimum wages, union impact on wages, innovation and firm growth, pay equity and employment equity. He has published in such journals as *Industrial Relations (Berkeley), Canadian Journal of Economics, Canadian Public Policy, British Journal of Industrial Relations, Journal of Labor Research, International Journal of Manpower, Journal of Management History, Social Indictors Research*, and *Perspectives on Labour and Income*. He also received numerous research grants and awards from Social Sciences and Humanities Research Council and Human Resources and Social Development Canada.

Bernie Michael Frolic is Professor Emeritus, Department of Political Science, York University, and Senior Research Fellow, Asian Institute, Munk School for Global Affairs, University of Toronto. He is Visiting Professor in

Canadian Studies at Beijing Foreign Studies (Beiwai) University Graduate Centre. He first visited China in 1965. In the 1970's he served as First Secretary in the Canadian Embassy in Beijing. His published works include books on Canada-PRC relations, the Cultural Revolution, civil society in China, and democracy and human rights in S.E Asia. He is currently completing a book on Canada-PRC relations since 1970 and working on a longer term study of political change in China.

Jack Jedwab is currently the Executive Director of the Association for Canadian Studies (ACS) and the newly established International Association for the Study of Canada (IASC). He has served as Executive Director since 1998. From 1994-1998 he served as Executive Director of the Quebec Branch of the Canadian Jewish Congress. Mr. Jedwab earned a BA in Canadian History with a minor in Economics from McGill University and went on to complete an MA and PhD in Canadian History from Concordia University. He was a doctoral fellow of the Social Sciences and Humanities Research Council of Canada from 1982-1985. He lectured at McGill University between 1983 and 2008 in the Quebec Studies Program, the sociology and political science departments and the McGill Institute for the Study of Canada where he taught courses on Official Language Minorities in Canada and Sports in Canada. He is the founding editor of the publication Canadian Diversity and the new Canadian Journal for Social Research. A former contributor to the Canadian edition of Reader's Digest, he has written several essays in books, scholarly journals and in newspapers across the country and has also authored various publications and government reports on issues of immigration, multiculturalism, human rights and official languages.

Ann H. Kim is an Assistant Professor in the Department of Sociology at York University, an Affiliate of *CERIS-The Ontario Metropolis Centre* and a Faculty Associate of the *York Centre for Asian Research*. Her research is largely motivated by questions related to the immigrant and ethnic integration process and the factors that contribute to differing paths of integration. She has published on ethnicity and residential patterns in Canada and the United States (a 2009 book with *LFB Publishing* and articles in the *American Journal of Sociology, Canadian Studies in Population* and *Sociological Methods and Research*), immigrant generations and homeownership (*Canadian Journal of Urban Research*), and international migration flows (*Canadian Studies in Population*). More recently, she has developed an expanding program of research on the Korean diaspora in Canada which encompasses ethnic entrepreneurship, immigrant seniors, new destinations, and transnational families, and currently, she is working on two major projects, one on Korean transnational families and another on the gendered and racialized patterns of economic security in later life.

Sonny Shiu-Hing Lo is Professor in the Faculty of Arts and Sciences at the Hong Kong Institute of Education and Co-Director of the Research Center for Greater China Studies there. He formerly taught political science at the University of Waterloo, University of Hong Kong, Hong Kong University of Science and Technology, Hong Kong Lingnan College, and the University of East Asia, Macau. In 1991-92, he was a research fellow at Murdoch University, Australia. His recent publications include *The Politics of Cross-Border Crime in Greater China* (M. E. Sharpe, 2009) and *The Dynamics of Bejing-Hong Kong Relations: A Model for Taiwan?* (Hong Kong University Press, 2008).

Guida C. Man is an Adjunct Professor in the Faculty of Liberal Arts and Professional Studies at York University, teaching in the Departments of Sociology, Equity Studies, and Women Studies. She is a Faculty Associate of the *Centre for Feminist Research* and the *York Centre for Asian Research*, and an Affiliate of *CERIS-The Ontario Metropolis Centre*. Her research interest encompasses the interactions of globalization, transnational migration, gender, work, and social inequality, as they are articulated to gender, race and class relations. She has conducted a number of research studies concerning Chinese immigrants in Canada, addressing such issues as transnationalism, families, gender relations, employment, and integration. Currently, she is the Principal Investigator of a research entitled *"Transnational Migration Trajectories of Immigrant Women Professionals in Canada: Strategies of Work and Family"* funded by SSHRC Standard Research Grant (2009-11), and another research on transnational linkages of Chinese immigrant women in Toronto funded by a York University research grant (2009-10). She has published extensively in her area of specialization, and is presently involved in a co-edited book project entitled *Transnational Voices: Global Migration and the Experiences of Women, Youth and Children.*

Errol P. Mendes is a lawyer, professor, author and advisor to corporations, governments, civil society groups, and the United Nations. His areas of expertise include corporate law, governance and social responsibility, international business, trade and public law, constitutional law, and human rights law and policy. He has taught in these areas at law schools across Canada and is presently a full Professor of law at the University of Ottawa. He has also been a human rights Tribunal member in Canada, acted as an international arbitrator and an advisor in Canada's Privy Council Office, and recently served as a Visiting Professional at the International criminal Court in The Hague. While his ethnic roots are from Goa, India, Professor Mendes was born in Kenya, East Africa. He obtained his Bachelor of Law degree from the University of Exeter in the UK, followed by a Master of Laws degree from the University of Illinois. In 1979, he emigrated to Canada and was called to the Bar of Ontario in 1986. Prof. Mendes has been a Project Leader for conflict resolution, governance and justice projects in Asia and Latin America, and has lectured and given media commentaries across Canada and throughout the world. He led a project on human rights in China in partnership with Beijing University, which produced three landmark books he co-edited on human rights that included contributions from leading Chinese and Canadian intellectuals and practitioners. He has authored, co-authored, or edited several other books, including the landmark constitutional law text, The Canadian Charter of Rights and Freedoms, 3rd Edition, Carswell, 1996. He is also Editor-in-Chief of Canada's leading constitutional law journal, The National Journal of Constitutional Law. In 2006, Prof. Mendes was awarded the Walter S. Tarnopolsky Human Rights Award by the Canadian Section of the International Commission of Jurists and the Canadian Bar Association.

Ghazy Mujahid, a former United Nations Advisor on Population Policies and Development for East and South-East Asia, is an Affiliate of *CERIS- The Ontario Metropolis Centre* and an Associate of the *York Centre for Asian Research*. He has focused his research increasingly on population ageing and issues of senior populations. He has published extensively on the subject and his major publications include *"Population Ageing in East and South-East Asia: Current Situation and Emerging Challenges"* (2006); *"The Impact of Social Pensions: Perceptions of Asian Older Persons"* (2008) and *"Demographic Prognosis for South Asia: a future of rapid ageing"* (2009), all published by the United Nations Population Fund (UNFPA). His most recent work *"The Senior Population in Peel Region: Trends, Characteristics and Issues (1996-2006)"* was published by the Social Planning Council of Peel in March 2010. He is currently working with Professor (Emerita) Kenise Murphy Kilbride on a project *"Immigrant Senior Men in Ontario: Understanding and Meeting Their Needs and Challenges"* based in Ryerson University, Toronto.

Jeremy Paltiel is professor of political science at Carleton University in Ottawa and was visiting professor at the department of international relations at Tsinghua University in Beijing in 2009. He previously taught at the University of Alberta (1984-1990), the University of Arizona (1983-84) and the University of California at San Diego (1981-83). He received his BA in East AsianStudies from the University of Toronto in 1974, a diploma in Philosophy from Beijing University in 1976, and his MA (1979) and his PhD (1984) in political science from the University of California, Berkeley.

Most recently he co-ordinated the Chinese domestic background theme of the Canadian International Council's China Working Group and authored two of its papers: "Canada in China's Grand Strategy" and "Structure and Process in China's Foreign Policy Making – implications for Canada". He is the author of *The Empire's New Clothes: Cultural Particularism and Universality in China's Rise to Global Status* (Palgrave, 2007), "China and the Six-Party Talks" (2007), "Mencius and World Order Theories" (2010), "China's Regionalization Policies: Illiberal internationalism or Neo-Mencian Benevolence?" (2009), "Peaceful Rise? Soft Power? Human Rights in China's New Multilateralism"(2007) as well as numerous other articles on Chinese politics, East Asian foreign relations and Sino-Canadian relations.

Yuen Pau Woo is President and CEO of the Asia Pacific Foundation of Canada. Mr. Woo is an advisor to the Shanghai WTO Affairs Consultation Centre and the Canadian Ditchley Foundation. He is also on the Global Council of the Asia Society in New York, a member of the Greater Vancouver Advisory Board for the Salvation Army, and a board member of the Mosaic Institute.

Since 2006, Mr. Woo has been coordinator of the State of the Region Report, the flagship publication of the Pacific Economic Cooperation Council (PECC). He is also on the editorial board of Pacific Affairs.

Qiang Zha is an Assistant Professor at the Faculty of Education, York University. He holds a PhD in Higher Education, earned at the Ontario Institute for Studies in Education of the University of Toronto (OISE/UT). As a Chevening Scholar, he received a Master of Art degree in Comparative Education from the University of London Institute of Education. In 2004, he was a co-recipient of the inaugural UNESCO Palgrave Prize on Higher Education Policy Research.

In recent years, Qiang Zha focused his research on two SSHRC-supported projects, "China's Move to Mass Higher Education: Implications for

Democratization and Global Cultural Dialogue" and "Canadian Universities and International Talent in a New Era of Global Geo-Politics." The first project shed light on China's move to mass higher education in terms of the policy making process and the empirical experience. Its major findings are to be reported in a book titled *Portraits of 21st Century Chinese Universities: In the Move to Mass Higher Education* (Springer and Comparative Education Research Centre, The University of Hong Kong, 2011), which Qiang Zha co-authored with Ruth Hayhoe, Jun Li, and Jing Lin. This second project explores Canadian universities' attractiveness to international talent, and in particular to university professors originating from China who now hold Canada Research Chairs (CRC). This study is situated in the current context of a global geo-political shift, with emerging powers such as China and India shaping global interactions in new ways.

Kenny Zhang is a Senior Project Manager at the Asia Pacific Foundation of Canada, which was created by an Act of Parliament in 1984, as an independent, not-for-profit think-tank on Canada's relations with Asia.

Mr. Zhang joined the Foundation in January 2003 and specializes in China and immigration topics. His main research interests include Canada-China trade and investment relations, economics of immigration of Canada with focus on the Canadians abroad. Mr. Zhang received his BA and MA degrees in economics from Fudan University, China and the Institute of Social Studies, The Netherlands, respectively. Prior to joining the Foundation, he worked as associate research professor at the Shanghai Academy of Social Sciences and senior researcher at the Centre of Excellence on Immigration Studies at Simon Fraser University, Vancouver.

Mr. Zhang is on the Board of Directors of Canada China Business Council (BC Chapter) and the Board of Directors of Metropolis British Columbia. He has been a member of Vancouver Mayor's Working Group on Immigration since 2005. He is also member on the Joint Federal Provincial Immigration Advisory Council and Immigrant Employment Council of British Columbia.

Appendix

Major Events in Sino-Canadian Relations since 1970

Cassandra Cao

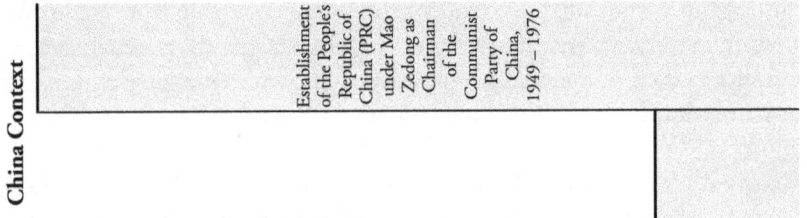

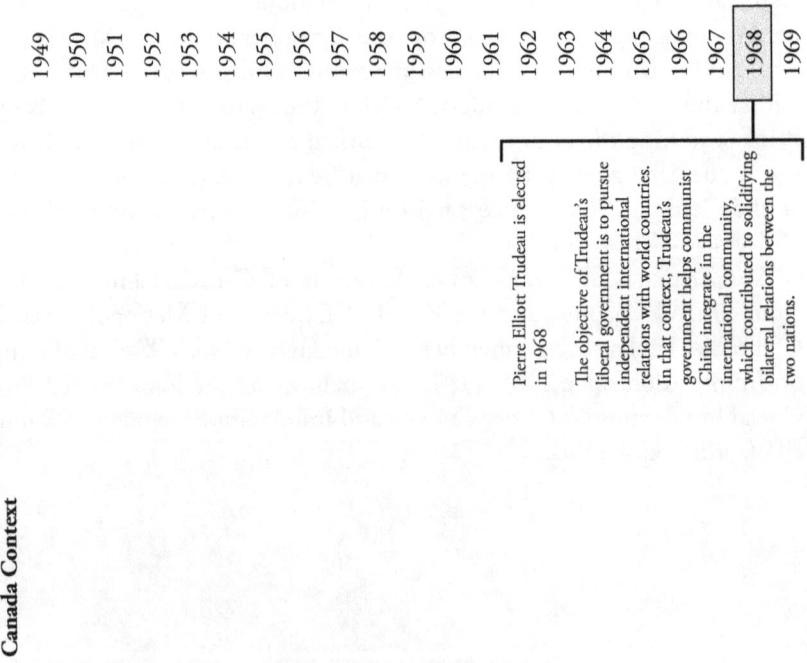

China Context

Establishment of the People's Republic of China (PRC) under Mao Zedong as Chairman of the Communist Party of China, 1949–1976

| 1949 | 1950 | 1951 | 1952 | 1953 | 1954 | 1955 | 1956 | 1957 | 1958 | 1959 | 1960 | 1961 | 1962 | 1963 | 1964 | 1965 | 1966 | 1967 | 1968 | 1969 |

Pierre Elliott Trudeau is elected in 1968

The objective of Trudeau's liberal government is to pursue independent international relations with world countries. In that context, Trudeau's government helps communist China integrate in the international community, which contributed to solidifying bilateral relations between the two nations.

Canada Context

China Context

The Cultural Revolution, 1966–1976

Hua Guofeng becomes Chairman of the Communist Party of China, 1976–1981

Beginning of economic reforms, 1978

Hu Yaobang becomes General Secretary of the Communist Party of China, 1981–1987

PRC under Deng Xiaoping as paramount leader, 1978–1997

Zhao Ziyang becomes General Secretary of the Communist Party of China, 1987–1989

Timeline (1970–1990)

1970	Formal diplomatic relations between Canada and China are established on October 13th, 1970
1971	PRC receives seat on UN Security Council, 1971
1972	
1973	Trudeau visits China, 1973
1974	
1975	
1976	Montreal Olympics 1976
1977	
1978	
1979	Chinese Premier Zhao Ziyang addresses a joint session of the Canadian Parliament, 1984 (This was the first leader of a communist country to address the Canadian House of Commons)
1980	Canada grants a 2 billion line of credit to China for expansion of economic reforms, 1980
1981	
1982	
1983	President of China Li Xiannian makes a state visit to Canada, 1985 (the first visit by the President of China to Canada after the establishment of diplomatic relations between the two countries) / Trudeau visits China, 1983
1984	
1985	Brian Mulroney visits China, 1986
1986	Canada announces a 350 million dollar expansion on top of a 2 billion line of credit to China to promote bilateral trade, 1986
1987	Establishment of Canada-China Strategy, 1987
1988	
1989	On June 30th, 1989, Canada imposes sanctions against China. / Tiananmen Square protests, 1989*
1990	

A general agreement is signed between Canada and China on Development Cooperation, 1983

CIDA aid program is doubled to 200 million dollars, 1986

On June 5th, 1989, the Canadian House of Commons unanimously condemns the Tiananmen incident.

Canada Context

Pierre Elliott Trudeau's liberal government 1970–1979

Joe Clark's conservative government 1979–1980

Pierre Elliott Trudeau's liberal government 1980–1984

Brian Mulroney's conservative government 1984–1993

* The Tiananmen Square protests, which took place in May and June 1989, involved millions of demonstrators, the majority of whom were university students, mobilizing on Tiananmen Square in Beijing, and in other major Chinese cities, against corruption and for democracy.

China Context

- Deng Xiaoping's southern tour, 1992
- Jiang Zemin becomes General Secretary of the Communist Party of China, 1989 – 2002
- Hong Kong returns to China, 1997
- Macau returns to China, 1999
- Hu Jintao becomes General Secretary of the Communist Party of China, 2002 – present

Timeline (upper / China-Canada relations):

- China participates for the first time in the UN Commission on Human Rights, 1996
- Foundation of the Canada-China Joint Committee on Human Rights, 1997
- China signs the UN's International Covenant on Civil and Political Rights, 1998
- China officially joins WTO, 2001
- Paul Martin visits China, 2005
- The extending of honorary Canadian citizenship to the Dalai Lama by a unanimous vote of the House of Commons, 2006

- Chinese Premier Li Peng visits Canada, 1995
- Jiang Zemin visits Canada, 1997
- Chinese Premier Zhu Rongji visits Canada, 1999
- Chinese Premier Wen Jiabao visits Canada, 2003
- Hu Jintao visits Canada, 2005
- Beijing Olympics, 2008
- World Expo, Shanghai, 2010
- Hu Jintao visits Canada, 2010

Years: 1991, 1992, 1993, 1994, 1995, 1996, 1997, 1998, 1999, 2000, 2001, 2002, 2003, 2004, 2005, 2006, 2007, 2008, 2009, 2010, 2011

Timeline (lower / Canada–China relations):

- Three Canadian Members of Parliament are expelled from China during an official visit to the country, 1992
- Team Canada to China, 1996
- Team Canada to China, 1998
- Team Canada to China, 2001
- Team Canada to China, 2003
- The Canadian government announces Canada's Asia-Pacific Gateway & Corridor Initiative in 2005
- Stephen Harper makes his first official visit to China, 2009

Canada Context

- Jean Chrétien leads the First Team Canada trade mission to China, 1994
- Jean Chrétien's liberal government's foreign policy vis-à-vis China is based on four main pillars: (1) economic partnership; (2) peace and security; (3) sustainable development; and (4) human rights.
- Canada decides to end the co-sponsoring human rights resolution on China at United Nations meeting and announces a bilateral package of human rights initiatives, 1997
- Paul Martin meets with the spiritual chief of Tibetans Dalai Lama in a non-official context in April 2004
- Stephen Harper formally meets the Dalai Lama in his Parliament Hill office, 2007
- Approved destination status for Chinese tourism to Canada is signed, 2010

- Kim Campbell's conservative government, 1993
- Jean Chrétien's liberal government 1993-2003
- Paul Martin's liberal government 2003-2006
- Stephen Harper's conservative government 2006-present

www.ingramcontent.com/pod-product-compliance
Lightning Source LLC
Chambersburg PA
CBHW020338270326
41926CB00007B/225